Communications
in Computer and Information Science 526

Editorial Board

Simone Diniz Junqueira Barbosa
  Pontifical Catholic University of Rio de Janeiro (PUC-Rio),
  Rio de Janeiro, Brazil
Phoebe Chen
  La Trobe University, Melbourne, Australia
Alfredo Cuzzocrea
  ICAR-CNR and University of Calabria, Cosenza, Italy
Xiaoyong Du
  Renmin University of China, Beijing, China
Joaquim Filipe
  Polytechnic Institute of Setúbal, Setúbal, Portugal
Orhun Kara
  TÜBİTAK BİLGEM and Middle East Technical University, Ankara, Turkey
Igor Kotenko
  St. Petersburg Institute for Informatics and Automation of the Russian
  Academy of Sciences, St. Petersburg, Russia
Krishna M. Sivalingam
  Indian Institute of Technology Madras, Chennai, India
Dominik Ślęzak
  University of Warsaw and Infobright, Warsaw, Poland
Takashi Washio
  Osaka University, Osaka, Japan
Xiaokang Yang
  Shanghai Jiao Tong University, Shangai, China

More information about this series at http://www.springer.com/series/7899

Terry Rout · Rory V. O'Connor
Alec Dorling (Eds.)

Software Process Improvement and Capability Determination

15th International Conference, SPICE 2015
Gothenburg, Sweden, June 16–17, 2015
Proceedings

Editors
Terry Rout
Griffith University
Brisbane
Queensland
Australia

Alec Dorling
Impronova AB
Lindome
Sweden

Rory V. O'Connor
Dublin City University
Dublin
Ireland

ISSN 1865-0929   ISSN 1865-0937   (electronic)
Communications in Computer and Information Science
ISBN 978-3-319-19859-0   ISBN 978-3-319-19860-6   (eBook)
DOI 10.1007/978-3-319-19860-6

Library of Congress Control Number: 2015939995

Springer Cham Heidelberg New York Dordrecht London
© Springer International Publishing Switzerland 2015
This work is subject to copyright. All rights are reserved by the Publisher, whether the whole or part of the material is concerned, specifically the rights of translation, reprinting, reuse of illustrations, recitation, broadcasting, reproduction on microfilms or in any other physical way, and transmission or information storage and retrieval, electronic adaptation, computer software, or by similar or dissimilar methodology now known or hereafter developed.
The use of general descriptive names, registered names, trademarks, service marks, etc. in this publication does not imply, even in the absence of a specific statement, that such names are exempt from the relevant protective laws and regulations and therefore free for general use.
The publisher, the authors and the editors are safe to assume that the advice and information in this book are believed to be true and accurate at the date of publication. Neither the publisher nor the authors or the editors give a warranty, express or implied, with respect to the material contained herein or for any errors or omissions that may have been made.

Printed on acid-free paper

Springer International Publishing AG Switzerland is part of Springer Science+Business Media
(www.springer.com)

Preface

On behalf of the SPICE 2015 conference Organizing Committee, we are proud to present the proceedings of the 15th International Conference on Software Process Improvement and Capability dEtermination (SPICE 2015), held in Gothenburg, Sweden, during June 16–17, 2015.

The SPICE Project was formed in 1993 to support the development of an international standard for software process assessment. The work of the project has eventually led to the finalization of ISO/IEC 15504 – Process Assessment, and its complete publication represented a climax for the work of the project. The standardization effort continues, with the publication of the first documents in the new ISO/IEC 330xx family of standards on process assessment.

As part of its charter to provide ongoing publicity and transition support for the emerging standard, the project organized a number of SPICE workshops and seminars, with invited speakers drawn from project participants. These have now evolved to a sustaining set of international conferences with broad participation from academia and industry with a common interest in model-based process improvement. This was the 15th in the series of conferences organized by the SPICE User Group to increase knowledge and understanding of the International Standard and of the technique of process assessment.

The conference program featured invited keynote talks, research papers, and industry experience reports on the most relevant topics related to software process assessment and improvement; a significant focus this year were detailed studies of aspects of process implementation, assessment, and improvement, and the expansion in the range and variety of relevant process models. The technical research papers were selected for presentation following peer review by members of the Program Committee. In addition, a number of tutorials were hosted.

SPICE conferences have a long history of attracting attendees from industry and academia. This confirms that the conference covers topics that are up to date, important, and interesting. SPICE 2015 offered a unique forum for industry and academic professionals to discuss their needs and ideas in the area of process assessment and improvement and in related aspects of quality management.

On behalf of the SPICE 2015 conference Organizing Committee, we would like to thank all participants. Firstly all the authors, whose quality work is the essence of the conference, and the members of the Program Committee, who helped us with their expertise and diligence in reviewing all of the submissions. As we all know, organizing a conference requires the effort of many individuals. We wish to thank also all the members of our Organizing Committee, whose work and commitment were invaluable.

June 2015

Terry Rout
Rory V. O'Connor
Alec Dorling

Organization

General Chair

Alec Dorling — Impronova AB, Sweden

Program Chair

Terry Rout — Griffith University, Australia

Local Organizing Chair

Alec Dorling — Impronova AB, Sweden

Proceedings Chair

Rory V. O'Connor — Lero, Dublin City University, Ireland

Program Committee

Béatrix Barafort	Luxembourg
Luigi Buglione	Italy
Aileen Cater-Steel	Australia
Melanie Cheong	Australia
Gerhard Chroust	Austria
François Coallier	Canada
Tony Coletta	Italy
Onur Demirors	Turkey
Fabrizio Fabbrini	Italy
Dennis Goldenson	USA
Christiane Gresse von Wangenheim	Brazil
Victora Hailey	Canada
Linda Ibrahim	USA
Jørn Johansen	Denmark
Ravindra Joshi	India
Ho-Won Jung	South Korea
Giuseppe Lami	Italy
Marion Lepmets	Ireland
Catriona Mackie	UK
Antonia Mas Pichaco	Spain

Fergal McCaffery   Ireland
Tom McBride   Australia
Antanas Mitasiunas   Lithuania
Takeshige Miyoshi   Japan
Risto Nevalainen   Finland
Mark Paulk   USA
Saulius Ragaisos   Lithuania
Alain Renault   Luxembourg
Patricia Rodriguez-Dapena   Spain
Clenio Salviano   Brazil
Jean-Martin Simon   France
Fritz Stallinger   Austria
Timo Varkoi   Finland
Bharathi Vijayakumar   India
Murat Yilmaz   Turkey

Local Organizing Committee

Alec Dorling   Impronova AB, Sweden
Dr. Maria Dorling   Impronova AB, Sweden
Dr. Miroslaw Staron   Chalmers | University of Gothenburg, Sweden

Acknowledgments

The conference organizers wish to acknowledge the assistance and support of the SPICE User Group, SPICE 2015 Program Committee, and reviewers in contributing to a successful conference.

Contents

Industrial Frameworks

An Empirical Study on Software Process Improvement in Automotive 3
    Fabio Falcini and Giuseppe Lami

Safety Critical Software Process Assessment: How MDevSPICE®
Addresses the Challenge of Integrating Compliance and Capability 13
    Paul Clarke, Marion Lepmets, Alec Dorling, and Fergal McCaffery

Software Process Improvement and Roadmapping – A Roadmap for
Implementing IEC 62304 in Organizations Developing and Maintaining
Medical Device Software. 19
    Peter Rust, Derek Flood, and Fergal McCaffery

Implementation and Assessment

Matching Context Aware Software Testing Design Techniques
to ISO/IEC/IEEE 29119. 33
    Santiago Matalonga, Felyppe Rodrigues, and Guilherme H. Travassos

The Development and Validation of a Roadmap for Traceability 45
    Gilbert Regan, Derek Flood, and Fergal McCaffery

Quantitative Requirements Prioritization from a Pre-development
Perspective. 58
    Enrico Johansson, Daniel Bergdahl, Jan Bosch,
    and Helena Holmström Olsson

Evaluation of Software Mediated Process Assessments for IT Service
Management. 72
    Anup Shrestha, Aileen Cater-Steel, Mark Toleman, and Terry Rout

Process Improvement

Emphasis on Personal Attributes/Skills to Produce 'Quality' Assessment
Outputs That Lead to Steady Generation of SPI Effects 87
    Takeshige Miyoshi

Proposing an ISO/IEC 15504 Based Process Improvement Method
for the Government Domain. 100
    Ebru Gökalp and Onur Demirörs

Evaluating VSEs Viewpoint and Sentiment Towards the ISO/IEC 29110
Standard: A Two Country Grounded Theory Study.................... 114
   *Mary-Luz Sanchez-Gordon, Rory V. O'Connor,
and Ricardo Colomo-Palacios*

Agile Processes

LAPIS – LOGO Agile Process Improvement System 131
   Tuğrul Tekbulut, Ayhan İnal, and Betül Doğanay

A Reference Model for Software Agility Assessment: AgilityMod 145
   Ozden Ozcan-Top and Onur Demirörs

Observations on Utilising Usability Maturity Model-Human Centredness
Scale in Integrating Agile Development Processes and User
Centred Design.. 159
   Dina Salah, Richard Paige, and Paul Cairns

Assessment and Maturity Models

Causes of Continuity and Participation Problems in Process Improvement
with Staged Maturity Models...................................... 177
   Algan Uskarci and Onur Demirörs

Towards a Maturity Model for ISO/IEC 20000-1 Based on the TIPA for
ITIL Process Capability Assessment Model 188
   Alain Renault, Stéphane Cortina, and Béatrix Barafort

Process and Education

Towards the Development of a Framework for Encouraging the Learning
of SPICE Model by Using Knowledge Graphs...................... 203
   Alvaro Fernández Del Carpio and Leonardo Bermón Angarita

Towards a Serious Game to Teach ISO/IEC 12207 Software Lifecycle
Process: An Interactive Learning Approach 217
   Ufuk Aydan, Murat Yilmaz, and Rory V. O'Connor

Short Papers

An Approach for Combining SPICE and SCRUM in Software
Development Projects 233
   Detlev Hantke

A Layered Framework for Managing Access to Customer-provided
Process Requirements 239
   Ricardo Eíto-Brun

How to Certify the Very Small Entity Software Processes Using
ISO/IEC 29110... 245
   Patricia Rodríguez-Dapena and Miguel Francisco Buitrago-Botero

Author Index 253

Industrial Frameworks

An Empirical Study on Software Process Improvement in Automotive

Fabio Falcini and Giuseppe Lami(✉)

Istituto di Scienza e Tecnologie della Informazione, Consiglio Nazionale delle Ricerche,
Via Moruzzi, 1 56124 Pisa, Italy
{fabio.falcini,giuseppe.lami}@isti.cnr.it

Abstract. This paper presents the results of an empirical study on process improvement initiatives linked to management of software developments for the automotive industry. In this context the software development is mainly demanded to specialized software suppliers that are required by car makers to improve and measure the process quality of their projects by applying process models such as Automotive SPICE®.

The authors, as Automotive SPICE assessors, have directly observed and analyzed specific software process improvement opportunities during a significant number of assessments performed at several organizations.

This paper, that focuses specifically on the project management process, is the initial step of a wider study. Such a study aims at identifying common weaknesses in industrial projects having negative impact according Automotive SPICE. The study relies on data taken from several assessments performed world-wide and it shows the most occurring weaknesses in terms of the project management process base practices – such recurrent weaknesses that are then clustered appropriately and analyzed to provide insight in this crucial process.

Keywords: Software process improvement · Automotive · Automotive SPICE® · Project management

1 Introduction

Car OEMs (Original Equipment Manufacturer) are now turning their vehicles from mechanical devices into elaborated electronically controlled systems. As a result the software (with increased demand in terms of size and complexity) is a crucial car component since it is part of embedded systems called Electronic Control Units (ECU) that control electronically a large number of the vehicle functions. The number of ECUs, both for economic to luxury vehicle models, is remarkably increased during the last fifteen/twenty years.

In general, the software development is demanded to software suppliers that range from small-medium organizations to large and structured ones. It is remarkable to notice that small and medium organizations represent currently a significant part of the players in this challenging arena. In such a context project management and software engineering, initially underestimated sides of the ECU development projects, are today considered as crucial in the automotive industry. Software projects are required to meet increasingly demanding timing and quality objectives - it is interesting to remark that budget efficiency is also important but mass production can partially mitigate this aspect in some circumstances. In particular, the market expectations (it is a fact that the bulk of car issues currently come from electronics and software issues) and technology advances have produced a real need for improvement at managerial and technical levels in order to keep software developments on track, especially for SME small and medium-sized enterprises (SME).

In automotive, beyond the complexities of the embedded development, SW suppliers needs to accommodate tights schedules and the peculiarities of the vehicle development process that at very high level reflects the following paradigm:

Fig. 1. High-level paradigm of vehicle development phases

The aim of this paper is to present the results of an empirical study conducted using the data from a sample of assessments performed on twenty-three (23) organizations by the authors worldwide in the last five years. The empirical study is aimed at making explicit and analyzing commonalities in Automotive SPICE assessment findings observed by the authors related to project management process as it is a key aspect of development.

More specifically this paper focuses on a specific area (i.e. process) of the software development as described later. The paper is structured as follows:

- Section 2: Notes on Automotive SPICE®
- Section 3: The Methodological Approach
- Section 4: Empirical Study Results
- Section 5: Conclusions

2 Notes on the Automotive SPICE™ Model

SPICE (Software Process Improvement and Capability dEtermination) is an acronym that identifies the ISO/IEC 33000 standard series (that recently substituted the former ISO/IEC 15504 standard) [3]. In early 2000s an initiative was launched by the Procurement Forum with the principal European Car Makers, their assessors and representative bodies to address the problems related to software assessments in automotive. In the framework of this initiative, a Special Interest Group (SIG) has been founded with the aim to design a special version of the SPICE model (called Automotive SPICE) tailored on the needs and peculiarities of the automotive business area. The first results of the initiative was to create consensus on commonality of approach in order to avoid that suppliers face multiple assessments from multiple manufacturers using different models and criteria and consume resources that put additional pressure on delivery times. Furthermore, the focus on software capability determination by means of software process assessment has determined a common trend among the European Car Makers in using Automotive SPICE^{TM} as a mean for determining a supplier's qualification mechanism.

Nowadays Automotive SPICE®, as a de-facto process standard, is used by car makers to push software process improvement among their ECU and software suppliers [4], [5]. Many of the car makers are using also this standard to assess supplier capabilities and are requiring the achievement of specific rating. Thus it provides both a scheme for evaluating the capability of software processes and a path for their improvement. In extreme synthesis the four basic pillars of Automotive SPICE® are: Process Reference Model (PRM) [2], Process Assessment Model (PAM) [1], Measurement Framework and Assessment Scope:

1. **PRM**: it is a model comprising definition of processes in a life-cycle described in terms of "process purpose" and "process outcomes", together with an architecture describing the relationships between processes. In practice, the PRM contains the set of the descriptions of the processes that should be assessed.

2. **PAM**: it is a model suitable for the purpose of assessing process capability, based on one or more PRMs with a two-dimensional view. In one dimension, it describes a set of process entities that relate to the processes defined in the specific PRM (it is called Process Dimension); in the other dimension the PAM describes capabilities that relate to the process capability levels and process attributes.

3. **Measurement Framework**: The rating of the "capability" starts from the lowest level (Level 0) means that not all processes in the scope are adequately performed. In Level 1 all important documents are available, in Level 2 everything is systematically planned and tracked, in Level 3 there are uniform guidelines for the complete organization, and in Levels 4 and 5 the processes are statistically measured and optimized. It is interesting to highlight that current industrial requirement ranges from Level 1 to Level 3. The determination of the capability of a process is obtained by means of the rating of process attributes (some process specific – the Base Practices - and others generic – the Generic Practices). The scale of such a rating is composed of four values: N (Not achieved), P (Partially achieved), L (Largely achieved), and F (Fully achieved).

4. **Assessment Scope**: it is a subset of the processes contained in Automotive SPICE® where each process is associated with a target process

capability level. In particular the Hersteller Initiative Software (HIS) Scope is a subset of the processes contained in Automotive SPICE®, which will be assessed by each manufacturer. In the meantime, the HIS Scope of the Automotive SPICE® has been adopted by other industries as a reference for process improvement initiatives and scope for assessments.

The following picture highlights the HIS scope of Automotive SPICE® in the context of all ISO/IEC IS 15504 and Automotive SPICE® processes.

In Table 1 the whole Automotive SPICE PRM is presented, the processes in bold are those belonging to the HIS assessment scope.

Table 1. HIS Assessment Scope

Process Id.	Process Name	Process Id.	Process Name
ACQ.3	Contract agreement	SUP.8	**Configuration Management**
ACQ.4	**Supplier monitoring**	SUP.9	**Problem resolution management**
ACQ.11	Technical requirements	**SUP.10**	**Change request management**
ACQ.12	Legal and administrative Requirements	PIM.3	Process improvement
ACQ.13	Project requirements	**ENG.1**	**Requirement elicitation**
ACQ.14	Request for proposals	**ENG.2**	**System requirements analysis**
ACQ.15	Supplier qualification	**ENG.3**	**System architectural design**
MAN.3	**Project management**	**ENG.4**	**Software requirements analysis**
MAN.5	Risk management	**ENG.5**	**Software design**
MAN.6	Measurement	**ENG.6**	**Software construction**
SPL.1	Supplier tendering	**ENG.7**	**Software integration test**
SPL.2	Product Release	**ENG.8**	**Software testing**
SUP.1	**Quality Assurance**	**ENG.9**	**System integration test**
SUP.2	Verification	**ENG.10**	**System testing**
SUP.4	Joint Review	REU.2	Reuse program management
SUP.7	Documentation		

From Table 1 results that processes in Automotive SPICE® (the ones with marked with the letter A on the left) are conveniently grouped and large in number. The rational behind the HIS scope is to limit the impact on the practitioners by selecting the core of the engineering processes and only other few fundamental processes. As a matter of fact MAN.3 is the only process in management process group.

3 The Methodological Approach

During the last five years the authors, in the capacity of qualified Automotive SPICE Principal Assessor (according to the IntACS international assessor certification scheme) [6], have performed more than thirty Automotive SPICE assessments of several organizations producing software-intensive systems for the automotive industry.

Typically these Automotive SPICE assessments have targeted the HIS scope (or variants of HIS scope) in several domain (e.g. body electronics, lighting, closures...) and they had one or more of the following purposes:

- ➢ Perform Gap Analysis for benchmarking
- ➢ Measure the progress after a SW Process Improvement effort
- ➢ Supplier process capability rating

as the typical software process improvement path follows the following pattern:

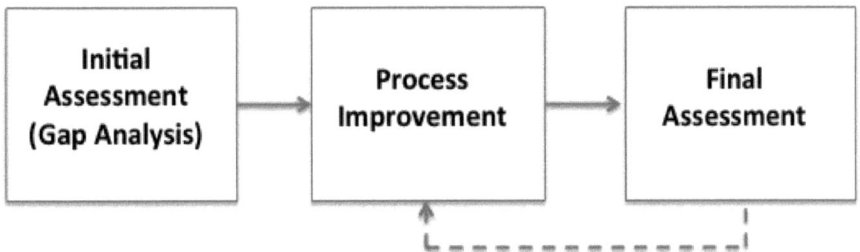

Fig. 2. Typical process Improvement path

Table A.1 in Annex A summarizes in anonymous way the database that supports this study – although the number is limited in number (23) and geographical distribution (Italy 18, China 2, Korea 2, Israel 1) it can be considered meaningful by all means due to the nature of the subject under analysis. Yet the following outcomes have not a statistical validity and are based on empirical observations.

It is key to remark that the organizations have been assessed:

- Before and after improvement (10 organizations) for a total of 21 assessments
- Before implementing a structured improvement initiative (6 organizations) for a total of 6 assessments
- After implementing a structured improvement initiative (7 organizations)

targeting a total of 42 projects (some of them with ISO 26262 norm requirements [8] for functional safety of road vehicles). From a size point of views the organizations ranges from small (6), medium (11), large (6) ones.

This empirical study, that focuses on Project Management process (MAN.3) only, represents the starting point of an wider analysis aiming at getting a complete "in practice" view of the software process improvement internals in the automotive industry.

During the assessments, data on the processes in scope are collected in different ways, including interviews and document analysis and these data are assessed (using their expert judgment) against a set of indicators provided by the Automotive SPICE model itself. These indicators are the so-called Base Practices (process-specific) and the Generic Practices (applicable to all processes). In context of process improvement it is important to remark that the assessment activity is not limited to a mere rating of process indicators, but it includes also the provision of high-level improvement guidance for the projects under assessment. Assessments also enrich the assessors by exposing them to precious "behind-doors" experience of real projects.

The following step-wise approach has been adopted in this study:

S.1 the organizations assessed by the authors are classified in terms of product domain, organization size (omitted from annex A for confidentiality), location, and type of assessment.

S.2 the assessment results have been analyzed in order to identify those Base Practices rated unsatisfactorily (N or L). Such Base Practices have been reported in tabular format.

S.3 The rationales of Base Practices weaknesses have been investigated and clustered, when possible, following homogeneity criteria.

Confidentiality issues has been considered and carefully addressed.

4 Empirical Study Evidences and Results

According to what stated in Section 3. in this paper the gaps related to the Project Management process (MAN.3) are taken into account. The Project Management process is a key process for an organization developing software because it addresses the *"identification, establishment, planning, co-ordination, monitoring and control of the activities, tasks, and resources necessary for a project to produce a product and/or service, in the context of the project's requirements and constraints"* [1], [7]. Consequently, this process allows an all-around view of the activities dealing with software development projects (in fact, MAN.3, usually the initial process to be addressed in a Automotive SPICE assessment, is used by assessors to get the complete picture of the project).

Table 2 reports the Base practices of the Project Management process (MAN.3) that have been found not fully achieved in the assessment performed on the Organizational Unit (OU) belonging to the study sample. The 'X' in a cell indicates that the rating of the corresponding Base practice has been not "Fully Achieved" or "Largely Achieved".

The weaknesses indicated in Table 2 have been analyzed in detail, according to the step S.3 of the study's methodological approach, and then the most recurrent one are linked to a clustering system built using the common basis of such process weaknesses that the authors call Gap Clusters (GC).

The data reported on Table 2 show a concentration of weaknesses for the following Base practices:

MAN.3 BP.3: Determine and maintain estimates for project attributes;

MAN.3 BP.6: Define and maintain project schedule;

MAN.3 BP.8: Establish project plan;

MAN. 3BP.10: Monitor project attributes.

Table 2. Best Practices weaknesses for MAN.3 process

OU Id.	MAN.3 Project Management											
	BP1	BP2	BP3	BP4	BP5	BP6	BP7	BP8	BP9	BP10	BP11	BP12
1	P	P	P	P	L	P	L	P	L	P	P	L
2	F	P	P	P	L	P	L	P	L	P	L	L
3	F	F	L	F	F	F	F	F	F	F	F	F
4	F	F	L	F	F	F	F	F	F	L	F	F
5	F	F	L	L	L	F	F	F	L	L	F	F
6	F	F	P	P	F	P	F	F	F	L	F	F
7	F	L	L	L	F	L	F	F	F	P	F	L
8	F	P	P	F	F	P	F	F	F	L	F	F
9	P	P	P	F	F	F	L	P	L	L	P	F
10	F	F	L	F	F	F	F	F	F	L	F	F
11	F	F	L	F	F	P	F	F	F	L	F	F
12	P	P	P	P	L	P	L	P	L	P	P	L
13	F	P	P	P	L	P	L	P	L	P	L	L
14	F	F	L	F	F	F	F	F	F	F	F	F
15	F	F	L	F	F	F	F	F	F	L	F	F
16	F	F	L	L	L	F	F	F	L	L	F	F
17	F	F	P	P	F	P	F	F	F	L	F	F
18	F	L	L	L	F	L	F	F	F	P	F	L
19	MAN.3 not in scope											
20	F	F	L	F	L	F	F	F	F	L	L	L
21	F	L	L	L	L	L	F	P	P	L	L	F
22	F	P	P	P	L	P	F	P	P	P	L	L
23	P	P	P	P	L	P	F	P	P	P	L	L

The investigation on the rationales of these Base Practices weaknesses on the basis of the assessment outcomes in Assessment Reports, determined the following gap clusters (GC):

GC a) Operative scheduling definition and control is informal [MAN,3 BP.6].

GC b) Poor project planning update and dissemination [MAN.3 BP.8].

GC c) Lack of estimations [MAN.3 BP.3].

GC d) Poor effort management [MAN.3 BP.8, MAN.3 BP.10].

In the following, the clusters listed above are discussed:

The gap clusters a) and b) are mainly due to the adoption of inadequate approaches, tools and means to support the planning and the monitoring of project activities are a substantial source of process issues. In fact such an inadequate infrastructural support often leads to a general habit to separate the actual project planning and control (performed informally and with few evidences) with respect to the documented project planning and control (documents and charts are not always used in practice and often are just maintained for process compliance reasons or for interfacing the customer). Such a habit causes two negative effects: 1) lack of evidences and poor availability of information about the actual planning (re-planning) and control of the project activities and tasks; 2) waste of effort for maintaining formal document and charts, not always actually used.

The cluster c) is primarily due to the fact that an estimation process is not explicitly established and made available. In particular, the estimations are often made (but not documented) by senior staff on the basis of their experience only, without any support of estimation methodologies nor historical data.

The cluster d) is mainly due to neglecting the effort (intended as man hours/days) as fundamental project attribute to control and predict the project performance; focus is often just on addressing timing and cost aspects of the projects.

In order to discuss the frequency of the Clusters above, their occurrence in the outcomes of the gap analysis/assessments performed on the OU belonging to study sample is represented in the Table 3. With reference to the Table in Annex A, the X means that, for a specific organization unit (OU) corresponding to a column some gaps related to the corresponding Gap Cluster (GC) have been pointed out during the gap analysis/assessment.

Table 3. Clusters occurring in OU assessment/gap analysis results

G	OU																						
	1	2	3	4	5	6	7	8	9	10	11	12	13	14	15	16	17	18	19	20	21	22	23
a)		X		X	X		X	X	X	X			X		X	X						X	X
b)		X		X	X	X	X	X	X				X		X	X		X			X	X	X
c)	X	X	X	X	X	X	X	X	X				X		X	X		X			X	X	X
d)	X		X	X	X			X	X							X						X	X

5 Conclusions and Next Steps

This paper contains the results of an empirical study aimed at identifying, on the basis of a sample of Automotive SPICE assessments, some common weaknesses related to the performance of the Project Management process (identified as MAN.3 in the Automotive SPICE terminology).

The study relies on data taken from a sample of 23 assessments performed by the authors world-wide, and follows a well defined the methodological approach.

The analysis of the most occurring weaknesses in terms of Base Practices rating allowed the identification of clusters of rationales of such weaknesses. The resulting set of rationales represent an useful insight (given the fact that related literature is almost totally missing) that can be beneficial for whole software process improvement community, because it can be used as a reference for process improvement efforts.

The study reported in this paper is to be considered as the starting point of a wider study involving, not only the MAN.3 process, but also the other processes belonging to the HIS scope of Automotive SPICE. Once the results of the full study will be available they may represent the first extensive analysis of improvement drivers for the automotive software community.

One of the objectives of the future deployments of this study is to extend the approach and the corresponding clustering, by including also additional dimensions such as the OUs and of the project types used in the assessments (as for instance the size of the OU, the geographical location, the domain of the projects).

References

1. Automotive SPICE, Process Assessment Model (PAM) v2.5 (2010)
2. Automotive SPICE, Process Reference Model (PRM) v4.5 (2010)
3. ISO/IEC 33000 – Information Technology – Process Assessment, International Organization for Standardization (2013)
4. Hoermann, K., Mueller, M., Dittman, L, Zimmer, J.: Automotive SPICE in Practice: Surviving Implementation and Assessment. Rocky Noor (2008). ISBN 978-1933952291
5. Fabbrini, F., Fusani, M., Lami, G., Sivera, E.: A SPICE-based Supplier Qualification Mechanism in Automotive Industry. Software Process Improvement and Practice Journal. **12**, 523–528 (2007). Wiley InterScience
6. www.intacs.info
7. Project Management Institute: A Guide to the Project Management Body of Knowledge, 4th edn. Project Management Institute, ANSI/PMI Standard 99-001-2008 (2008)
8. ISO 26262 - Road Vehicles - Functional Safety, International Organization for Standardization (2011)

Annex A

Table 4. A.1 Synthetic representation of the empirical study sample.

OU Id.	Product Domain	OU Size	Project Team Size	Company Size	Location	Gap An. Assessm.	Year Scope
1	Body electronics	10	7		Italy	YY	2013 ENG.4, ENG.5, ENG.6, ENG.8, MAN.3, SUP.1, SUP.8, SUP.9, SUP.10 (CL2)
2	Infotainment & Telematics	27	12		China	NY	2014 ENG.2, ENG.3, ENG.4, ENG.5, ENG.6, ENG.7, ENG.8, ENG.9, ENG.10, MAN.3, MAN.5, MAN.6, SUP.1, SUP.8, SUP.9, SUP.10 (CL2)
3	Electric vehicle Control	1000	15		South Korea	YY	2014 ENG.2, ENG.3, ENG.4, ENG.5, ENG.6, ENG.7, ENG.8, ENG.,9, ENG.10, MAN.3, SUP.1, SUP.8, SUP.9, SUP.10 (CL2)
4	Electric vehicle Control	18	15		South Korea	YY	2014 ENG.2, ENG.3, ENG.4, ENG.5, ENG.6, ENG.7, ENG.8, ENG.9, ENG.10, MAN.3, SUP.8, SUP.9, SUP.10 (CL2)
5	Electric Steering	10	5		Italy	YN	2014 ACQ.4, ENG.1, ENG.2, ENG.3, ENG.4, ENG.5, ENG.6, MAN.3, MAN.5, SUP.1, SUP.4, SUP.8, SUP.9, SUP.10, SPL.2 (CL2)
6	Body electronics	5	5		Italy	NY	2013 ENG.1, ENG.2, ENG.3, ENG.4, ENG.5, ENG.6, ENG.7, ENG.8, ENG.,9, MAN.3, MAN.5, SUP.1, SUP.4, SUP.8, SPL.2 (CL2)
7	Body electronics	31	12		Italy	NY	2012 ACQ.4, ENG.1, ENG.2, ENG.3, ENG.4, ENG.5, ENG.6, ENG.7, ENG.8, ENG.9, ENG.10, MAN.3, MAN.5, SUP.1, SUP.8, SUP.9, SUP.10 (CL2)
8	Cooling Fan	10	8		Italy	YN	2011 ENG.2, ENG.3, ENG.4, ENG.5, ENG.6, ENG.7, ENG.8, ENG.,9, ENG.10, MAN.3, SUP.1, SUP.8, SUP.9, SUP.10 (CL2)
9	Motor Control	15	10		Italy	YN	2011 ENG.2, ENG.3, ENG.4, ENG.5, ENG.6, ENG.7, ENG.8, ENG.,9, ENG.10, MAN.3, SUP.1, SUP.8, SUP.9, SUP.10 (CL2)
10	Cooling Fan	10	9		Italy	YY	2013-2014 ENG.2, ENG.3, ENG.4, ENG.5, ENG.6, ENG.7, ENG.8, ENG.,9, ENG.10, MAN.3, SUP.1, SUP.8, SUP.9, SUP.10 (CL2)
11	Lighting Control	10	6		Italy	YY	2013-2014 ENG.2, ENG.3, ENG.4, ENG.5, ENG.6, ENG.7, ENG.8, ENG.,9, ENG.10, MAN.3, SUP.1, SUP.8, SUP.9, SUP.10 (CL3)
12	Window lift	50+	10		China	YY	2014 ENG.2, ENG.3, ENG.4, ENG.5, ENG.6, ENG.7, ENG.8, ENG.,9, ENG.10, MAN.3, SUP.1, SUP.8, SUP.9, SUP.10 (CL2)
13	Driving Assistance	100+	20+		Israel	NY	2013 ENG.2, ENG.3, ENG.4, ENG.5, ENG.6, ENG.7, ENG.8, ENG.,9, ENG.10, MAN.3, SUP.1, SUP.8, SUP.9, SUP.10 (CL2)
14	Closures	10	7		Italy	NY	2013 ENG.2, ENG.3, ENG.4, ENG.5, ENG.6, ENG.7, ENG.8, ENG.,9, ENG.10, MAN.3, MAN.5, MAN.6, SUP.1, SUP.8, SUP.9, SUP.10 (CL2)
15	Electric Pumps	10	7		Italy	YY	2013 ENG.2, ENG.3, ENG.4, ENG.5, ENG.6, ENG.7, ENG.8, ENG.,9, ENG.10, MAN.3, SUP.1, SUP.8, SUP.9, SUP.10 (CL2)
16	Cooling Fan	5	5		Italy	YY	2012 ENG.2, ENG.3, ENG.4, ENG.5, ENG.6, ENG.7, ENG.8, ENG.,9, ENG.10, MAN.3, MAN.5, MAN.6, SUP.1, SUP.8, SUP.9, SUP.10 (CL2)
17	Instrument Cluster	6	7		Italy	NY	2011 ENG.2, ENG.3, ENG.4, ENG.5, ENG.6, ENG.7, ENG.8, ENG.,9, ENG.10, MAN.3, SUP.1, SUP.8, SUP.9, SUP.10 (CL2)
18	Body electronics	20	7		Italy	NY	2012 ENG.2, ENG.3, ENG.4, ENG.5, ENG.6,, ENG.7, ENG.8,, ENG.9, ENG.10, SUP.1, SUP.8, SUP.9, SUP.10, MAN.3 (CL3)
19	Window lift	5	4		Italy	YY	2012 ENG.4, ENG.5, ENG.6, ENG.7, ENG.8 (CL2)
20	Electric vehicle Control	20	8		Italy	YY	2010-2012 ENG.2, ENG.3, ENG.4, ENG.5, ENG.6, ENG.7, ENG.8, ENG.,9, ENG.10, MAN.3, SUP.1, SUP.8, SUP.9, SUP.10 (CL2)
21	Instrument Cluster	10	5		Italy	YN	2010 MAN.3, SUP.1, SUP.8, SUP.9, SUP.10, ENG.4, ENG.5, ENG.6, ENG.7, ENG.8 (CL1)
22	Instrument Cluster	10	5		Italy	YN	2010 MAN.3, SUP.1, SUP.8, SUP.10 ENG.2, ENG.3, ENG.9, ENG.10 (CL1)
23	Electric vehicle Control	10	6		Italy	YN	2010 ENG.2, ENG.3, ENG.4, ENG.5, ENG.6, ENG.7, ENG.8, ENG.,9, ENG.10, MAN.3, SUP.1, SUP.8, SUP.9, SUP.10 (CL1)

Safety Critical Software Process Assessment: How MDevSPICE® Addresses the Challenge of Integrating Compliance and Capability

Paul Clarke[✉], Marion Lepmets, Alec Dorling, and Fergal McCaffery

Regulated Software Research Centre, Dundalk Institute of Technology, Dundalk, Ireland
{paul.clarke,marion.lepmets,alec.dorling,
fergal.mccaffery}@dkit.ie

Abstract. One of the primary outcomes of a software process assessment is visibility of the capability of a software process which among other things, informs us of the ability of a process to deliver consistent product quality levels. In safety critical domains, such as the medical device sector, high product quality – and particularly high product safety - is an important consideration. To address this safety concern, the medical device sector traditionally employs audits to determine compliance to software process standards and guidance. Unlike an audit which results in a pass/fail outcome, an assessment provides a process capability profile which identifies areas for improvement and enables a comparison with broader best practice. MDevSPICE® integrates the various medical device software standards and guidance within the infrastructure of a SPICE assessment model, thus encompassing aspects of compliance and capability. This paper describes some of the key enablers of this integration.

Keywords: Safety critical software · Medical device software · Software process improvement · Software process assessment · MDevSPICE®

1 Introduction

Safety critical software is software which if not operating correctly can result in harm or even death to humans [1]. It is therefore the case that safety critical software development should take additional steps beyond general software development to specifically address safety considerations. Medical device software is of a safety critical nature and regulators have implemented legal requirements (or regulations) which must be met prior to placing a device on the market. Whereas general software development studies have demonstrated that software developers may be unwilling to embrace a strong software process focus [2], such processes are a mandatory requirement in the medical device sector. These regulations are typically regional in application, with the Food and Drug Administration (FDA) and the European Commission (EC) regulating for the US and EU respectively.

In the case of the EU, medical device regulation is contained in the Medical Device Directive (MDD) 93/42/EEC [3], the Active Implantable Medical Device Directive

(AIMDD) 90/385/EEC [4], and the In-vitro Diagnostic (IVD) Medical Device Directive 98/79/EC [5] – with MDD 2007/47/EC [6] amending these earlier directives. In the US, the FDA advances medical device regulation through Code of Federal Regulation (CFR) Title 21, Chapter I, Subchapter H, Part 820 [7]. In both the EU and the US regulations, provisions are made for classifying medical devices depending on the role of the device, ranging from Class I to Class III depending on the extent of the role of the device in supporting or sustaining human life. Various standards and guidance exists to support manufacturers developing medical devices in adhering to the regulations, and compliance to these standards will generally enable market access. Primary among these standards are ISO 14971 [8], ISO 13485 [9], IEC TR 80002-1 [10], IEC 62304:2006 [11], IEC TR 80002-3 [12], IEC 62366 [13], IEC 60601-1 [14], IEC 82304 [15]), the FDA guidance documents on premarket submission [16], off-the-shelf software use [17] and software validation [18]. These standards and guidance documents are presented in Figure 1 and in further detail in [19].

Despite the existence of regulation, standards and guidance for medical device software, the proportion of medical devices being recalled owing to software errors is growing. From a base of less than 10% for most of the 1990s, the proportion of medical device recalls attributable to software errors hit 24% in 2011 [20] and this trend would appear to be set to continue upwards. Although one of the reasons for this growth is undoubtedly the increasing use of software in medical devices, other factors such as inadequacies in the software development process could have a role to play. To help address this undesirably upward trend in the proportion of medical device recalls attributable to software errors, the introduction of a SPICE-based process assessment may be of benefit, especially given the significant positive impact that SPICE models have had within other safety critical sectors, e.g. Automotive SPICE [21].

2 Integrating Medical Device Standards into SPICE

While there are potentially significant benefits to be derived from the use of SPICE based assessment in the medical device sector, the task of integrating the existing medical device standards and guidance into the SPICE framework is a challenging one. Medical device standards and guidance are rich in detail, varied in origin, and sometimes with overlapping content. As a result, a significant burden of effort is required to integrate these disparate sources into a single, comprehensive framework. Furthermore, SPICE frameworks do not typically trace the origin of different process requirements – rather, a SPICE assessment is performed against the accumulated best practice that is incorporated into the framework. Therefore, the following significant challenge emerged during the development of MDevSPICE®:

> **Challenge:** How can the origin of different process requirements be carried forward into a SPICE framework such that assessments can also assist manufacturers in addressing their basic standards compliance requirements?

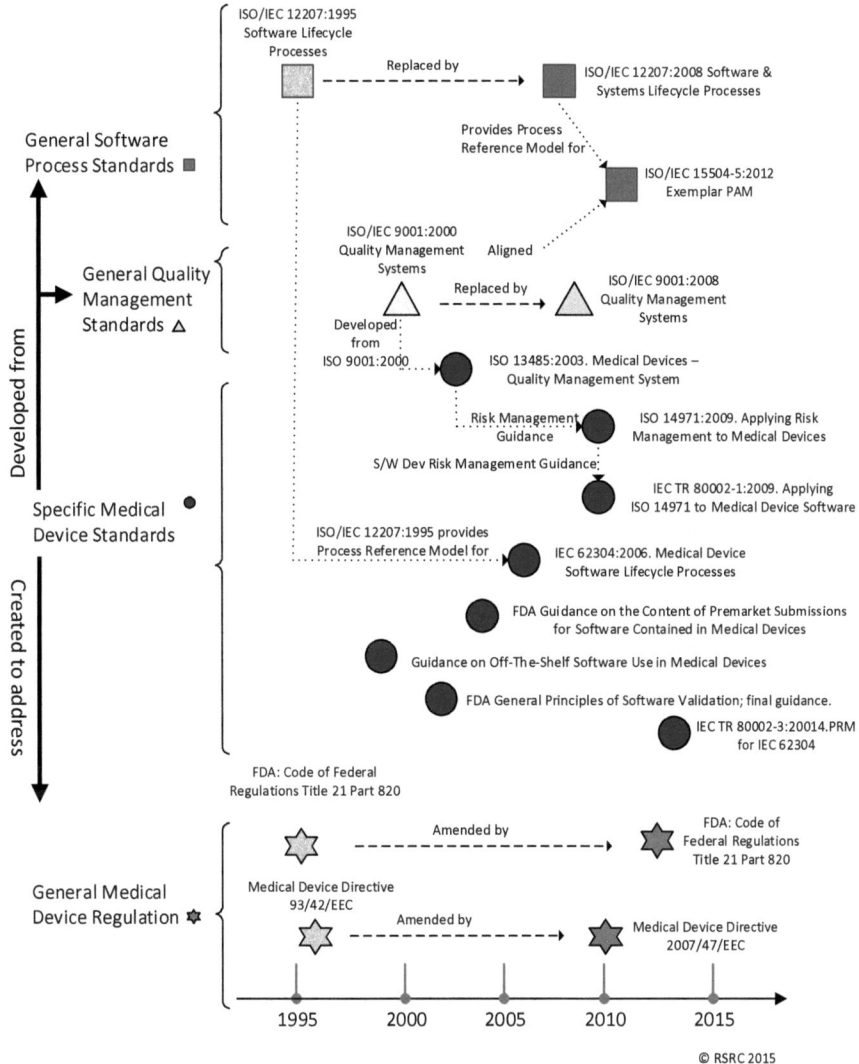

Fig. 1. Medical Device Standards and Regulation

2.1 Process Lineage

To address the challenge identified above, we determined to identify the source for various specific standards and guidance contained within the MDevSPICE® Process Assessment Model (PAM). All MDevSPICE® assessments operate upon the basic assumption that IEC 62304 is within the scope of an assessment – as it is the globally recognised standard that should be adopted when performing medical device software development. Therefore, IEC 62304 requirements form the foundation of MDevSPICE® [22]. In fact, an important foundation to this was the publication of IEC 80002-3 [12] by the developers of MDevSPICE® as a Process Reference model for IEC 62304. IEC 80002-3 was then used as the starting point for the development of the MDevSPICE® PAM. Software safety classification (detailed in IEC 62304) is a concept similar to medical device classification, with three classes existing and these being determined based upon the worst possible consequence in the case of a software failure.

Building on IEC 62304, additional details incorporated from aligned standards and guidance documents retain information regarding the source of such details. For example, in the case of the Software Architectural Design process, when describing the software architecture (which is the first base practice for this process), there is an explicit reference to an item of FDA Guidance on the use of off the shelf software, specifically addressing the treatment of Software Of Unknown Provenance (SOUP) as follows:

> **FDA on OTS:** *identify the expected design limitations of the SOUP Software.*

There are many further examples of such additions and indications in the MDevSPICE® PAM, for instance, in the Software Requirements Analysis process, there is an addition to base practice five *Verify Software Requirements*, as follows:

> **FDA on Validation:** *A software requirements traceability analysis should be conducted to trace software requirements to (and from) risk analysis results.*

While software process adaptation is considered advantageous in a general sense [23], it is however a requirement for medical device manufacturers since regulation (and corresponding standards and guidance) is subject to change. In this respect, MDevSPICE® is of particular benefit to manufactures. Through our work in the Regulated Software Research Centre, the creators of MDevSPICE® will continue to work with the international standards organisations to develop and improve standards and guidance, with corresponding updates being further applied to the MDevSPICE® framework. Thus, manufacturers can continually adopt MDevSPICE® for the purpose of staying abreast of standards and guidance evolution.

2.2 Assessment Questions

To further aid MDevSPICE® Assessors, a suite of detailed questions has been developed as a counterpart to the PAM. The detailed questions are directly linked to the PAM, with specific questions designed to address aspects of the PAM that have been incorporated from sources other than IEC 62304 and which therefore could be important within the context of determining approximate standard or guidance compliance. It should be noted that it is not the intention to use MDevSPICE® assessments to certify compliance to individual standards. Instead, MDevSPICE® is used to determine the capability of the software development process relative to the accumulated best practice information available. Having process lineage to individual source standards and guidance, and providing a set of corresponding questions does however permit a reasonably accurate approximation to standards compliance and it is possible that in the fullness of time and subject to robust validation, MDevSPICE® could concurrently address the capability consideration that is central to all SPICE assessments (and which enables targeted process improvement and supplier selection) in tandem with undertaking a compliance audit (which would enable market access).

3 Conclusion

Safety critical software development is often subject to regulation, with that regulation being realized through the implementation of associated standards and guidance. The aim of regulations is to reduce the risk of harm to humans in so far as is possible. This is achieved through the adoption of a robust software development process – with such a process effectively increasing product quality and thereby safety. Process assessment frameworks such as SPICE have been designed to achieve (among other things) higher levels of product quality and have been used to good effect in safety critical domains such as the automotive sector. Therefore, MDevSPICE® was developed for the medical device sector to deliver a view on process robustness though the capability lens, while simultaneously providing an approximation to standards and guidance compliance. However, standards compliance and process capability are not necessarily natural bed-fellows, and the creation of MDevSPICE® has had to incorporate some innovations to enable the integration of both concerns. Specifically in this respect, MDevSPICE® retains linkage to the source standards. To further enable the harmonization of compliance and capability considerations, the MDevSPICE® PAM has an associated set of questions that align with the process components in the PAM. Through the MDevSPICE® process question set, MDevSPICE® Assessors can consistently examine both process capability and standards alignment in a single engagement, and this, we believe, represents an important step forward for medical device software development.

Acknowledgments. This research is supported by Enterprise Ireland and the European Regional Development Fund (ERDF) under the National Strategic Reference Framework (NSRF) 2007-2013, grant number CF/2012/2631, and in part by the Science Foundation Ireland Principal Investigator Programme, grant number 08/IN.1/I2030 and by Lero - the Irish Software Research Centre (http://www.lero.ie) grant 10/CE/I1855 & 13/RC/20194.

References

1. Turk, D., France, R., Rumpe, B.: Limitations of agile software processes. In: Proceedings of Third International Conference on eXtreme Programming and Agile Processes in Software Engineering Italy (2002)
2. Clarke, P., O'Connor, R.V., Yilmaz, M.: A hierarchy of SPI activities for software SMEs: results from ISO/IEC 12207-based SPI assessments. In: Mas, A., Mesquida, A., Rout, T., O'Connor, R.V., Dorling, A. (eds.) SPICE 2012. CCIS, vol. 290, pp. 62–74. Springer, Heidelberg (2012)
3. European Commission: Directive 93/42/EEC of the European Parliament and of the Council concerning medical devices, in OJ o L 247 of 2007-09-21. EC, Brussels, Belgium (1993)

4. European Commission: Council directive 90/385/EEC on active implantable medical devices (AIMDD). Brussels, Belgium (1990)
5. European Commission: Directive 98/79/EC of the European parliament and of the council of 27 October 1998 on in vitro diagnostic medical devices. Brussels, Belgium (1998)
6. European Commission: Directive 2007/47/EC of the European Parliament and of the Council concerning medical devices, OJ no L247 2007-09-21. EC: Brussels, Belgium (2007)
7. FDA: Chapter I - Food and drug administration, department of health and human services subchapter H - Medical devices, Part 820 - Quality system regulation. http://www.accessdata.fda.gov/scripts/cdrh/cfdocs/cfcfr/CFRSearch.cfm?CFRPart=820 (cited June 03, 2015)
8. ISO 14971:2007, Medical Devices — Application of risk management to medical devices. ISO, Geneva (2007)
9. ISO 13485:2003, Medical devices — Quality management systems — Requirements for regulatory purposes. ISO, Geneva (2003)
10. IEC/TR 80002-1:2009, Medical device software Part 1: Guidance on the application of ISO 14971 to medical device software. BSI, London (2009)
11. IEC 62304:2006, Medical device software—Software life cycle processes. IEC, Geneva (2006)
12. IEC/TR 80002-3:2014, Medical Device Software - Part 3: Process reference model for medical device software life cycle processes (IEC 62304). ISO: Geneva, Switzerland (2014)
13. IEC 62366:2007, Medical devices - Application of usability engineering to medical devices. IEC, Geneva (2007)
14. BS EN 60601-1:2005 Medical electrical equipment – Part 1: General requirements for basic safety and essential performance. IEC, Geneva (2005)
15. IEC/CD 82304:2014, Health Software - Part 1: General Requirements for Product Safety. ISO, Geneva (2014)
16. US FDA Center for Devices and Radiological Health: Guidance for the Content of Premarket Submissions for Software Contained in Medical Devices. CDRH, Rockville (2005)
17. US FDA Center for Devices and Radiological Health: Off-The-Shelf Software Use in Medical Devices; Guidance for Industry, medical device Reviewers and Compliance. CDRH, Rockville (1999)
18. US FDA Center for Devices and Radiological Health: General Principles of Software Validation; Final Guidance for Industry and FDA Staff. CDRH, Rockville (2002)
19. Lepmets, M., Clarke, P., McCaffery, F., Finnegan, A., Dorling, A.: Development of MDevSPICE® - the Medical Device Software Process Assessment Framework. Journal of Software: Evolution and Process (To appear)
20. FDA: FDA News on Software Failures Responsible for 24% of all Medical Device Recalls (2012). http://www.fdanews.com/newsletter/article?articleId=147391&issueId=15890 (cited June 03, 2015)
21. Automotive SIG, Automotive SPICE Process Assessment V 2.2 (August 21, 2005)
22. McCaffery, F., Clarke, P., Lepmets, M.: A lightweight assessment method for medical device software processes. In: Mitasiunas, A., Rout, T., O'Connor, R.V., Dorling, A. (eds.) SPICE 2014. CCIS, vol. 477, pp. 144–156. Springer, Heidelberg (2014)
23. Clarke, P., O'Connor, R.V.: An approach to evaluating software process adaptation. In: O'Connor, R.V., Rout, T., McCaffery, F., Dorling, A. (eds.) SPICE 2011. CCIS, vol. 155, pp. 28–41. Springer, Heidelberg (2011)

Software Process Improvement and Roadmapping – A Roadmap for Implementing IEC 62304 in Organizations Developing and Maintaining Medical Device Software

Peter Rust[✉], Derek Flood, and Fergal McCaffery

Regulated Software Research Centre and Lero,
Dundalk Institute of Technology, Dundalk, Ireland
{peter.rust,derek.flood,fergal.mccaffery}@dkit.ie

Abstract. Organizations engaged in medical device software are required to demonstrate compliance with a set of medical device standards and regulations before the device can be marketed. One such standard *IEC 62304, Medical device software – Software life cycle processes*, is a standard that defines the processes that are required to be executed in order to develop safe software. Demonstrating compliance with IEC 62304 can be problematic for organizations that are new to or have limited experience in the domain. The standard defines what processes must be carried out, but does not state how. This paper presents a research method for generating a roadmap that will guide organizations in the implementation of IEC 62304.

Keywords: Medical device software · Medical device standards · Regulatory compliance · Software roadmap · Software process improvement · Software process improvement roadmaps · IEC 62304

1 Introduction

Developing safe medical device software is critical, especially considering the number of recalls of medical devices and the number of deaths and serious injuries caused by failure of software in medical devices [1][2]. Alemzadeh et al.[2] describe how 33.3% of Class I (presenting a high risk of severe injury or death to patients) recalls between 2006 and 2011 were software related.

Authorities around the world, charged with the regulation of medical devices, have recognized the importance of standards adoption in the development and manufacture of medical devices. ISO 13485 [3], ISO 14971 [4] and IEC 62366 [5] form a suite of standards introduced to help improve the development of safe medical devices, including software.

Software is now also deemed to be a medical device in its own right [6]. IEC 62304 [7] identifies the processes that need to be carried out but do not say how the processes should be carried out. The existing Software Process Improvement (SPI) models, such as the Capability Maturity Model® Integration (CMMI®) [8] and ISO/IEC 15504-5:2012 (SPICE) [9] are directed to the general software development domain and do not provide sufficient coverage to achieve medical device regulatory compliance [10]. MDevSPICE® (formally known as Medi SPICE) has been developed to fill this gap [10]. MDevSpice® is based on ISO/IEC 15504-5:2012 [9], IEC 62304:2006 [11] and ISO/IEC 12207:2008 [12] and has being developed in line with the requirements of ISO/IEC 15504-2:2003 [13] and contains a Process Reference Model (PRM) and Process Assessment Model (PAM). However, these models only identify the gaps in an organizations processes but not how to fill them. The aim of this project is to develop a set of tailored "How To" SPI roadmaps for medical device companies to both improve their software development practices and assist them to achieve regulatory compliance. To meet this aim, this paper describes the creation of a roadmap for the implementation of IEC 62304.

The remainder of this paper is structured in the following manner: Section 2 outlines the related work carried out with regard to the use of roadmapping in general, in the SPI field and in the medical device standards domain. Section 3 discusses the importance of the software development lifecycle within the medical device domain. Section 4 describes the research method used in developing roadmaps while section 5 details the generation of the IEC 62304 roadmap. Section 6 discusses the experience of generating the roadmap. Section 7 outlines the future work before the paper is concluded in section 8.

2 Related Work

The roadmapping process is established and proven in the technology domain and continues to be adopted in many other fields of endeavour. Phaal [14] lists over 2000 public domain roadmaps organized by topic including chemistry, construction, defence, energy, transport and many more. A number of large companies use roadmapping to develop their strategic planning going forward. NASA embraced roadmapping in 2005[15] arising out of a number of cost overruns in their development budgets.

Within the SPI domain, the number of published roadmaps is limited. McFeeley et al.,[16] have developed a high level process improvement roadmap and describe how their roadmap is intended to provide an organization with a guide to forming and carrying out an SPI program.

Höss et al.,[17] launched a pilot project to acquire skills in implementing IEC 62304 in a hospital-based environment (in-house manufacture). They concluded that the pilot project carried out at their facility clearly demonstrated that the interpretation and implementation of IEC 62304 is not feasible without appropriately qualified staff. They recognized that it could be carried out by a small team with limited resources although the initial effort is significant and a learning curve must be overcome.

It can be seen that applying the roadmapping process to IEC 62304 and generating a roadmap that will aid medical device software development organizations in the implementation of IEC 62304 is a necessary and justified step.

Flood et al. [18][19] have already applied the roadmapping process to ISO 14971 and IEC 62366 and these roadmaps have been validated with industry experts. A roadmap has also been developed for traceability in the medical device domain leaving the development of an IEC 62304 roadmap as the last piece of the puzzle.

3 Software Development Lifecycle in the Medical Device Domain

Safe medical device software requires risk management, quality management and good software engineering [20]. IEC 62304 does not prescribe a specific lifecycle model, but rather the standard provides a framework of life cycle processes with activities and tasks that are necessary for the safe design and maintenance of medical device software. IEC 62304 is not a standalone standard and the manufacturer of a medical device is responsible for ensuring compliance with the other relevant standards. Irrespective of the lifecycle model chosen, the processes defined in the standard must form part of the model and be implemented during the development of the medical device software. One method organizations have of doing this is through mapping the standard to their particular life cycle model. The IEC 62304 implementation roadmap will remove this step in the software development process as the requirements of IEC 62304 are already mapped to the defined processes, identified as Activities and any gaps that exist in the organizations processes will be detected.

4 Research Method

The aim of the paper is to describe the roadmapping process undertaken to develop an SPI roadmap for IEC 62304. The method chosen has already been used successfully in developing roadmaps for ISO 13485, ISO 14971 and IEC 62366[18][21].

4.1 Overview

The definition of a Roadmap for the purposes of applying the roadmapping process to this and the other standards in the domain is *"A series of Milestones, comprised of Goals that will guide an organization through the use of specific Activities towards compliance with regulatory standards"*[18].

After evaluation of the IEC 62304 standard it was found that the existing terminology used in the roadmap definition was inappropriate. The use of milestone, goal and activity conflicted with their use in IEC 62304. Therefore the definition of a roadmap in this context has been redefined. The definition now reads *"A series of Activities, comprised of Tasks that will guide an organization through the use of specific "How To's" towards compliance with regulatory standards"*. All further references in this paper will use this new terminology.

4.2 Roadmap Development Method

To generate the roadmap for IEC 62304 the roadmap development method described by Flood et al [19] has been applied. This method, described below, has been revised in light of the changes to the definition of a roadmap.

- Identify requirements of the standard and rephrase them as Tasks;
- Group the Tasks into logical Activities;
- Order the Activities into a sequence by which they can be introduced into an organization in a rational manner;
- Validate the generated roadmap;
- Identify the "How To's" that can meet the identified Tasks;
- Validate the "How To's" in a host organization.

5 Roadmapping and Roadmaps

5.1 Roadmap Generation

In step 1 as described above the standard was decomposed into its elementary requirements and a total of 172 elementary requirements were identified. The requirements were then transformed into Tasks by the application of an action verb.

Taking as an example of the transformation process requirement 5.3.5 which states that *"the manufacturer shall identify the segregation between software items that is essential to risk control, and state how to ensure that the segregation is effective"*. This was transformed into a Task defined as ***"Identify the segregation between software items that is essential to risk control and state the measures taken that ensure the segregation is effective."***

In step 2 when the transformation of all the requirements was complete, the Tasks were analysed for particular keywords that would aid their grouping into logical Activities. The above Task was assigned the keyword "Software Detailed Design". A total of five Tasks were grouped according to this keyword and an Activity created titled "Software Detailed Design". This process continued until all Tasks were grouped resulting in sixteen Activities. These are detailed in Table 1.

ISO/IEC TR 24774:2010 Systems and software engineering — Life cycle management — Guidelines for process description [22] recommends that the number of outcomes for a process should fall within the range 3 to 7. Considering this criteria and adapting it to arrive at the optimum range that should apply to the number of tasks in any given activity, the range between 1 and 7 inclusive was chosen. As can be seen from Table 1, some of the Activities have a number of Tasks far in excess of the optimum. The Tasks were re-analysed a further three times and a number of them reconstituted from their elemental parts. This resulted in 91 Tasks being attributed to the same sixteen Activities. This outcome is detailed in Table 2.

As can be seen from the table, the number of Tasks per activity was still problematic. T-Plan the Fast Start to Technology Roadmapping [23] describes the approach for developing technology roadmaps. The approach consists of four structured and facilitated workshops that guide an organization through the process of developing a technology roadmap. Four workshops titled Market, Product, Technology and Charting are conducted where the relevant managers from the organization gather together to identify the needs of the market, a product that might satisfy that need, the technology required to build the product and finally to chart the way forward once a decision is made to follow the strategy developed. The charting workshop brings all the

Table 1. Number of Tasks per Activity

Ref	Title	No of Tasks	Ref	Title	No of Tasks
1	Prerequisites.	2	9	Software Detailed Design Process	5
2	Software Development Planning Process	16	10	Software Unit Implementation and Verification Process	28
3	Software Documentation.	25	11	Software Integration and Integration Testing Process	7
4	Software Risk Management Process	13	12	Software System Testing Process	7
5	Software Requirements Analysis Process	16	13	Software Release Process	4
6	Software Architectural Design Process	6	14	Software Archive	2
7	Software Safety Classification.	4	15	Software Problem Resolution Process	18
8	Software Configuration Management Process	11	16	Software Maintenance Process	8

mangers together and a plan is drawn up as to how the strategy will be implemented. This is achieved by the use of a wall chart divided into layers and then a series of post-its are written up and pinned to the wall chart in the most appropriate layer. The managers can immediately visualize the plan as the workshop proceeds and the roadmap is produced by the end of the workshop. Due to the similarity of the two processes it was decided to try and utilize this workshop method to resolve the issues that arose with the generation of the IEC 62304 Roadmap using Step 2 of the original roadmap development method.

5.2 Roadmap Workshop

In preparation for the workshop each of the 91 Tasks were pre-printed on "post-its", as illustrated in Figure 1. The activity number and title were used as per the Activities identified during the initial generation. During the workshop these were not used and all Tasks were arranged as per the sections contained within the IEC 62304 standard. After each workshop these were updated to reflect the outcomes of the workshop.

To aid in the identification of individual Tasks, each one was assigned a unique Task Ref Number in the range of 1 to 91 and detailed on the post-its. In addition, to aid in traceability to the original standard, the IEC ref number and section title of each Task was recorded on the post-its.

Table 2. Number of Tasks per Activity after Reconstitution of Tasks.

Ref	Title	No of Tasks	Ref	Title	No of Tasks
1	Prerequisites.	2	9	Software Detailed Design Process	5
2	Software Development Planning Process	3	10	Software Unit Implementation and Verification Process	9
3	Software Documentation.	13	11	Software Integration and Integration Testing Process	5
4	Software Risk Management Process	9	12	Software System Testing Process	2
5	Software Requirements Analysis Process	5	13	Software Release Process	3
6	Software Architectural Design Process	6	14	Software Archive.	2
7	Software Safety Classification.	3	15	Software Problem Resolution Process	11
8	Software Configuration Management Process	6	16	Software Maintenance Process	7

```
Activity: 13

Activity Title:  Software Release

IEC Ref 5.8.5     IEC Title: Document how released software
was created.

Task Ref Number          62

Task Text:  Document the procedure and environment used to
create the released software.
```

Fig. 1. Example of Printed Post-it

Each activity was assigned a title and then each Task was assigned to an activity. The IEC 62304 reference and title from the standard were recorded on the post-it along with the Task text as detailed in figure 1. A room was laid out with a table on which the post-its were arranged as per the sections of IEC 62304 (see Photograph 1). A wall was designated on which the post-it's would be pinned in their final designated Activities (see Photograph 2). A number of three hour workshops were then conducted where a facilitator and three experts gathered to go through each Task and determine to which activity they belonged.

Photograph 1: Table laid out with arranged post-its

Photograph 2: Post-its pinned to wall under Activities

The facilitator introduced the aim of the workshop and gave a broad overview of the roadmapping process and what the output – the roadmap – might look like. A detailed discussion on each Task and which activity it belonged to took place and when agreement was arrived at, the new Task was pinned to the wall under the appropriate activity. This process continued until all the individual post-it's were allocated to Activities.

Due to the extent of the standard, three such workshops were used to finally determine the grouping of the Tasks to their Activities. The number of Tasks now totals 82, quite a number were combined on the basis of one of the underpinning ideas behind the standard – "if a process is undertaken then document it." To give an example, Tasks 7.1.2 and 7.1.4 were combined as "Identify and document in the risk management file potential causes of the software item identified in the medical device risk analysis activity (of ISO 14971) contributing to a hazardous situation."

5.3 Ordering the Activities

Step 3 of the method requires that the Activities be ordered in a manner by which they can be introduced to a medical device software development organization. Table 3 details the Roadmap that was developed during the course of the workshops and compares it to the one prior to the workshops. The Tasks associated with the Activities of Software Documentation and Software Archive were redistributed to other Activities as an outcome of the workshops. The consensus of the experts at the workshop was that as documentation plays a crucial role in the demonstration of compliance that the Tasks associated with documentation should be integrated into the performance of the Task rather than keeping them as a separate Task. In addition the experts concluded that it would be more beneficial to merge the Tasks of Software Archive with Software Release to optimise the implementation of the roadmap.

The Change Request Process was added as an Activity and covers Tasks from section 5, 6, 7 and 8 of the IEC 62304 standard and now includes seven Tasks. These Tasks came from a range of other Activities, including Software Maintenance, Software Risk Management and Software System Testing. After a lengthy discussion the experts agreed that the Change Request Tasks would be implemented together rather than in their respective original Activities and therefore should be implemented as an Activity in their own right.

The Software Risk Management Process with nine, Software Architectural Design Process with ten and Software Problem Resolution Process with eight Tasks remain with their total number of Tasks above the optimum. However this is unavoidable due to the complex and rigorous nature of these Activities.

Table 3. Final Order of the Activities and the Number of Tasks

Ref	Activity	No of Tasks prior to Workshops	No of Tasks after Workshops
	Software Documentation	13	redistributed
	Software Archive	2	redistributed
1	QMS	1	1
2	RMS	1	1
3	Software Safety Classification	3	3
4	Software Development Planning Process	3	5
5	Software Configuration Management Process	6	4
6	Software Risk Management Process	9	9
7	Software Requirements Analysis Process	5	4
8	Software Architectural Design Process	6	10
9	Software Detailed Design Process	5	4
10	Software Unit Implementation and Verification Process	9	5
11	Software Integration and Integration Testing Process	5	6
12	Software System Testing Process	2	3
13	Software Release Process	3	6
14	Software Problem Resolution Process	11	8
15	Change Request Process	n/a	7
16	Software Maintenance Process	7	6

Software Process Improvement and Roadmapping – A Roadmap for Implementing

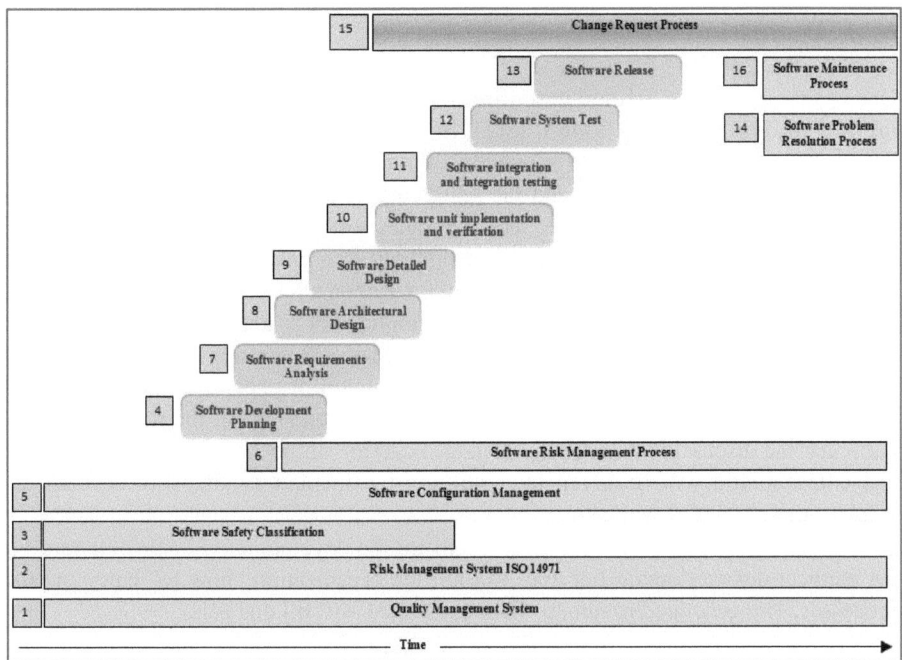

Fig. 2. Metaphor for the Roadmap

During the final workshop a discussion was held on the ordering of the Activities with particular reference as to how the roadmap might be graphically represented. Concern was expressed that the tabular representation with the Activities numerically identified might give an impression that one process must be complete before the next process can be undertaken. In consideration of this and with regard to the form of roadmaps that are generated in the technology domain a metaphor for the roadmap was generated and is detailed in figure 2.

The metaphor presented above was designed to highlight the stage at which each of the Activities may be applied during the development of a medical device software project. It can be seen that a number of the processes above may be ongoing for the duration of the software development process.

During the initial phase of the development of the product, a software safety classification of C is assigned to the device. During the architectural phase this may be revised in light of the risks posed by various components of the system therefore the software safety classification is ongoing right through the software architectural design phase.

Each of the phases in the software development lifecycle is depicted to overlap as a number of Tasks may be performed in parallel. Taking an example of the Software Unit Implementation and Verification Process and the Software Detailed Design Process, it is feasible that during the second Task of the Software Detailed Design Process – *"Document a design with enough detail to allow correct implementation of each software unit"*, the organization may commence the first Task of the Software Unit Implementation – *"Implement each software unit"*.

6 Discussion

One of the reasons the method described in previous works [18][21] used in developing SPI roadmaps for ISO 13485, ISO 14971 and IEC 62366 achieved a successful outcome was due to the limited size and extent of the standards. IEC 62304 covers a much broader set of processes and the scalability of the method was not there when applied to IEC 62304. Three other methodologies were identified, "STAR "[24], Qupar [25] and "T-Plan the fast start to Technology Roadmapping" [26]. The work of Phaal et al. was of the greatest interest as it has gained a lot of traction in the technology roadmapping domain. A method for developing SPI roadmaps for the implementation of the regulatory standards which includes a workshop element can only enhance the roadmapping process. Having the opinion of experts in the medical device software development domain during the generation stage of the roadmap and in particular the discussion that was held on the ordering of the Activities was invaluable and consideration will be given to modifying the method to take into account the value of these types of workshop.

IEC 62304 defines the processes required for the development of safe software for the medical device domain but does not tell the organization "how to" carry out the processes. The generated roadmap when completed will fill this gap.

7 Future Work

The next stage of this work is to validate the roadmap through expert review. A number of experts will be recruited for the validation from a diverse range of backgrounds including those who work in the medical device domain and use the standards on a regular basis, assessors who regulate organizations using the standard, academics with the appropriate expertise, and members of the standards committee.

Once the roadmap is validated, work will commence on the identification of the "how to's" for the achievement of the Tasks defined in the generated roadmap and the building of a repository to house them. This will be achieved through interaction with organizations that are close to regulatory compliance and assessment of their processes. This will enable future implementations in medical device organizations.

The roadmap will be evaluated within medical device organizations of varying maturity. For each organisation the roadmap will be customized to suit their own circumstances including criteria such as the lifecycle that is being employed, the size of the organisation and their existing process. This will enable the method to be truly tested and validated in a real world setting.

8 Conclusions

Organizations that are engaged in or wish to become engaged in the medical device software development domain are placed under a high level of scrutiny by the regulatory bodies tasked with ensuring that the medical device organization is compliant with all the standards. These standards identify the requirements the medical device organization must satisfy without telling them how to achieve compliance. This can hinder both the development of new medical devices and existing software houses entering the medical device domain due to the range of methods available for implementing the standards.

Building on previous work in the area, which developed a set of SPI roadmaps for ISO 14971 and IEC 62366, this paper has introduced a roadmap for the implementation of IEC 62304. To develop this roadmap a number of workshops were conducted with experts in IEC 62304 which examined not only the arrangement of Tasks into Activities, but also examined the order in which these Activities should be introduced into an organization. Through this roadmap, organizations that are entering the medical device domain will be guided through the process of implementing the IEC 62304 standard in an efficient and effective manner.

Acknowledgement. This research is supported by the Science Foundation Ireland Principal Investigator Programme, grant number 08/IN.1/I2030 and by Lero - the Irish Software Research Centre (http://www.lero.ie) grant 10/CE/I1855 & 13/RC/20194.

References

1. Ward, J.R., Clarkson, P.J.: An analysis of medical device-related errors: prevalence and possible solutions. J. Med. Eng. Technol. **28**(1), 2–21 (2004)
2. Alemzadeh, H., Iyer, R.K., Kalbarczyk, Z., Raman, J.: Analysis of Safety-Critical Computer Failures in Medical Devices. IEEE Secur. Priv. **11**(4), 14–26 (2013)
3. ISO 13485:2003 - Medical devices – Quality management systems – Requirements for regulatory purposes. ISO, Geneva (2003)
4. ISO 14971:2007 - Medical devices – Application of risk management to medical devices. ISO, Geneva (2007)
5. IEC 62366-1:2007 - Medical devices – Part 1: Application of usability engineering to medical devices. ISO, Geneva (2007)
6. McHugh, M., McCaffery, F., Casey, V.: Standalone software as an active medical device. In: O'Connor, R.V., Rout, T., McCaffery, F., Dorling, A. (eds.) SPICE 2011. CCIS, vol. 155, pp. 97–107. Springer, Heidelberg (2011)
7. IEC 62304:2006 - Medical device software – Software life cycle processes. ISO, Geneva (2006)
8. Team, C.P.: CMMI for Development, Version 1.3. Carnegie Mellon Univ., no. (November 2010)
9. ISO/IEC 15504-5, Information technology - Process Assessment - Part 5: An Exemplar Process Assessment Model. ISO, Geneva (2012)
10. McCaffery, F., Dorling, A.: Medi SPICE Development. Softw. Process Maint. Evol. Improv. Pract. J. **22**(4), 255–268 (2010)
11. IEC 62304:2006: Medical device software—Software life cycle processes. IEC, Geneva, vol. 3 (2006)
12. ISO/IEC 12207:2008, Systems and software engineering — Software life cycle processes. ISO, Geneva (2008)
13. ISO/IEC 15504-2:2003, Software engineering — Process assessment — Part 2: Performing an assessment. ISO, Geneva (2003)

14. Phaal, R.: Public Domain Roadmaps. Centre for Technology Management, University of Cambridge (2011)
15. Hall, L.: Space Technology Roadmaps: The Future Brought To You By NASA. Brian Dunbar, June 07, 2013
16. McFeeley, R., McKeehan, D., Temple, T.: Software Process Improvement Roadmap. Software Engineering Institute (1995)
17. Höss, A., Lampe, C., Panse, R., Ackermann, B., Naumann, J., Jäkel, O.: First experiences with the implementation of the European standard EN 62304 on medical device software for the quality assurance of a radiotherapy unit. Radiat. Oncol. **9**, 79 (2014)
18. Flood, D., Caffery, F.M., Casey, V., Regan, G.: A methodology for software process improvement roadmaps for regulated domains – example with IEC 62366. In: McCaffery, F., O'Connor, R.V., Messnarz, R. (eds.) EuroSPI 2013. CCIS, vol. 364, pp. 25–35. Springer, Heidelberg (2013)
19. Flood, D., Mc Caffery, F., Casey, V., McKeever, R., Rust, P.: A Roadmap to ISO 14971 Implementation. J. Softw. Process Evol. Accept. Awaiting Publ.
20. 62304 and TIR32 Training Slides - Eagles_Dundalk_04Sept13.pdf. https://www.dkit.ie/system/files/Eagles_Dundalk_04Sept13.pdf (accessed: March 12, 2015)
21. Regan, G., Casey, V., Flood, D., Mc Caffery, F.: A critical evaluation of a methodology for the generation of software process improvement roadmaps. In: Barafort, B., O'Connor, R.V., Poth, A., Messnarz, R. (eds.) EuroSPI 2014. CCIS, vol. 425, pp. 36–47. Springer, Heidelberg (2014)
22. ISO/IEC TR 24774:2010 - Systems and software engineering – Life cycle management – Guidelines for process description. ISO, Geneva (2010)
23. Farrukh, C.J.P., Phaal, R., Probert, D.: Technology roadmapping: linking technology resources into business planning. Int. J. Technol. Manag. **26**, 2 (2003)
24. Gindy, A.H.N.N.Z., Morcos, M.S., ulent Cerit, B.: Strategic Technology Alignment Roadmapping STAR® Aligning R&D Investments with Business Needs – document. International Journal of Computer Integrated Manufacturing, Taylor & Francis, STM, Behavioural Science and Pub- lic Health Titles (2008)
25. Regnell, B., Svensson, R.B., Olsson, T.: Supporting Roadmapping of Quality Requirements. IEEE Softw. **25**(2), 42–47 (2008)
26. Phaal, R., Farrukh, C.J.P., Probert, D.R.: T-plan: The Fast Start to Technology Roadmapping. Planning Your Route to Success. University of Cambridge. Institute for Manufacturing (2001)

Implementation and Assessment

Matching Context Aware Software Testing Design Techniques to ISO/IEC/IEEE 29119

Santiago Matalonga[1(✉)], Felyppe Rodrigues[2], and Guilherme H. Travassos[2]

[1] Universidad ORT Uruguay, Cuareim 1471, 11100 Montevideo, Uruguay
smatalonga@uni.ort.edu.uy
[2] Programa de Engenharia de Sistemas e Computação,
Universidade Federal do Rio de Janeiro, Rio de Janeiro, Brazil
felyppers@cos.ufrj.br

Abstract. A software system is context aware when it uses contextual information to help actors (users or other systems) to achieve their tasks. Testing this type of software can be a challenge since context and its variabilities cannot be controlled by the software tester. The ISO/IEC/IEEE 29119 intended to cover testing of any software system. It provides a common language and process for testing software systems, including a categorization of conventional testing techniques. This paper contains the initial results of our ongoing efforts to understand the testing of context aware software, Specifically, we evaluate whether the observed techniques for testing context aware software can be matched against the ISO/IEC/IEEE 29119 categories or if they represent a new breed of testing techniques. The results indicate that using conventional techniques variations to test context aware software systems does not produce evidence on their feasibility to test the context awareness features in such systems.

Keywords: Context awareness · Testing · ISO 29119:2013 · Systematic literature review

1 Introduction

The ISO/IEC/IEEE 29119 is a novel standard that covers software and systems engineering testing. It was published in 2013, and some parts have not been approved yet. The purpose of the series of software testing standards is to define an internationally-agreed set of standards for software testing that can be used by any organization when performing any form of software testing[1]. It means it should be suitable to adapt the testing techniques not only to different organizational scenarios, but also to keep pace with technological advances of software systems. Although relevant, its scope seems to be broad and ambitious, considering the reality of contemporary software.

Context aware software systems are a relatively new breed of software applications. As a result of the evolution of ubiquitous and pervasive computing, context aware applications take advantage of the myriad of sensors available in mobile devices and use that information to serve their actors (users or other systems). The verification and validation of this type of system is an area where software technologies have yet to be investigated [2]. Since the context of the application varies, testing all possible alternatives is not feasible. Context aware applications and their correspondent context states can explode the permutation of available test space for a software application. It is likely that coverage or other test completeness techniques might not be useful in the realm of context aware software system.

The ISO/IEC/IEEE 29119:2013, particularly part 4, defines software test design techniques. By taking into account the novelty of both domains, the ISO/IEC/IEEE 29119:2013 international standard test design techniques and context aware software testing techniques identified during a *quasi* Systematic Literature Review [3], this paper describes the observed equivalence among Test Types and Test Design Techniques defined in the ISO standard and such testing techniques.

Considering the features of context aware applications, the results point out that most of the reviewed technical literature uses conventional testing techniques to test context aware software. In our opinion, this is an indication that either the testing of context aware software systems is no different from testing conventional software, or that there are still software technologies targeting at context aware software systems to be developed . We believe these results are important for the practitioners and software industry, because if they can only rely on traditional testing techniques to test context aware software systems, they are bound to keep taking tradeoff decisions between feasibility and coverage of their testing effort. It is unlikely that a conventional testing strategy can be comprehensive enough to execute all possible context variations throughout testing execution, increasing the risk of failures in such applications after they are delivered.

This article is organized as follows; Section 2 summarizes our research project in testing context aware software systems. Section 3 presents a summary of the ISO/IEC/IEEE 29119:2013 family of standards. In Section 4the matching methodology and results are presented. Section 5 discuss our findings and provide hypothesis for understanding the results. Finally we discuss the threats to validity in Section 6 and summarize our conclusions in Section 7.

2 Acquiring Knowledge Regarding the Testing of Context-Aware Software Systems

Context Aware Testing for Ubiquitous Systems (CAcTUS) is an ongoing research project involving researchers from three universities (Universidade Federal do Rio do Janeiro, Universidade Federal do Ceará – both in Brazil – and University of Valenciennes and Hainaut-Cambresis in France). The objective is to understand test strategies for the quality assessment of actor-computer interaction in ubiquitous systems. The initial tasks for the CAcTUS' researchers are concerned with the identification of relevant knowledge in the area. Therefore, there are three teams undertaking secondary studies (*quasi* systematic literature reviews - qSLR [4]) to reveal evidence on testing techniques, test case design, test case documentation, and interoperability testing concerned with context aware software systems. Particularly, this paper presents some results of the qSLR whose objective was to identify techniques reported in the technical literature for testing context aware software systems For the sake of simplicity, only the main features of the qSLR protocol is going to be presented. A complete description can be obtained in [3].

The search string used was interactively organized by using the PICO approach [5]. Table 1 presents the components of the search string, which had been applied to the Web of Science, Scopus and IEEE Xplore databases. The use of these databases can be justified by their stability and coverage of technical literature they provide.

Table 1. qSLR's Search String

Population	Context Aware Software Systems
	"context aware" OR "event driven" OR "context driven" OR "context sensitivity" OR "context sensitive" OR "pervasive" OR "ubiquitous" OR "usability" OR "event based" OR "self adaptive" OR "self adapt"
Intervention	Software Testing
	"software test design" OR "software test suite" OR "software test" OR "software testing" OR "system test design" OR "system test suite" OR "system test" OR "system testing" OR "middleware test" OR "middleware testing" OR "property based software test" OR "property based software testing" OR "fault detection" OR "failure detection" OR "GUI test" OR "Graphical User Interfaces test".
Comparison	-
Outcome	Testing approaches
	"model" OR "metric" OR "guideline" OR "checklist" OR "template" OR "approach" OR "strategy" OR "method" OR "methodology" OR "tool" OR "technique" OR "heuristics"

From the 1680 different articles retrieved, 110 were selected after evaluating their title and abstract. These were then narrowed down to the 11 technical papers ([6], [7], [8], [9], [10], [11], [12], [13], [14], [15] and [16]) used in this work as input to evaluate the testing of context aware software in section IV.

3 Acquiring Knowledge Regarding the Testing of Context-Aware Software Systems

The ISO/IEC/IEEE 29119:2013 [1] represents a relatively new series of international standards whose purpose is to provide governance of processes of software testing. The series encompasses the following four parts:

- Part 1 purpose is to present the definitions of testing terms and some discussions on key concepts to the understanding of the ISO/IEC/IEEE 29119 series of software testing international standards [1].
- Part 2 purpose is to specify test processes that can be used to govern, manage and implement software testing for any organization, project or smaller testing activity. It comprises generic test process descriptions defining the soft-

ware testing processes. Supporting informative diagrams describing the processes are also provided [17].
- Part 3 specifies software test documentation templates that can be used by any organization, project or smaller testing activity [17].
- Part 4 defines software Test Design Techniques that can be used during the test design and implementation processes defined in ISO/IEC/IEEE 29119-2 Test Processes [18]. This standard part is currently in ISO review process draft stage.
- Part 5 is in even early stages of the ISO review process. It will specifically target processes and techniques for keyword based testing.

A recurring topic through the different standards' parts is that the series of international standards were designed to be suitable for *any* type of organization, following *any* software development lifecycle. In this paper, we focus on Part 4: Test Design Techniques.

3.1 ISO/IEC/IEEE 29119-4-DIS. Test Design Techniques

The standard classifies the Test Design Techniques to achieve the testing process requirements (Part 2) in three broad categories:

1. Specification based techniques: the test basis (e.g. requirements, specifications, models or user needs) is used as the main source of information to design test cases.
2. Structure based techniques: the structure of the test item (e.g. source code or the structure of a model) is used as the primary source of information to design test cases.
3. Experience based techniques: Tester's knowledge and experience are used as primary sources of information to design test cases.

Table 2 presents ISO/IEC/IEEE 29119-4-DIS's Test Design Techniques grouped by these three categories.

Table 2. ISO/IEC/IEEE 29119 Test Design Techniques

Test Design Technique Category	Test Design Technique
Specification based testing	Equivalence partitioning; Classification tree method; Boundary value analysis; Syntax testing; Combinatorial test design techniques; Decision table testing; Cause-Effect graphing; State Transition Testing; Scenario Testing, and; Random Testing.

Table 2. (*continued*)

Structure based testing	Statement Testing; Branch Testing; Decision Testing; Branch Condition Testing; Modified Condition Testing, and; Data Flow Testing Test Design Techniques.
Experience based testing	Error Guessing

3.2 ISO/IEC/IEEE 29119-4-DIS and ISO 25010 Test Type

While ISO/IEC/IEEE 29119 defines the Test Design Techniques, it relies on a previously defined standard – the ISO/IEC 25010 Systems and Software Quality Requirements and Evaluation (SQuaRE) -- System and software quality models – for the definition of Test Types.

As a quick introduction, the ISO/IEC 2510:2011 [19] is the current standard where quality attributes are defined. A quality attribute is a factor affecting the run-time behavior, system design and user experience. The ISO/IEC 2510:2011 defines Test Types aiming at the quality attribute the test is intended to evaluate. Table 3 presents the test types defined in this standard, which will be used for the mapping presented in the following section.

Table 3. ISO/IEC 25010 Test Types

ISO/IEC 25010 Test Types	
Accessibility Testing;	Maintainability Testing;
Backup/Recovery Testing;	Performance-Related Testing;
Compatibility Testing;	Portability Testing;
Conversion Testing;	Procedure Testing;
Disaster Recovery Testing;	Reliability Testing;
Functional Testing;	Security Testing;
Installability Testing;	Stability Testing, and;
Interoperability Testing;	Usability Testing.
Localization Testing;	

4 On Matching Testing Context Aware Software Systems Testing Techniques and ISO/IEC/IEEE 29119:2013

4.1 Matching Methodology

Mapping the Test Design Techniques, as it was initially our intention, was not possible since most of the identified authors did not make an explicit reference to the design techniques used in their work. Therefore, for our purposes we studied and named the techniques that, to the best of our knowledge, the authors seemed to have used (see 4).

In contrast, it was possible to extract names for the test types that the authors defined to be using (presented in Table 5). However, to map these types also represented a challenge, since the names they used to use do not have a literal correspondence to the types described in the standard. Therefore, we provided this matching by interpreting the intention of each test type in the standard to what the authors have reported.

For instance, Merdes et al. [11] define the test type as being "run time testing", while our interpretation is that run time is the means to achieve interoperability testing ("run time testing" is not a valid category in ISO/IEC/IEEE 29119). Meanwhile, She et al. [14] define that their tools provide functional testing, which we agree and maintained the authors classification in our matching.

4.2 Matching Rationale

This section describes the 11 identified technical papers concerned with the testing of context aware software systems.

Alsos and Dhal [6] presents a case study for usability testing of context aware systems in healthcare. The observational cases were designed by physically designing new scenarios in their environment. They present three prototypes to be used by each participant in a sequential order. The definition of Scenario Testing according to the ISO/IEC/IEEE 29119-4 says that scenario testing uses a model of the sequences of interactions between the test item and other systems (in this context users are often considered to be other systems) for the purpose of testing usage flows involving the test item. Test conditions shall either be one sequence of interactions (i.e. one scenario) or all sequences of interactions (i.e. all scenarios)[18].

Merdes et al. [11] present a proposal for fidgeting with resource sensors in mobile devices at runtime. They present a XML-based-tool for helping with this intervention. This XML layer enables the user to configure run time scenarios where the Test suites for the application will be executed. The approach presented in the article and its practical examples are pre-established scenarios created with the proposed XML based-tool, similar to Alsos and Dhal[6].

Canfora et al. [9] present a case study where they recorded the users reactions to a mobile context aware application. Their aim was to build an automated workbench for mobile usability testing. The authors described their experimental design as a set of testing scenarios, in which each of them was created in order to attend a different user level of knowledge (normal user, smart user and businessman). This kind of approach is characterized as scenario testing.

Jiang et al.[8] and She et al. [14] presented an automated testing environment for testing mobile applications. Both environments allow the definition of context variables to be used in the test case design. Jiang et al.[8] separated the population on teams, all the teams were given the same tasks to be followed step-by-step (just as the previous presented scenario testing papers). However, in contrast to [8], She et al.[14]

do not provide any indication of what is the technique the subject used to generate the test cases. The authors propose a framework to aid the testers and try to compare what they call "manual testing" with the presented approach. Nevertheless, none of these approaches were detailed, making the ISO/IEC/IEEE 29119-4 classification unfeasible.

In similar fashion, Amalfitano et al. [7] present an app running on the Android platform. This app juggles the input received by the device sensors and feeds it to the application under test. The authors define their Test Design Technique as "exploration-based technique". The ISO/IEC/IEEE 29119-4 defines the Error Guessing Technique as the design of a checklist of defect types that may exist in the test item, allowing the tester to identify inputs to the test item that may cause failures, if those defects exist in the test item. Each defect type shall be a test condition. Considering Amalfitano et al. [7]'s features, we matched their approach to the error guessing Test Design Technique according to the ISO/IEC/IEEE 29119-4.

Ryan and Gonsalves[12] present an experiment to evaluate the usability of context aware applications in different device types. In this study, the authors adapt the same application to run on four different device types and then evaluate them for Usability related quality attributes (for instance, learnability and ease of use). Similarly to the previously presented scenario testing papers, the population group had a list of steps to follow during the experimentation.

Satoh[13] defines the aim of the study as interoperability test of context aware applications. The author's strategy is to emulate several sensors thus creating a sandbox for the context aware application to run in. Even though the proposed emulator seems to be promising, the test descriptions were not detailed enough for making the matching against the ISO/IEC/IEEE 29119-4.

Tse et al. [15] coin the term "methamorphic testing" to describe their approach. The approach is based on specifying the context variables and sensors to which the application is aware, and then use mutation operators to juggle that initial specification in order to find defects. An initial database contains the input/output variables and the approach presented selects different combinations of inputs to check if the outputs remains the same in different input sequences of execution. ISO/IEC/IEEE 29119-4 defines Random Testing as a model of the input domain of the test item that defines the set of all possible input values. An input distribution for the generation of random input values shall be chosen. The domain of all possible inputs shall be the test condition for random testing.

Finally, Wang and Chan [16] propose a metric for evaluating how exposed a test suite is to context variables. Their approach hypothesizes that maximizing test suit development for that metric will improve coverage of the context of the application. Lu et al. [10] present a similar measurement concept, and provide a laboratory proof of concept of their approach that is used to help them identify challenges in testing context-aware software systems. Both of the authors try to observe the context-awareness testing problem as a structure-based problem, instead of specification-based (approach used by the previously cited papers). Even though testing all possible context variable combinations being unfeasible, the authors show different arrangements resulting in distinct coverage criteria for white-box testing. According to the ISO/IEC/IEEE 29119-4, Branch Testing is a control flow model that identifies branches in the control flow of the test item shall be derived. Each branch in the control flow model shall be a test condition. Even though the authors' proposals are different; both of them are executing branch testing.

4.3 Matching Results

This section presents the results of identifying approaches to context aware software testing. Table 4 summarizes our classification of the sources against the standards Test Design Techniques, according to the rationale explained in the previous section.

Table 3. Papers Classification by ISO/IEC/IEEE 29119 Test Design Technique

Article	ISO/IEC/IEEE 29119 part 4 Test Design Technique
Alsos and Dhal[6]	Scenario Testing
Amalfitano et al. [7]	Error Guessing
Jiang et al.[8]	Scenario Testing
Canfora et al.[9]	Scenario Testing
Lu et al.[10]	Branch Testing
Merdes et al.[11]	Scenario Testing
Ryan and Gonsalves[12]	Scenario Testing
Satoh[13]	None
She et al.[14]	None
Tse et al.[15]	Random Testing
Wang and Chan[16]	Branch Testing

In contrast to the Test Design Technique classification, in Table 5 is possible to observe the comparison between the ISO/IEC 25010 (referenced standard for Test Types in ISO/IEC/IEEE 29119) and the authors own classification.

Table 4. Comparision of Authors' vs ISO/IEC's Test Type

Article	ISO/IEC 25010 Test Type	Authors defined Test Type
Alsos and Dhal[6]	Usability Testing	Usability Comparative Testing
Amalfitano et al. [7]	Procedure Testing	Exploratory Testing
Jiang et al.[8]	Compatibility Testing	None
Canfora et al.[9]	Usability Testing	User Experience Testing
Lu et al.[10]	Functional Testing	Functional Testing
Merdes et al.[11]	Interoperability Testing	Run-Time Testing
Ryan and Gonsalves[12]	Usability Testing Functional Testing	Usability Testing
Satoh[13]	Compatibility Testing Interoperability Testing	Interoperability Testing
She et al.[14]	Functional Testing	Functional Testing
Tse et al.[15]	Functional Testing	Metamorphic Testing
Wang and Chan[16]	Branch Testing	Coverage-based Testing

5 Discussions

The results in **Table** 5 show that five out of the 11 references use the same name for Test Type. Taking into consideration the novelty of the standard it could be an indication that the community did not have enough time to adopt the terms yet. In contrast, given that software testing is a long standing area of practice in Software Engineering, it is still striking that researchers are still using such diverse names to describe the same things.

Regarding the applicability of the proposed techniques for context-aware software testing, it seems clear that most authors have taken the approach of treating context awareness as another dimension which must be taken into account when designing test cases. This means, authors are using context variables as input, variables which should be defined in the test case and not influencing the testing scenario, according their perspectives.

With the exception of Satoh[13] and She et al. [14], all other authors are using Test Design Techniques that can be mapped to the Standard. Furthermore, the majority of the approaches presented are using Scenario Testing as its Test Design Technique, i.e. the approach guides the tester in which way and with what perspective it should execute the test. If we consider that the context variations may occur at any time and without control, whether the approach limits the way of testing, it is reasonable to believe that the approach will not support the test of context-awareness features.

However, since nine out of 11 studies can be classified regarding the international standard, it seems that either (a) testing context-aware software is no different from testing of conventional – not context aware – software, for this group of papers; or (b) the novelties of the issues associated with this specific type of software system (context awareness) have yet not been explored. We argue in favor of the second hypothesis, since it spite of having achieved nine classifications, this have not been straight forward. And in addition to this, there is no evaluation of the suitability of the test design techniques for the test of context aware software systems.

Another observation is that the authors in the reviewed technical literature have distinct perceptions of software testing. For instance, four out of 11 references do not include the need of an oracle or specification as an integral part of the construction of test cases. The international standards wording for the definition of test cases is rather ambiguous in this subject. The standard puts the focus on the dynamic execution of the unit under test with the aim of evaluating its quality, and gives the oracle a nice-to-have status.

6 Threats to Validity

We understand that there are two main threats to the validity of the discussions presented in this work. One is regarding the draft status of part 4 of the ISO/IEC/IEEE 29119 international standard. In our experience with other ISO standards, there can be significant changes between the DIS and the final approved version of the standard. This means that it is likely that the Test Design Techniques classification might not be stable yet. In contrast, the Test Types are taken from the ISO/IEC 25010:2011 that is stable. On the other hand, it is also possible that we might have overlooked some concept during the matching process or that other researchers performing the same matching process can come up with different classifications for the same sources. This might have impact on the conclusions and results presented in this paper.

Another source of threat to validity is inherent to the research method applied for identifying the relevant technical literature. The qSLR research protocol [3] documents the research process and results, which for the sake of brevity are not discussed but mentioned here:

- Threats of missing literature and Selection Bias: both are always a threat in qSLR studies and are mitigated by a rigorous research protocol [3].
- Inaccuracy of data extraction and bias on synthesis of information: there is always the threats that we could have misunderstood the intention of the authors whose work we have study. The readers of this paper can evaluate the summary of this papers in the section 4.2.

7   Conclusion

In this paper we have presented the Standard for Testing Software Systems (ISO/IEC/IEEE 29119) and its matching with currently used testing techniques for context awareness software systems. The scope of this standard is broad and ambitious; it seeks to define processes and techniques for testing all types of software systems. Being context aware software systems a relatively new type of software, our aim with this paper was to evaluate whether this new international standard could cover the testing of context aware applications.

Therefore, this paper classified the identified technical literature on testing context aware software by using the ISO/IEC/IEEE 29119 Test Design Techniques and ISO/IEC 25010 Test Types. The relevant technical literature included in this work resulted from a qSLR undertaken in the context of CAcTUS project.

The testing of context aware applications brings on the challenges associated with an ever changing context in which the application is executed. Therefore, context can become an ever increasing source of possible input spaces for defining test cases.

The results presented in this paper show that most of the identified technical literature reports to be using traditional testing techniques to test context aware software and that they are using techniques which can be classified using the international standard. However, as far as we could investigate, we have not been able to identify a test design technique that specifically targets at context variables in its conception.

Nonetheless, the question still remains whether the reason this is so is that the challenges and issues associated with testing context aware software are still so new that they haven't been explored yet or that they are no different than the testing of regular (or non context aware) software. Nonetheless, we believe that further evidence is needed to evaluate this claim.

Acknowledgements. This work was supported by the "CAcTUS - Context-Awareness Testing for Ubiquitous Systems" project partially financed by CNPq – Universal 14/2013 Number 484380/2013-3. Prof. Matalonga is supported by Banco Santander Uruguay grant for young researchers.

References

1. Software and systems engineering Software testing Part 1:Concepts and definitions. ISO/IEC/IEEE 29119-1:2013. 1–64 (2013)
2. Malik, N., Mahmud, U., Javed, Y.: Future challenges in context-aware computing. In: Proc. IADIS Int. Conf. 306–310 (2007)
3. Rodrigues, F., Matalonga, S., Travassos, G.H.: Systematic literature review protocol: Investigating context aware software testing strategies.Rio de Janeiro (2014) www.cos.ufrj.br/~ght/cactus_pr012014.pdf
4. Travassos, G.H., Santos, P.S.M. dos, Mian, P.G., Neto, A.C.D., Biolchini, J.: An Environment to Support Large Scale Experimentation in Software Engineering. In: 13th IEEE International Conference on Engineering of Complex Computer Systems (ICECCS 2008), pp. 193–202. IEEE (2008)
5. Pai, M., Mcculloch, M., Gorman, J.D., Pai, N., Enanoria, W., Kennedy, G., Tharyan, P., Colford Jr, J.M., Colford, J.M.: Systematic reviews and meta-analyses: an illustrated, step-by-step guide. Natl. Med. J. India **17**, 86–95 (2004)
6. Alsos, O.A., Dahl, Y.: Toward a best practice for laboratory-based usability evaluations of mobile ICT for hospitals. In: Proc. 5th Nord. Conf. Human-computer Interact. Build. Bridg. – Nord, 3 (2008)
7. Amalfitano, D., Fasolino, A.R., Tramontana, P., Amatucci, N.: Considering Context Events in Event-Based Testing of Mobile Applications. In: 2013 IEEE Sixth International Conference on Software Testing, Verification and Validation Workshops, pp. 126–133 (2013)
8. Jiang, B., Long, X., Gao, X.: MobileTest: A tool supporting automatic black box test for software on smart mobile devices. In: Proceedings of the International Conference on Software Engineering (2007)
9. Canfora, G., Mercaldo, F., Visaggio, C.A., D'Angelo, M., Furno, A., Manganelli, C.: A case study of automating user experience-oriented performance testing on smartphones. In: Proceedings of the IEEE 6th International Conference on Software Testing, Verification and Validation, ICST 2013. pp. 66–69 (2013)
10. Lu, H., Chan, W.K., Tse, T.H.: Testing context-aware middleware-centric programs. In: Proceedings of the 14th ACM SIGSOFT International Symposium on Foundations of Software Engineering, SIGSOFT 2006/FSE-14. p. 242. ACM Press, New York (2006)
11. Merdes, M., Malaka, R., Suliman, D., Paech, B., Brenner, D., Atkinson, C.: Ubiquitous RATs: How Resource-Aware Run-Time Tests Can Improve Ubiquitous Software System. In: 6th International Workshop on Software Engineering and Middleware, SEM 2006, pp. 55–62 (2006)
12. Ryan, C., Gonsalves, A.: The effect of context and application type on mobile usability: An empirical study. In: Conferences in Research and Practice in Information Technology Series, pp. 115–124 (2005)
13. Satoh, I.: Software testing for mobile and ubiquitous computing. In: The Sixth International Symposium on Autonomous Decentralized Systems, ISADS 2003 (2003)

14. She, S., Sivapalan, S., Warren, I.: Hermes: A tool for testing mobile device applications. In: Proceedings of the Australian Software Engineering Conference, ASWEC, pp. 121–130 (2009)
15. Tse, T.H., Yau, S.S.: Testing context-sensitive middleware-based software applications. In: Proceedings of the 28th Annual International Computer Software and Applications Conference, COMPSAC 2004, pp. 458–466. IEEE (2004)
16. Wang, H., Chan, W.K.: Weaving Context Sensitivity into Test Suite Construction. In: 2009 IEEE/ACM International Conference on Automated Software Engineering, pp. 610–614. IEEE, Auckland (2009)
17. Software and systems engineering Software testing Part 2:Test processes. ISO/IEC/IEEE 29119-3:2013(E). 1–138 (2013)
18. IEEE Draft International Standard for Software and Systems Engineering–Software Testing–Part 4: Test Techniques. ISO/IEC/IEEE P29119-4-DISMay2013. 1–132 (2014)
19. Systems and software engineering – Systems and software Quality Requirements and Evaluation (SQuaRE) – System and software quality models. ISO/IEC 25010:2011. 1–34 (2011)

The Development and Validation of a Roadmap for Traceability

Gilbert Regan[✉], Derek Flood, and Fergal McCaffery

Regulated Software Research Centre and Lero, Dundalk
Institute of Technology, Dundalk, Ireland
{gilbert.regan,derek.flood,fergal.mccaffery}@dkit.ie

Abstract. Organisations who operate in the safety critical domains such as the medical device, avaition, and automotive domains must ensure their software is safe and provide objective evidence to this effect. One way of achieving this is by adhering to domain specific regulations and guidelines which specify a comprehensive implementation of traceability. However there is a gap between regulatory traceability requirements and what is implemented in practice. This lack of compliance means that organisations find it difficult to assess the safety of their software and thus ensure its safety. One reason for non-compliance with regards to traceability is a lack of guidance on what traceability to implement or how to implement it. In this paper we present the development and validation of a roadmap for the implementation of traceability in the medical device domain. The roadmap will provide medical device organisations with a pathway for effective traceability implementation.

Keywords: Software traceability · Medical device · Roadmap · Compliance · Safety critical software · Standard · Guideline

1 Introduction

Developing software in the safety critical domain is a difficult task as manufacturers must comply with numerous regulations and guidelines. Additionally, it is incumbent on the manufacturers of such software to prove that their software is safe. This involves submission of a safety case which is a reasoned argument supported with objective evidence proving that the software is safe for its intended use [1]. Establishing effective software development processes that are based on recognised engineering principles appropriate for safety critical systems will greatly contribute towards the safety of the software. At the heart of such processes they must incorporate traceability.

Traceability is the ability to establish links (or traces) between source artefacts and target artefacts [2]. Tracing, which is the process of developing traces, is an important technique that can help to ensure that the right system is being designed and implemented. It is important to implement "just the right amount" of traceability in "just the right way" so that the risk-to-reward ratio benefits a project's circumstances. Otherwise, you may find that:

1. A project suffers from excessive overhead without commensurate quality improvement.
2. The project fails to deliver the requisite quality

Neither of these outcomes is desirable therefore it is beneficial to define and implement the right traceability strategy from the beginning. In the medical device domain, the "right amount" of traceability is determined by the medical device standards and guidelines. These standards require traceability between each phase of the Software Development Lifecycle (SDLC), Risk Management and Change Management processes, e.g. traceability between software requirements and software architectural design. This standards' traceability requirements ensure verification of inputs to outputs. Additionally, the "right way" is influenced by traceability best practices.

However despite the regulatory requirements for traceability and the many benefits it has to offer, most existing software systems lack explicit traceability links between artefacts [3] and required phases. This leads to difficulties in verifying and validating the software. Numerous reasons have been identified for reluctance in implementing traceability, including a lack of guidance in terms of what traces to implement and how to implement them. As a result practitioners are ill informed as to how best to accomplish this task [4, 5]. To assist medical device organisations in addressing the lack of guidance on how to implement effective traceability, this paper presents the development and validation of a traceability roadmap.

While there is no standard definition of a roadmap, many definitions do exist, for example a roadmap is *'the view of a group of stakeholders as to how to get where they want to go to achieve their desired objective'*[6], or a roadmap is *'a series of milestones, comprised of goals, that will guide an organisation, through the use of specific activities, towards compliance with regulatory standards'*[7]. In effect a roadmap is a plan that allows organisations put solutions in place in order to achieve specific goals.

The remainder of this paper is structured as follows: Section 2 outlines various types of roadmaps and roadmap development methodologies while Section 3 outlines the development methodology used to develop the roadmap presented in this paper.

Section 4 details the structure of the developed roadmap while Section 5 presents the findings of an expert evaluation of the roadmap and a discussion of those findings, while Section 6 concludes the paper.

2 Related Work

Robert Phaal et al., [8] leading authorities in the world of roadmapping (the process of developing a roadmap), examined approximately 40 roadmaps and categorised them into 8 types of roadmap (in terms of purpose) and 8 formats of roadmap (in terms of graphical format). Based on the purpose that they serve, the following 8 types of roadmap have been identified: Product planning; Service/capability planning; Strategic planning; Long range planning; Knowledge asset planning; Program planning; Process planning; and Integration planning. Based on the graphical format, the following 8 formats of roadmap have been identified: Multiple layers; Single layer; Bars; Tables; Graphs; Pictorial representations; Flow Charts; and Text.

Phaal et al. note that a range of roadmaps observed may be partially due to a lack of an accepted standard for roadmap development, or may be due to the fact that organisations need to adapt their approach to suit their particular situation i.e. business purpose, available resources etc. The authors also note that roadmaps can contain elements of more than one type of roadmap resulting in many hybrid forms of roadmap, which can result in organisations finding them difficult to use.

As a result of challenges organisations encountered when developing roadmaps Phaal et al. developed a fast start approach called T-Plan to support the rapid initiation of roadmapping [9]. These challenges included: keeping the roadmapping process "alive" on an ongoing basis; starting up the process; and developing a robust method. The T-Plan approach is based on four facilitated workshops. The first workshop ("Market") aims to establish a set of prioritized market and business drivers for the future, reflecting external and internal factors. The second workshop ("Product") aims to establish a set of "product feature concepts" that could satisfy the drivers identified in Workshop 1. The third workshop ("Technology") aims to identify possible technological solutions that could deliver the desired product features. The fourth workshop ("Charting") draws the marketing and technology strands together to produce the first roadmap. Its format is defined in terms of time scales, levels and product strategy.

The Software Engineering Institute in collaboration with Carnegie Mellon University and the Hewlett-Packard Company have developed a Software Process Improvement (SPI) Roadmap [10]. This roadmap is a generic long range integrated plan for initiating and managing a SPI program. Its purpose is to provide a generic description of the steps involved in implementing a SPI program, at both a strategic level and an operational level. The roadmap describes a process improvement program that occurs in three phases, made up of six major activities within these phases. The three phases are analogous to the SEI's IDEAL model (Initiating, Diagnosing, Establishing, Acting and Learning) for software process improvement. The phases are:

- Initiate process improvement;
- Baseline the current processes and opportunities;
- Implement process improvement by developing and sustaining improvements within the organization.

Flood et al., [11] have developed a SPI roadmap for the implementation of medical device standards. The goal of this roadmap is to implement the processes necessary to meet the requirements of specific medical device standards, and not to improve existing processes as in traditional SPI models. The methodology used to develop the roadmap is similar to the methodology used by Barafort et al., [12] for the construction of ISO/IEC 15504-2 [13]compliant process assessment and process reference models. The methodology contains seven steps as follows:

1. Identify requirements of the standards;
2. Logically group all goals;
3. Separate grouped goals in line with ISO/IEC 15504 capability levels. These grouped goals form milestones;
4. Order the milestones based on capability levels and logical groupings;
5. Validate the generated roadmap;
6. Identify activities that can meet the identified goals;
7. Validate activities in host organisation.

While there are numerous publications on roadmap development methodologies [14-17], the most common methodology is a three phase approach: an initiation phase which includes defining the scope and boundaries of the technology roadmap, a development phase, and a follow up phase which includes roadmap validation and implementation plan.

3 Methodology

To develop a roadmap it is necessary to answer the following three questions: Where are we now? Where are we going? and How do we get there?

The objective of this roadmap is to provide a pathway for the implementation of traceability in a manner which is compliant with the medical device standards requirements for traceability, and also to provide a pathway that adopts the best practices for traceability implementation. These requirements and best practices provide an answer to the question 'Where are we going?' An analysis of the medical device standards (which included ISO/IEC 62304 [18], ISO/IEC 14971[19], ISO/IEC 13485 [20], and the FDA guidance documents [21-23]) yielded 26 requirements for traceability. These requirements were then transformed into a ISO/IEC 15504-2 [13] compliant process assessment and process reference model using the TIPA transformation process [12]. The application of this process assessment model (PAM), developed prior to this roadmap [24], provides a baseline of an organisation's current state with regards to traceability and answers the question 'Where are we now?'. To determine the best practices for implementing traceability a literature review was conducted which yielded 23 best practices [25]. These 23 best practices were categorised under the 6 headings of: Traceability Policy; Traceability Information Model; Resources; Appropriate Techniques; Standard Operating Procedure and Communication Method.

Now that the requirements and best practices for traceability implementation were identified a decision as to the type and format of the roadmap was required. In contemplating the taxonomy of roadmap types and formats identified by [8] it was considered that the traceability roadmap aligned with the 'Process planning' type of roadmap. This type supports the management of knowledge, focusing on knowledge flows that are needed to facilitate effective traceability implementation. In addition to, and perhaps more important than roadmap type, the format of the roadmap was then considered. It was decided that the roadmap should be a hybrid version entailing both the 'single layer' and 'text' formats. This hybrid version was chosen for the following reasons:

- Combinations of pictorial information with text-only information facilitate significant improvements in understanding [26];
- The single layer roadmap is a graphical format and can present a lot of information in a readily understandable format;
- The traceability roadmap needed to present a lot of information such as base practices and the benefits that an organisation could leverage through each phase of the implementation. In addition, it was felt that an implementation case study would be of great benefit to organisations that do not have expertise in the area of traceability. Therefore it was decided that the best way to present this information would be in text format.

4 Roadmap Overview

The roadmap contains three separate sections. Section 1 contains an overview (see Figure 1) of the steps an organization should take when implementing an effective traceability process. During the **pre-production stage** 'Plan for Traceability', an organisation should decide at an organisation level, or the project manager should decide at the project level which of the traceability best practices to implement. The best practices are numbered from 2.4.1 to 2.4.6 and this is the suggested order of implementation as there are certain dependencies between them, for example the Traceability Information model details the traces to be implemented and this information should be known before deciding on required resources.

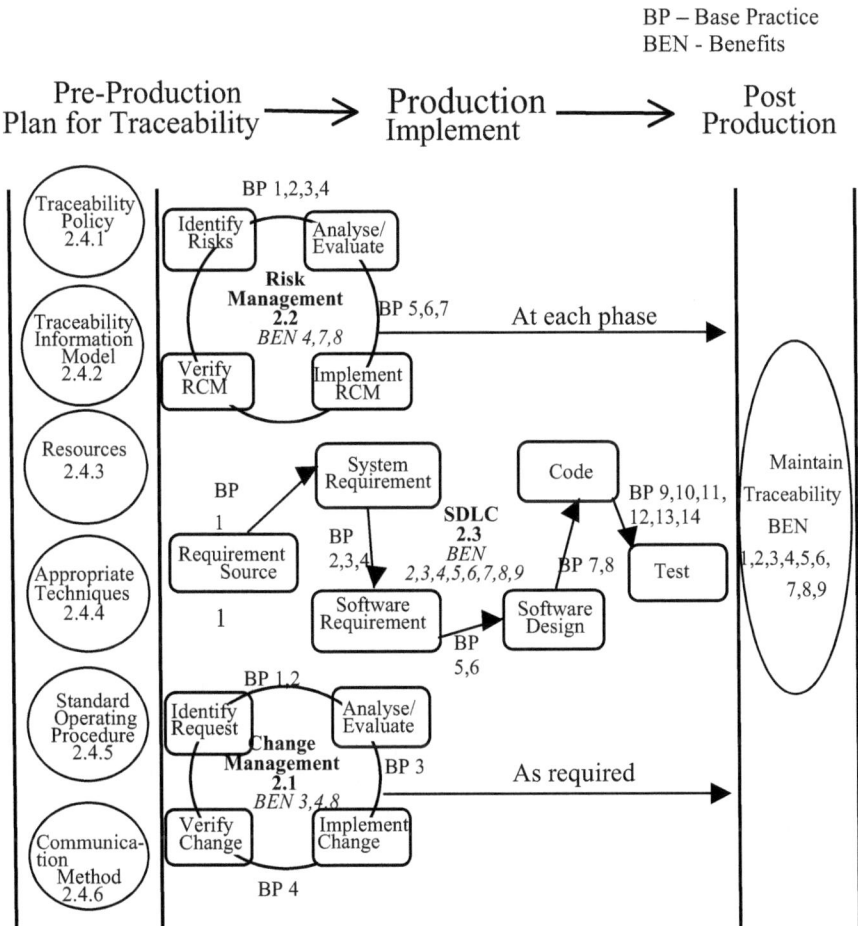

Fig. 1. Traceability Roadmap Overview

The **Production stage** in Figure 1 indicates implementation of traceability through the Software Development Lifecycle (SDLC) and the supporting processes of Risk Management and Change Management. The SDLC, Risk Management and Change Management processes respectively contain 14, 7 and 4 base practices (as distinct from best practices identified in Pre-Production). Figure 1, indicates at what stage during these processes the base practices should be exercised. These base practices have been extracted from the traceability PAM developed in conjunction with this roadmap [24]. Risk Management and thus risk management traceability should be implemented at each stage of the SDLC and through the maintenance lifecycle whereas Change Management and thus change management traceability should be implemented whenever a change is required through the SDLC and maintenance lifecycle.

Traceability needs to be maintained throughout Production and **Post-Production** or it will degrade and become untrustworthy. Maintaining traceability through Post-Production requires exercising the same development processes (i.e. SDLC, Risk Management and Change Management) and same base practices exercised during the production stage.

Section 2 of the roadmap contains details of the base practices for implementing traceability through the SDLC, Change Management, and Risk Management processes in addition to the best practices for implementing traceability. These base practices, are the activities that contribute to achieving the effective implementation of traceability through the SDLC, Risk Management and Change Management processes. For example Base Practice 1 (BP1) of the SDLC is: Establish bi-directional traceability between System requirement and their source.

Section 3 of the roadmap contains an implementation case study which guides the reader through the implementation of traceability in a fictional organization and is thought to be of particular benefit to organisations with little experience in software process improvement or implementation of traceability.

Figure 1 also indicates the benefits that can be leveraged during the SDLC and supporting processes of risk management and change management e.g. benefits 4, 7 and 8 can be leveraged through Risk Management traceability. The benefits are:

Benefit 1: Maintenance. Accurate traceability information facilitates making changes correctly and completely during maintenance, thus improving productivity.

Benefit 2: Reuse of components. The traceability matrices facilitate reusing product components from past projects and thus increasing productivity.

Benefit 3: Impact Analysis. Traceability information can be used to quickly and accurately identify the impact of any proposed change to the system.

Benefit 4: Project Management. Traceability information allows project managers to have current data on the progress of the project. By analysing the traceability matrices, the project manager can quickly determine which artefacts have been implemented and thus determine if schedule is on target.

Benefit 5: Customer confidence. The traceability matrices can be presented to the customer as reassurance that the customer is getting the product that they requested.

Benefit 6: Verification and Validation. The SDLC traceability matrix can be used to prove that a requirement has been designed into the system and implemented in the code. This validates the requirement. Similarly the trace matrix can be used to prove that the requirement, design and code have been tested which verifies the requirement, design and code.

Benefit 7: Certification. Regulation normally requires critical systems are certified before entering service. This involves submission of a safety case. A good safety case encompasses an effective risk mitigation process which is highly dependent on requirements traceability.

Benefit 8: Key personnel leaving. Documenting the links between artefacts through the traceability matrices reduces the risks of information being lost if key personnel leave the project/organisation.

Benefit 9: Test failures. If tests fail, the SDLC traceability matrix can be used to identify the artefacts that potentially cause the failures, as requirements, design and code are linked to software requirements test.

5   Validation of the Roadmap

5.1   Research Method

An initial validation of the traceability roadmap has been conducted by expert review. Eight experts agreed to participate and were chosen based on their expertise in one or more of the following: a) roadmap development, b) medical device standards, c) requirements traceability, d) medical device software development and e) software process improvement. A brief overview of the experts credentials include:

Expert 1 has seven years in industry and seven years in academia researching traceability;

Expert 2 has more than thirty years' experience in software development, is a consultant of a major medical device manufacturer, is a member of the ISO/IEC JTC1 WG10 (Process assessment), and is the author of the addendum of IEC 62304:2006 showing the mapping between 62304 and 12207;

Expert 3 has worked in the software industry for about 12 years as programmer, analyst, project manager and database administrator and is Chief Scientist with a major software research centre;

Expert 4 has forty years' experience in software development, the last ten of which have been in medical device software specialising in integration of traceability;

Expert 5 has twenty years' experience in software development in roles such as Quality manager, and Lean and Agile coach. He has established a UML modelling concept to support 100% traceability;

Expert 6 has managed software design and development processes for a medical device manufacturer. This role included oversight of software quality assurance;

Expert 7 develops software for laboratory testing in a medical device company and has experience with tests and requirements traceability according to IEC 62304;

Expert 8 has experience in industry software development, open source software development and roadmap development.

Each reviewer was sent a copy of the roadmap along with a questionnaire which focused on the roadmaps 'fit for purpose'. Some of the questions asked for an opinion based on the 5 level Likert scale [27] including a rationale for their response, while some of the questions asked for an opinion (without the Likert scale) and a rationale for their opinion. The questions requiring a Likert scale response are listed in Table 1. An example of a question without the Likert scale asked in the questionnaire is: Do you agree with the order of implementation depicted in Figure 1? Please give a short rationale for your opinion.

After all responses were received they were tabulated and a focus group consisting of four members from the Regulated Software Research Centre based in Dundalk Institute of Technology, Ireland was then convened to discuss the responses and arrive at a general consensus as to what changes should be made to the roadmap.

5.2 Findings

The eight experts were asked three questions which required a response rated on a five point Likert scale where 1 = Strongly Disagree, 2 = Disagree, 3 = Neither Agree or Disagree, 4 = Agree and 5 = Strongly Agree. The questions and responses are shown in Table 1.

Table 1. Reviewers responses rated on Likert scale

Questions	Rating				
	1	2	3	4	5
To what extent do you agree that the traceability implementation roadmap is usable in practice?		2	1	3	2
To what extent do you agree that the traceability roadmap is adaptable and customisable to different company settings (size, culture, resources etc.)?	1		2	5	
To what extent do you agree that the traceability roadmap is useful in practice?		1	2	4	1

The table indicates for example that in response to the question, 'To what extent do you agree that the traceability implementation roadmap is usable in practice?', two reviewers *strongly agreed* that it did while three reviewers *agreed* that it did etc. So while the table indicates an overall positive response, a series of further questions in the questionnaire elicited a total of 42 comments/suggestions for improvement. These comments were categorized under three main headings of Structure, Content, and Rationale as shown in Table 2.

The Structure category contained 7 comments about the structure of the roadmap. These comments related to:
- the order of the best practices under Pre-Production in Figure 1;
- a comment stating that references to medical device standards should be in an Appendix;
- 2 comments stating that the benefits of traceability should be in the introduction.

Table 2. Categorisation of Reviewer Comments

EXPERT	STRUCTURE			CONTENT							RATIONALE			
	Figure 1 Structure	Regulatory Location Reference	Traceability Location Benefits	Less Content/ Complexity	Tools/ Automation	Implementation Detail	Adaptability/ Flexibility	Additional Benefits	Content Applicability	Additional Content	Signposting	Overview Explanation	Base Practice v Best Practice	Tracing Rationale
1			1								1		1	
2	2	1	1	3	1				1	1		1		
3	1													1
4	1				2		1		2	4				
5				1	1	1				1				
6				1	2		1		2	1		1		
7								1						
8				1				1				1		
Total Comments	4	1	2	6	6	1	2	3	5	6	1	3	1	1

The majority of received comments were categorized under the Content category. This category contains 29 comments which were generally focused on the substance of the roadmap. These comments related to:

- Six comments stated that they thought the roadmap had too much content and was too complex e.g. "*I would have like to make it much shorter with better visualizations*".
- Six comments were also made with regard to tools and automation, suggesting that while the roadmap offers both automated and manual options, the roadmap would be better served if it '*encourages automation more*'.
- One comment on implementation detail suggests that a better explanation of how to complete matrices is required;
- Three comments suggested that a number of additional benefits of traceability could be added to the roadmap;
- Two reviewers thought that the roadmap could be improved if it was more flexible and that the methods suggested for implementing traceability should be marked as exemplar;
- Five comments were made with regard to the applicability of some of the content in the roadmap. These comments questioned the best practice of not using traceability in performance reviews, and if there is a need for a Standard Operating Procedure;
- Six comments were made with regard to adding additional content to the roadmap. These comments included adding additional columns to the trace

matrix, adding a section stating how the roadmap is applicable to different SDLC types e.g. Agile, Spiral, Iterative, and finally one reviewer thought that *'in order to be persuasive it is important to sell traceability'* .

The Rationale column contained 6 comments relating to the reviewers understanding of the roadmap and are summarised as:

- One reviewer thought that the roadmap could be improved with better 'signposting' to direct the reader through the document;
- Three reviewers thought that the Overview section was not self-explanatory and needed more detail;
- One reviewer was confused with the terms best practice and base practice;
- One reviewer considers that the rationale for traceability in the Introduction section could be improved.

5.3 Discussion

As a result of the comments/suggestions for improvement the focus group, which was convened after all the comments were received, came to a decision regarding changes to be made to the roadmap. The changes are listed under the Structure, Content and Rationale categories.

Structure Category. One comment thought that references to the standards which were in Section 2 of the roadmap should be put in an Appendix. This comment is related to six other comments categorised under the Content column which refer to the roadmap having too much content. The focus group agreed that the references to the regulations were not necessary for the implementation of the roadmap and were for informative purposes only and so agreed that they should be put in an appendix.

Two comments thought that the Introduction to the roadmap should contain the benefits of traceability. These comments relate to a comment under the Content category which states that it is important to sell traceability, and also relates to a comment under the Rationale column which states that the rationale for traceability in the Introduction could be improved. The focus group considered that putting the benefits of traceability in the Introduction would inappropriately extend the Introduction. It was agreed that the benefits and barriers section should be moved to an Appendix and referenced in the Introduction.

Content Category. Six comments under the Content section stated that the use of automatic tools should be encouraged more (as against manual methods which were described in Section 2 of the roadmap). These comments are related to two other comments under the Content section which state that the manual methods should be marked as exemplar. The focused group agreed with these comments and so the manual methods are marked as exemplar and moved to an appendix, which has the additional benefit of making the roadmap less complex. Additionally the use of automated trace tools will be highlighted in the roadmap overview along with a tool decision flowchart in Appendix D.

Three comments stated that a number of additional benefits of traceability could be added to Figure 1 e.g. benefits 5, 6 and 7 should be added to Change Management.

The focus group considered that these three benefits were generic across the three processes and so it was agreed to add them to the three processes.

A number of comments were made with regard to adding additional content to the roadmap. The focus group considered these comments and agreed to add a paragraph in the Introduction to address how the roadmap is applicable to different SDLC types e.g. Iterative, Spiral, Agile etc.

Rationale Category. The focus group agreed that adding hyperlinks to the roadmap would improve the readability of the document. This was in response to one reviewer's comment about improving the 'signposting' throughout the roadmap.

One reviewer stated that using the two terms 'best practice' and 'base practice' was confusing. The focus group agreed not to change these terms as 'base practice' is the term used in ISO/IEC 15504 and this is the standard on which the PAM related to this roadmap complies with. Additionally the term 'best practice' is a term used throughout the literature and is generally known. It was however agreed that a distinction between the terms should be made in the Introduction of the roadmap.

5.4 Complete Roadmap

A table of contents of the completed roadmap is shown in Table 3. The main body of the roadmap now contains three relatively short sections with a lot of informative material referenced in the Appendix.

Table 3. Completed Roadmap Table of Contents

Introduction	**Appendix A** Barriers and possible solutions Leveraging traceability benefits
Scope	**Appendix B** Difference between IEC 62304 and ISO 12207
Section 1 Roadmap Overview	**Appendix C** Traceability links and references to Standards

Section 2 Traceability Milestones, Outcomes and Base Practices for each of the processes:
    Change management
    Risk management
    SDLC
	Appendix D
	Exemplar traceability methods and tasks

Section 3 Implementation Case Study	**Appendix E** Traceability Best Practices in detail

6 Conclusion

To assist medical device organisations improve their traceability, a roadmap for the implementation of traceability has been developed. This roadmap is based on a ISO/IEC 15504 compliant Process Assessment Model (PAM) developed by the authors prior to this roadmap. The PAM will assist medical device organisations understand their actual traceability performance and management of activities, and the potential for improvement. The roadmap will then provide the pathway to that improvement and ensure compliance with the medical device standards and traceability best practices.

Eight experts reviewed the roadmap. While the response was mostly positive they made a total of forty two comments suggesting fourteen areas for change. A focus group reviewed these comments and through consensus agreed to make two changes to the structure of the roadmap, four changes to the content of the roadmap, and two changes to aid understanding (rationale) of the roadmap. Based on the review feedback and resulting amendments which have resulted in its enhancement, the roadmap is now ready for pilot assessment within two medical device organisations.

Acknowledgement. This research is supported by the Science Foundation Ireland Principal Investigator Programme, grant number 08/IN.1/I2030 and by Lero - the Irish Software Research Centre (http://www.lero.ie) grant 10/CE/I1855.

References

1. Mason, P.: On traceability for safety critical systems engineering. In: Proceedings of the 12th Asia-Pacific Software Engineering Conference, pp. 272-282. IEEE Computer Society (2005)
2. Gotel, O., Mader, P.: Acquiring tool support for traceability. In: Cleland-Huang, J., Gotel, O., Zisman, A. (eds.) Software and Systems Traceability. Springer, Heidelberg (2012)
3. Lucia, A.D., Marcus, A., Oliveto, R., Poshyvanyk, D.: Information retrieval methods for automated traceability recovery. In: Cleland-Huang, J., Gotel, O., Zisman, A. (eds.) Software and Systems Traceability, pp. 71–98. Springer, London (2012)
4. McCaffery, F., Casey, V.: Med-Trace: Traceability Assessment Method for Medical Device Software Development. EuroSPI pp. 1.1 - 1.8, Denmark (2011)
5. Mader, P., Gotel, O., Philippow, I.: Motivation matters in the traceability trenches. In: Proceedings of the 2009 17th IEEE International Requirements Engineering Conference, RE, pp. 143-148. IEEE Computer Society (2009)
6. Probert, D., Radnor, M.: Technology roadmapping: frontier experiences from industry-academia consortia. Research-Technology Management **46**, 27–30 (2003)
7. Flood, D., Caffery, F.M., Casey, V., Regan, G.: A methodology for software process improvement roadmaps for regulated domains – example with IEC 62366 In: European Systems and Software Process Improvement and Innovation Conference, EuroSPI - See more at (2013)
8. Phaal, R., Farrukh, C., Probert, D.: Technology roadmapping—A planning framework for evolution and revolution. Technological Forecasting & Social Change **71**, 5–26 (2003)

9. Phaal, R., Farrukh, C., Mitchel, R., Probert, D.: Technology roadmapping: Starting-up roadmapping fast. Research Technology Management **46**, 52–58 (2003)
10. McFeeley, R.S., McKeehan, D.W., Temple, T.: Technical Report CMU/SEI-95-UG-001 - Software Process Improvement Roadmap. SEI (1995)
11. Regan, G., Casey, V., Flood, D., Mc Caffery, F.: A critical evaluation of a methodology for the generation of software process improvement roadmaps. In: Barafort, B., O'Connor, R.V., Poth, A., Messnarz, R. (eds.) EuroSPI 2014. CCIS, vol. 425, pp. 36–47. Springer, Heidelberg (2014)
12. Barafort, B., Renault, A., Picard, M., Cortina, S.: A transformation process for building PRMs and PAMs based on a collection of requirements – Example with ISO/IEC 20000. SPICE, Nuremberg, Germany (2008)
13. ISO/IEC: 15504-2: Process assessment — Performing an assessment. ISO, Switzerland (2003)
14. Bray, O.H., Garcia, M.L.: Technology roadmapping: the integration of strategic and technology planning for competitiveness. International Conference on Management and Technology. IEEE, Portland, Oregon (1997)
15. Petrick, I.J.: Developing and Implementing Roadmaps – A Reference Guide (2008)
16. Garcia, M., Bray, O.: Fundamentals of Technology roadmapping. Sandia National Laborities (1997)
17. Smith, D.: Strategic Roadmaps (2005)
18. ANSI/AAMI/IEC: 62304:2006 Medical device software—Software life cycle processes. AAMI, Arlington, VA (2006)
19. ISO: ISO 14971:2007 Medical devices — Application of risk management to medical devices. ISO, Switzerland (2007)
20. ISO: ISO 13485:2003, Medical Devices-Quality Management Systems-Requirements for Regulatory Purposes. ISO, Geneva, Switzerland (2003)
21. FDA: Guidance for the Content of Premarket Submissions for Software Contained in Medical Devices. CDRH, Rockville (2005)
22. FDA: General Principles of Software Validation; Final Guidance for Industry and FDA Staff. CDRH, Rockville (2002)
23. FDA: Off-The-Shelf Software Use in Medical Devices; Guidance for Industry, FDA Reviewers and Compliance. CDRH, Rockville (1999)
24. Regan, G., McCaffery, F., McDaid, K., Flood, D.: The development and validation of a traceability assessment model. In: Mitasiunas, A., Rout, T., O'Connor, R.V., Dorling, A. (eds.) SPICE 2014. CCIS, vol. 477, pp. 72–83. Springer, Heidelberg (2014)
25. Regan, G., Mc Caffery, F., Mc Daid, K., Flood, D.: Implementation of traceability best practices within the medical device domain. EuroSPI 2013. DELTA, Dundalk, Ireland (2013)
26. Pekerti, A.A.: Augmentation of information in educational objects: Effectiveness of arrows and pictures as information for actions in instructional objects. Australasian Journal of Educational Technology 29, (2013)
27. Jamieson, S.: Likert scales:how to (ab) use them. Medical Ecducation **38**, 1217–1218 (2004)

Quantitative Requirements Prioritization from a Pre-development Perspective

Enrico Johansson[1(✉)], Daniel Bergdahl[1], Jan Bosch[2], and Helena Holmström Olsson[3]

[1] Sony Mobile Communications Inc, Lund, Sweden
{Enrico.Johansson,Daniel.Bergdahl}@sonymobile.com
[2] Department of Computer Science and Engineering,
Chalmers University of Technology, Gothenburg, Sweden
Jan.Bosch@chalmers.se
[3] Department of Computer Science, Malmö University, Malmö, Sweden
Helena.Holmstrom.Olsson@mah.se

Abstract. Feature content in system releases tends to be prioritized using limited amounts of qualitative user input and based on the opinions of those in product management. This leads to several problems due to the wasteful allocation of R&D resources. In this paper, we present the results of our efforts to collect quantitative customer input before the start of development using mock-ups and surveys for a mobile application developed by Sony Mobile. Our research shows that (1) collecting quantitative feedback before development is feasible, (2) the data collected deviates from the original feature prioritization, i.e. it is beneficial and (3) the data gives further insight in requirement prioritization than a qualitative method could have provided.

Keywords: Requirements engineering · Customer data · Survey · Mock-up · Data-driven development · Case study

1 Introduction

In most software development companies, the pre-development is the phase in which decisions are taken on whether to develop a feature or not. In this phase, during requirement prioritization, the expected value of a feature is estimated and if the outcome is positive the feature is developed. There are, however, a number of problems associated with this.

First, the estimated value of a feature is typically based on very limited data that can prove whether the estimation is correct. As a result, feature prioritization becomes an opinions-based process [1].

Second, the estimations that are done in the pre-study phase are typically based on limited amounts of qualitative feedback from customers. Data is collected by asking customers what they want and by observing what they do and the output is a limited set of individual customer opinions and experiences regarding product use. While this feedback is valuable, it does not represent a large customer base and it does not reveal actual product usage. Ideally, qualitative customer feedback in the pre-development phase should be complemented with quantitative data that confirm individual perceptions but this has proven difficult to accomplish [2]

Third, due to lack of mechanisms to measure feature usage, companies invest in developing features that have no proven customer value. Often, and as recognized in previous research [3], the majority of features in a system are never, or only very seldom, used. This situation could be avoided if accurate data collection mechanisms were in place, allowing companies to allocate resources to development with proven customer value.

There is a need to overcome these problems to stay competitive. The one who makes the best prediction (by prioritizing the features with highest value) not only wins the market shares but also reduces waste in the development cycle. However, prioritization is a challenging part of the requirement engineering processes since it is trying to predict the future. This is especially true in a market driven context addressing end-users as customers.

A number of qualitative prioritization methods are defined in requirement engineering processes. Qualitative prioritization methods are often by nature subjective and involve for example guessing or weighing requirements against each other. An alternative approach to find the requirement priority is to quantitatively measure usage by introducing mock-ups to collect what users find interesting.

The paper does an assessment if it is valuable to include quantitative prioritization methods in the overall requirement engineering process during pre-development. The assessment is based on a case study conducted at Sony Mobile Communications Inc. We explore data collection techniques that allows for collection of quantitative data in the pre-development phase, i.e. before development of a feature starts. The exploration is done by assessing the possibility of pre-development quantitative data collection as outlined by a specific model for quantitative and qualitative data collection. Our research shows that (1) collecting quantitative feedback before development is feasible, (2) the data collected deviates from the original feature prioritization, i.e. it is beneficial, and (3) the data gives further insight in requirement prioritization than a qualitative method could have provided.

The remainder of this paper is organized as follows. The next section presents the background research for this paper. Section 3 describes the problem statements that can be addressed via quantitative data collection methods before the start of development. Section 4 describes the method used to assess the pre-development phase. Section 5 describes the case study and data collected. Section 6 contains final analysis and discussion of the result and possibilities for further work.

2 Background

Companies use a range of techniques to collect customer feedback in the early stages of product development. In the pre-development phase, techniques such as customer interviews, customer observation and customer surveys are typically used to get an understanding for customer perceptions of new product functionality [2][4][5][6][7][8]. Furthermore, mock-ups and different prototyping techniques are common to have customers try early versions of the product and for evaluating e.g. user interfaces.

Typically, these techniques provide a limited set of qualitative data reflecting individual customer needs [2]. In addition, there exist a number of techniques that can be used to validate customer needs during the development process, e.g. the HYPEX model [1]. Inspired by the 'Build-Measure-Learn' loop as outlined in the Lean Startup literature [9], they emphasize the need to build smaller increments of features that can be frequently validated by customers to avoid developing features that are not appreciated by customers. In a number of recent studies [1][10][11], the notion of frequent customer validation is described as 'innovation experiment systems' in which the R&D organization responds based on instant feedback from customers. This requires features and products with instrumentation for data collection so that product use can be continuously monitored. In this way, companies can learn about customer behaviors on a continuous basis and improve their products accordingly. In addition, and similar to common practice in the Web 2.0 and the SaaS domain [12], companies can run feature experiments, e.g. A/B or split testing, in which different customer groups receive different versions of the same feature and where data is collected to determine which version is the most appreciated one. In [11], this is referred to as the most efficient way to learn about customers. According to this author, the faster an organization learns about its customer and the ways in which they use the products, the more value it will provide. In [1] the process for feature experiments is further elaborated upon, and the authors present the HYPEX model, i.e. a process model for initiating, running and evaluating feature experiments. Similar to [1], [13] describe this as continuous experimentation and emphasize that customer experiment results need to be closely linked to feature prioritization and road mapping in order to support a more flexible business strategy.

As one attempt to capture the wide range of available customer feedback techniques, [2] present a model in which they identify different techniques, the type of data that is collected and the development phases in which the techniques are typically used. They picture the early development stages as characterized by direct customer feedback, and with small amounts of qualitative data being collected. In later stages, and after commercial deployment of the product, companies observe customers and use indirect feedback techniques to collect large sets of quantitative data. In ongoing work, and as a way to further detail qualitative and quantitative customer feedback techniques, [14] present the 'Qualitative/quantitative Customer-driven Development' (QCD) model. In this model, qualitative and quantitative customer feedback techniques are used to validate hypotheses derived from a backlog representing product concepts and ideas. The model suggests an approach in which requirements are treated as hypotheses that are continuously validated with customers, and only those that prove customer value are fully developed and deployed.

However, despite a wide range of available techniques, there are few techniques that help companies collect quantitative customer data already before investing in development of a feature. In what follows, we detail the problems that we encountered in previous research and in the interactions with companies in the software development domain, and we explore techniques that allow for the collection of qualitative data also before investing in the idea.

3 Problem Statement

Based on the research presented above, we have identified three problems often occurring in companies developing software-intensive systems. Below we describe each problem in more detail.

3.1 Release Content Cast in Stone

Most companies use a release model where the feature content for each release is decided upon before the start of development. Companies lack mechanisms to continuously validate feature content with customers, and find it difficult to re-prioritize pre-study outcomes. This causes companies to complete the building of features even if during development it becomes obvious that the feature clearly doesn't provide value to customers. This causes a sizeable part of the R&D resources to be allocated to wasteful activities and deteriorates the competitive position of companies over time.

3.2 Featuritis

There is evidence that a majority of features are seldom or never used and that customers seldom use the full potential of the functionality they receive [3]. Often referred to as "featuritis" [15], this means half or more of the R&D effort of a company is wasted on non-value adding activities. Similar to the previous problem, if competitors manage to have less waste in their R&D activities, over time the market position of the company is affected negatively.

3.3 Everything and the Kitchen Sink

Although often treated as atomic in research, features can be implemented iteratively and to a lesser or greater extent. Engineers often have a tendency to build features such that all use cases, exceptions and special situations are taken into account. Often, however, the value of a feature to customers is already accomplished after building a small part of the feature that provides the greatest value. Further development does not lead to (much) more value for customers. However, companies find it difficult to decide on when and how to stop building a feature when further iterations fail to add value to customers due to a lack of mechanisms for collecting feedback before, during development and after deployment of functionality [2].

In the remainder of the paper, we present a case study in which we evaluate two techniques that help companies validate customer value already in the pre-development phase before R&D investment has been made.

4 Research Method and Process

The research reported in this paper is based on a case study conducted at Sony Mobile. In our study, we focus on the data collection practices, and especially how to collect quantitative data already in the pre-development phase. To study this, and to evaluate two techniques that allow for this, we conducted case study research [17][18] based on interviews, workshop sessions, participant observations and active interventions in the case company where two of the authors are also employed. As a research method, case study research is typically used to contribute to our knowledge of individual, group, organizational and social phenomena, and is typically used to explain 'how' and 'why' and questions that require an extensive and in-depth understanding of the phenomenon [17][18]. Below, we describe how we selected an appropriate product and application for our study, and how to assess the data collection practices in the pre-development phase. As can be seen below, the first step is to select a product and application that meets the requirements to make the assessment possible. The second step is to identify what aspects of the pre-development phase the assessment should target. The final step involves how the assessments are performed and evaluated.

4.1 Choice of Product and Application

The choice of product landed on Sony Xperia™ phone and a specific Android application. This choice of product and application has been governed by compliance with three main requirements.
1. Large number of interactions with end consumers
2. Main assumption and statistics is that people using the app are first time users.
3. Possibility to change the feature set for selected users by showing a mock-up of a new feature set.

Requirement 1 targets the external validity [16][17] of the study. External validity refers to how well data and theories from one single case study can be generalized. Requirement 2 targets the internal [16][17] validity of the study. Internal validity refers to how well the case study is designed to avoid confounding factors. A confounding factor can be described as possible independent variable causing the effect, rather the variable concerned in the case study.

Requirement 3 targets the technical aspects of the android applications. The challenge was to create a mock-up of an existing application and replace the application in the already deployed product.

4.2 Assessment of Pre-development Phase

Two aspects of the pre-development phases are within the assessment scope of the case study. These two aspects are:
1. How well can we rely on pre-development quantitative data?
2. Is it possible to use pre-development quantitative data to give input to the hypothesis used for further experimentation?

By exploring the result from three data sets an assessment can be made of how valuable quantitative data collection in pre-development phases. One data set (FS-I) collects data from the real customer usage, the second data set (FS-II) is collected through a on-line survey on the web and the third data set (FS-III) is collected by mockup of the application presenting possible features considering the branding and name of the application. The criteria for giving a positive assessment result for aspect 1 is if the mockup (FS-III) and real application (FS-II) show similar pattern in customer usage for similar features. The criteria for giving a positive assessment result for aspect 2 is if new, edited, deleted hypothesis are elicited with use of the data collected (FS-II and FS-III).

5 The Sony Mobile Case

The case study has been performed at Sony Mobile Communications Inc. (Sony Mobile). Sony Mobile is a wholly owned subsidiary of Tokyo-based Sony Corporation, a leading global innovator of audio, video, game, communications, key device and information technology products for both the consumer and professional markets. Due to confidentiality reasons we cannot reveal the actual application. However, we can provide the following base data: The application was first deployed to live users in January 2013 and at present it is available in approximately 40M devices globally. With a few exceptions, the application is shipped with every mobile phone and tablet that Sony Mobile ships. Every month the application is in use approximately 3.5M times where every use on average involves three main use cases. The original application provides 4 + 1 features (see description of feature set one (FS-I) below) where each feature requires two to five interactions in the normal case and based on collected data we know that the application has approximately 9,5M interactions per month. The use of the application is consistent over the year and does not show e.g. seasonal variations or variations due to product releases. The application is considered to be one of the base line applications delivered with Sony Mobile products.

5.1 Application Features

In order to not break confidentiality we have coded the available and possible features into feature types (FT) and enumerated these from FT01 to FT12. Of particular interest for this study are the "no feature" id est users that are not using the application for any particular reason, rather just exploring the application. This feature was added to Feature Set II and Feature Set III. The "nothing feature" is enumerated as FT13.

Throughout this study we have used three methods to capture what the user really wants to use; actual usage, survey and mock-up. Due to limitations, technical possibilities and semantic limitation in the three methods all features could not be made available in all three methods. Instead a selection had to be made. An explanation of what features were selected in respective feature set follows.

5.1.1 Feature Set I – (FS-I)

The first feature set to be evaluated is what was actually deployed in the first version of the application. The application itself contains a tracking mechanism that collects usage data into Google analytics. Hence the data was readily available for our study.

During the measured time frame the application was used 3.652.796 times. The application did at that time present four main features (FT01 - FT04) as well as a less prominently displayed feature (FT05). During that period the features were used a total of 2.618.513 times. All other usage of the application a total of 1.034.283 are considered to be in FT13 group (no usage/nothing group)

Expressed as percentage of usage the distribution of the six identified feature types looks like in Table 1 below:

Table 1. Response distribution FS-I

Feature	Relative Usage
FT01	28,56%
FT02	21,53%
FT03	11,49%
FT04	6,79%
FT05	3,31%
FT13	28,31%
Total	100,00%

5.1.2 Feature Set II – (FS-II)

As we were looking to extend the feature set for the product, but wanted to collect quantitative data on the customer needs we employed two techniques. The first, a survey, is discussed in this section. The second, a mockup, is discussed in the next section.

The second feature set to evaluate is what users answers when prompted in a survey. Users visiting a specific site were randomly selected to answer a survey about their reason for using the application. A total of seven (7) different features where selectable and only one answer could be given. The question was formulated as "What is the primary feature you are looking for", thereby forcing the user to give a distinct answer even if the user had several reasons for using the application.

The selectable features were basically the same as in the original application however the least prominent feature (FT05) was not included and two more features (FT06 and FT07) were possible to select. However FT01 through FT04 were selected to be same as well as the nothing feature (FT13). This slight separation between features was necessary in order to be able to present the various features in a sensible manner and not making it obvious to the user that additional data was collected so that we could get a clear user aware set-up. A total of 119.370 survey answers were collected during one month. The answer relative distribution can be seen in Table 2 below.

Table 2. Response distribution FS-II

Feature	Relative Usage
FT01	24,39%
FT02	33,55%
FT03	11,62%
FT04	13,09%
FT06	1,77%
FT07	2,50%
FT13	13,07%
Total	100,00%

5.1.3 Feature Set III – (FS-III)

Based on the two first feature sets, basically collected from existing data and/or without modifying the actual application it was seen that additional features could be possible candidates for further development. In line with the HYPEX model [1], we designed a new version of the application as a mockup that would allow for serving a very large number of features. Imperative was that the new design should be the minimal (least expensive/requiring the least effort) viable feature (MVF). In order to find possible features, in addition to the existing (FS-I) and the ones found when doing the survey (FS-II) a third feature set FS-III was constructed. To find additional possible features, similar applications from other manufacturers were surveyed. The features FT08 through FT12 were added. FT06 had to be excluded from the application due to its nature and in the context of the application it was too similar to FT07. In the choice between FT06 and FT07 it was judged that FT07 was a better match.

The application was modified to present the newly designed feature set and in order to keep the development and implementation as minimal as possible but still viable for use the underlying functionality was strictly limited, in fact so much that it just barely resembled the promised feature. To mitigate the risk of causing damage to the product extra work was put into making sure that any given user would be exposed to the new design only once.

As we presented a much larger feature set in the mockup and rather than implementing each feature, by and large linked to existing features or served rather simple screens, we view this as a pre-development activity as the features are not actually developed. Rather the mockup was "inserted" in front of the normal application and linked to existing functionality where possible.

The new design of the application forced the user to make a selection upfront leaving out all other elements of the application at this stage. The order in which the features were presented was randomized in order to avoid the risk of the user selecting e.g. the first or last feature.

The prototype was launched into production for a period of 10 days, during this time we collected 34.393 interactions. The relative distribution of answers is shown in table 3 below.

Table 3. Usage distribution FS-III

Feature	Relative Usage
FT01	27,08%
FT02	9,68%
FT03	9,79%
FT04	4,20%
FT05	4,57%
FT07	6,57%
FT08	8,90%
FT09	8,42%
FT10	3,63%
FT11	3,43%
FT12	2,26%
FT13	11,46%
Total	100,00%

5.2 Feature Set Usage Description

In the previous section, we introduced the features that were used for the baseline activity, the survey approach and the mockup approach. In this section, we present in more detail the usage of features for each approach and indicate relevant aspects of each step in our research process.

5.2.1 Feature Set – I (FS-I)

Looking at FS-I, with its limited number of features FT01, FT02 and FT13 together amounts for almost 80%, noting as well that the nothing feature (FT13) is almost as large as the real feature FT01, 28,31% for FT13 as compared to 28,56% for FT01. FT05 in FS-I is the feature that has a less prominent display in the application that could explain its very low usage (3,31%).

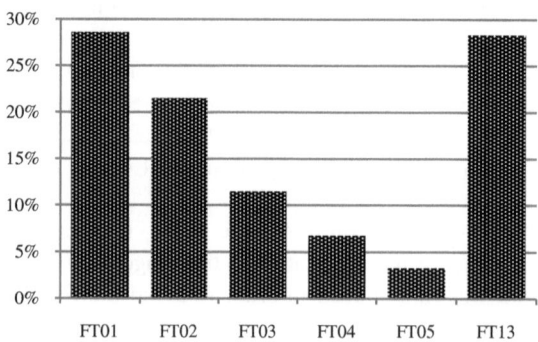

Fig. 1. FS-I Relative distribution of feature usage

5.2.2 Feature Set – II (FS-II)

In FS-II where the user was asked to actively participate in a survey the distribution of answers can be illustrated in figure 2. When asked the users appear to favor FT02 though the difference to FT01 is not that large. Looking at the graph it may appear such that the features group (FT01 and FT02, FT03 and FT04, FT06 and FT07), however looking at the underlying features no such grouping makes sense and this grouping is random rather than a true correlation. To our surprise FT013 stands out in this feature set as well: even in a survey, users of the app were willing to indicate that they were not looking for anything in particular.

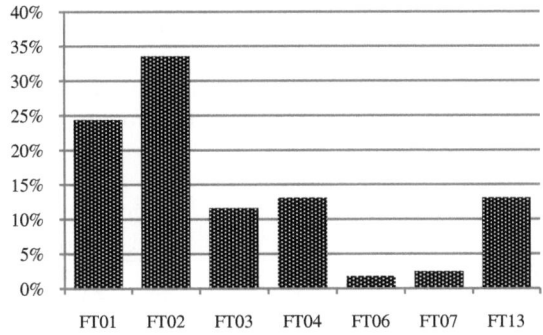

Fig. 2. FS-II relative distribution of feature type usage

5.2.3 Feature Set – III (FS-III)

Using the mock-up application, the large number of available features seems to have leveled out the choice users make, though FT01 as well as FT13 stands out. The relative usage is depicted in Fig 3 below.

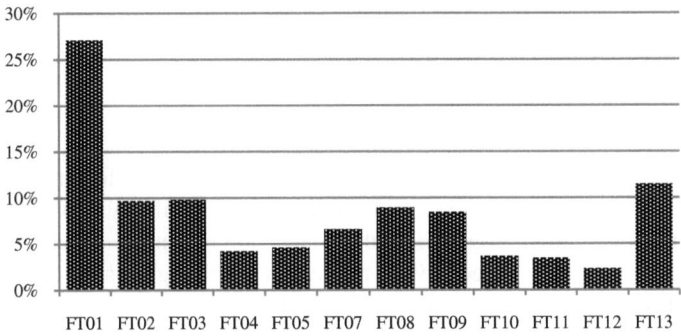

Fig. 3. FS-III relative distribution of feature usage

5.3 Feature Comparison Between Collection Methods

Looking at the differences between the three methods it can be clearly seen that the results match well between the various methods. The overall distribution is depicted in Fig. 4. below. In all three collection methods, FT01 and FT13 have high usage. An obvious conclusion from this is that carefully selecting the feature to put first as well as designing a good user experience for users that arrive at the app without a clear goal in mind is particularly important. When a wider selection is available as in FS-III the user preference for the other features is more nuanced and requires more careful interpretation of the data. For instance, the selection frequency for FT02 and FT04 is very different for the survey and the mockup. As the survey asks customers explicitly for a choice, the technique measures what users say they want. The mockup, on the other hand, is concerned with measuring what users will actually do in practice. The latter is obviously more relevant but understanding why the gap between espoused and enacted behavior in users exists is important for product management and R&D to understand.

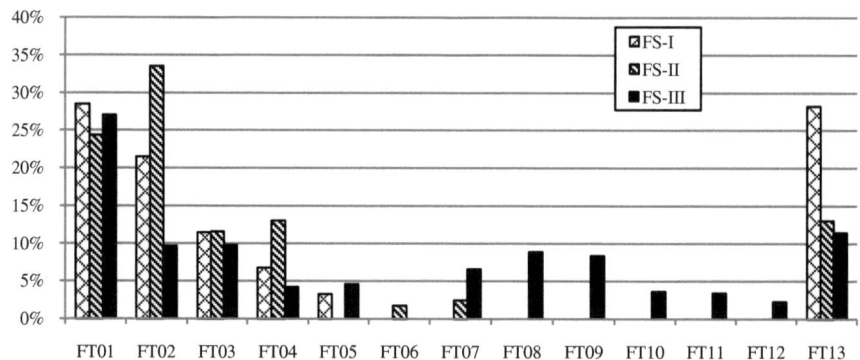

Fig. 4. Comparison of the feature types between the feature sets

6 Analysis and Discussion

6.1 Assessment of Aspect 1

The data collected from all set can be visualized by ordering the feature in descending order concerning the usage percentage. Considering the similarity in patterns especially with features with high usage is that the conclusion is that pre-development collection methods are valid for especially for the features with high usage.

For the different sets (FS-I, FS-II, FS-III) the lists are the following:
  i. :{FT01, FT13, FT02, FT03, FT05, FT04}
  ii. :{FT02, FT01, FT04, FT13, FT03, FT07, FT06}
  iii. :{FT01, FT13, FT03, FT02, FT08, FT09, FT07, FT06, FT05, FT04, FT10, FT11, FT12}

Table 4. Feature usage in usage order

FS-I	FS-II	FS-III
FT01	FT02	FT01
FT13	FT01	FT13
FT02	FT04	FT03
FT03	FT13	FT02
FT04	FT03	FT08
FT05	FT07	FT09
	FT06	FT07
		FT05
		FT04
		FT10
		FT11
		FT12

6.2 Assessment of Aspect 2

Interviews have been held with senior staff members at Sony Mobile. The scope of the interviews has been to study and compare the different data set to evaluate if hypothesis can been elicited. These hypotheses would be candidates to populate new, edit or delete hypotheses to be used as experiments in the product development. The result of the interviews is that it was possible to elicit hypothesis. The following hypotheses were elicited. FT07, FT08, FT09 are not available in existing application (FS-III) and have a relative high usage percentage in the mockup. Therefore they are considered valid entries to the hypothesis backlog as additional features. FT10 has a low usage rate in the mockup and the hypothesis is that there are a number of better features to invest in. FT13 is a special case since it defines a usage where the customer opens the application but does not take any actions. A hypothesis is that there is an opportunity to capture this kind of users and turn them to active users within the application.

6.3 Discussion

In this paper, we present a case study conducted at Sony Mobile in which we explore the feasibility to collect quantitative customer data also before development starts, i.e. in the pre-development phase. While this has proven difficult, we evaluate two techniques that allow for assessment of whether a feature is worthwhile developing or whether R&D resources should be allocated somewhere else. Our case study shows that collection of quantitative data in the pre-development phase is both feasible and useful in the feature prioritization process, and that this data is also reliable. In addition, the combination of techniques where users are aware that they are asked for input (espoused behavior) [19], and techniques where enacted user behavior is captured provides for valuable insight in to the difference between the two. This allows for further hypothesis development to explain the gap between espoused and enacted behavior.

In our study, the frequent use of the "do nothing" feature indicates that there are additional opportunities to engage users than the basic "select a feature" functionality. As the user opened the app without a clear goal in mind, the app can propose and nudge users to engage with the app or other Sony Mobile applications, as the user almost seems to expect the app to take the initiative. These types of insights, i.e. those user behaviors that are not necessarily captured by qualitative data collection techniques, are extremely valuable for product managers and R&D teams. Also, if these can be captured already before development starts, as shown in our study, product managers and R&D teams can act pro-actively and, if needed, re-prioritize feature content.

Finally, there are a number of opportunities for further study that we are considering, especially concerning the empirical design. For example, expanding the analysis to more applications, and other types of applications, making the feature sets in pre-development more comparable by using same number of features. Also, we plan to assess other pre-development quantitative methods.

Acknowledgments. The development work needed for of the case study has been funded and supported by Sony Mobile. This research was in part funded by Software Center (www.software-center.se).

References

1. Olsson, H.H., and Bosch, J.: From opinions to data-driven software R&D: a multi-case study on how to close the 'Open Loop' problem. In: Proceedings of EUROMICRO, Software Engineering and Advanced Applications (SEAA), Verona, Italy, 27-29 August 2014
2. Bosch-Sijtsema, P., Bosch, J.: User Involvement throughout the Innovation Process in High-Tech Industries. Journal of Product Innovation Management. (2014). doi:10.1111/jpim.12233
3. Backlund, E., Bolle, M., Tichy, M., Olsson, H.H., Bosch, J.: Automated user interaction analysis for workflow-based web portals. In: Lassenius, C., Smolander, K. (eds.) ICSOB 2014. LNBIP, vol. 182, pp. 148–162. Springer, Heidelberg (2014)
4. Hofman, H.F., Lehner, F.: Requirements engineering as a success factor in software projects. IEEE Software **18**, 58–66 (2001)
5. Kabbedijk, J.; Brinkkemper, S.; Jansen, S.; van der Veldt, B.: Customer Involvement in Requirements Management: Lessons from Mass Market Software Development, Requirements Engineering Conference (2009)
6. Yiyi, Y., Rongqiu, C.: Customer Participation: Co-Creating Knowledge with Customers- Wireless Communications, Networking and Mobile Computing (2008)
7. Olsson H.H., Bosch, J.: 2013a. Towards data-driven product development: a multiplecase study on post-deployment data usage in software-intensive embedded systems. In: Proceedings of the Lean Enterprise Software and Systems Conference (LESS), Galway, Ireland, 1-4 December 2013

8. Holmström Olsson, H., Bosch, J.: Post-deployment data collection in software-intensive embedded products. In: Herzwurm, G., Margaria, T. (eds.) ICSOB 2013. LNBIP, vol. 150, pp. 79–89. Springer, Heidelberg (2013)
9. Ries, E.: The Lean Startup: How Constant Innovation Creates Radically Successful Businesses. Penguin Group, London (2011)
10. Olsson, H.H., Alahyari, H., Bosch, J.: Climbing the "Stairway to Heaven": a multiple-case study exploring barriers in the transition from agile development towards continuous deployment of software. Proceedings of the 38th Euromicro Conference on Software Engineering and Advanced Applications, September, pp. 5–7. Cesme, Izmir (2012)
11. Bosch, J.: Building products as innovations experiment systems. Proceedings of 3rd International Conference on Software Business, pp. 18–20. Massachusetts, Cambridge (2012)
12. Kohavi, R., Crook, T., Longbotham, R.: Online experimentation at microsoft. In: Third Workshop on Data Mining Case Studies and Practice Prize (2009)
13. Fagerholm, F., Sanchez, G., Mäenpää, H., Münch, J.: Building blocks for continuous experimentation. In: The Proceedings of the RCoSE 2014 Workshop, Hyderabad, India, 3 June 2014
14. Olsson, H.H., Bosch, J.: The QCD Model: From Requirements To Continuous Reprioritization Of Hypotheses. Submitted to an international software engineering conference (Submitted)
15. Wikipedia. http://en.wikipedia.org/wiki/Feature_creep
16. Campbell, D.T., Stanley, J.C.: Experimental and quasi-experimental designs for research, p. 1983. Houghton Mifflin Company. Clark, R. E, Boston (1966)
17. Robson, C.: Real World Research, 2nd edn. Blackwell, Oxford (2002)
18. Runesson, P., Höst, M.: Guidelines for conducting and reporting case study research in software engineering, Empirical Software Engineering, vol, 14 (2009)
19. Argyris, C., Schön, Donald, A.: Organizational learning II. Reading, MA: Addison-Wesley (1996)

Evaluation of Software Mediated Process Assessments for IT Service Management

Anup Shrestha, Aileen Cater-Steel^(✉), Mark Toleman, and Terry Rout

School of Management and Enterprise, University of Southern Queensland,
Toowoomba, Australia
{Anup.Shrestha,Aileen.Cater-Steel,
Mark.Toleman,Terry.Rout}@usq.edu.au

Abstract. IT service organisations are cognisant that continual service improvement can be achieved by conducting regular process assessments. However, such assessments are expensive and so we have developed a Decision Support System (DSS) tool which uses the international standard for process assessment ISO/IEC 15504 to offer a transparent and efficient approach. This paper provides evidence of evaluation of this software-mediated process assessment (SMPA) approach which was based on ISO/IEC 15504, ISO/IEC 20000 and the IT Infrastructure Library (ITIL®). In a usability evaluation of the online tool, participants reported largely positive experiences finding the online survey easy to use trustworthy, comfortable, generally effective, and more transparent and less costly to implement than a manual assessment. However, to engage in process improvement, human judgment, and possibly expert assessment facilitators are necessary for assessment validation and improvement, that is, a fully automated online survey that is strictly standard-based is not very useful. Further clarification of the survey questions with relevant examples, clearer answer options and having more visible goal statements on every question page were suggested.

Keywords: ITSM process assessment · ISO/IEC 15504 · Evaluation · IT service management · Process improvement

1 Introduction

The increasing role of IT Service Management (ITSM) in facilitating business requires continual improvement of IT service processes [1]. In the current ITIL framework, Continual Service Improvement (CSI) has been proposed as an important service lifecycle phase. CSI emphasises that there should be an ongoing effort to identify opportunities for improvement in ITSM processes [2]. The CSI concept further stresses that "continual assessment" is important to identify improvement opportunities for all processes [3]. In performing CSI activities many organisations have adopted process assessment techniques that employ a systematic measurement of processes [3]. The measurement results are then used to determine the capability of each process and monitor improvements.

An alternative to reliance on expensive consultants with proprietary process assessments is for the organisation to carry out a standard process assessment itself using software tools that may be integrated with a knowledge base of ITSM best practices. To explore this alternative, we developed a novel approach for ITSM: *Software-mediated Process Assessment (SMPA)*. The SMPA approach is a standards-based process assessment approach by which organisations can self-assess their processes using a DSS tool to determine process capabilities. A decision support system (DSS) tool facilitates the SMPA approach to collect data for process assessments and analyses process capabilities to recommend process improvements.

To lend objectivity and consistency to the SMPA approach, its activities are aligned with the international standard for process assessment: ISO/IEC 15504 [4]. The application of the standard in ITSM is relatively new [5]. An exemplar process assessment model for ITSM has been published as a part of the international standard for process assessment [6]. This paper illustrates results and evaluation of the SMPA approach for ITSM.

Before a detailed account of the evaluation, we briefly explain the relevance of the SMPA approach in ITSM. ITSM is a service-oriented IT management framework that advocates best practice IT service processes based on IT Infrastructure Library (ITIL®) and the international standard for ITSM ISO/IEC 20000 to ensure that IT delivers quality service to businesses. The design and architecture of the SMPA approach was previously published [7].

One of the challenges in the ITSM industry is the lack of uniformity and transparency in the way IT service processes are assessed for improvement [3]. Existing ITSM process assessment frameworks such as Tudor's IT Process Assessment [1], CMMI for Services process appraisals [8] and ITIL Assessment Services [9] use proprietary assessment models and follow indistinct assessment activities. The issue of transparency is therefore a significant hurdle in conducting an objective process assessment. The SMPA approach, being software-mediated, uses an online survey tool to collect process assessment data.

Moreover, process assessments are conducted by expert assessors by gathering a variety of objective evidence such as documents and interviews of process stakeholders [4]. Efficiency can be achieved in process assessments since a number of process assessment activities can be automated with the use of a survey with questions aligned to the standard assessment model in order to collect data from process stakeholders instead of conducting interviews. This approach can translate to significant cost savings from not using expensive assessors and consultants while enabling repeated self-assessments for IT service organisations.

While most of the existing process assessments rely on process-specific indicators that demonstrate objective evidence of process capabilities, the SMPA approach facilitates a top-down approach where assessment at each level of process capability is conducted through online surveys. In the SMPA approach, explicit questions based on the standard indicators are presented. Every question is rated using the scale: "Not", "Partially", "Largely", "Fully" and "Not Applicable" as defined in the standard. All responses for survey questions are stored in order to calculate process capability scores. Rather than the assessment team making a subjective choice of the testimony of process stakeholders, the online survey collects and objectively measures[10] feedback from the process stakeholders directly from the responses to the questions. The approach of asking questions directly in a web-based survey environment represents a faster and more efficient data collection method compared to assessment interviews [10]. Figure 1 shows the structure of the SMPA approach.

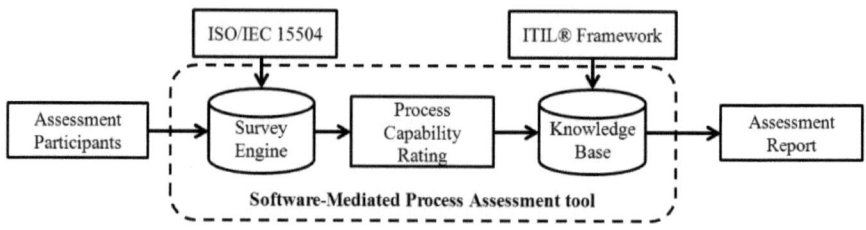

Fig. 1. Structure of SMPA approach

A literature review on ITSM process assessment is presented next to articulate the research problem. Research methodology is then discussed before a detailed account of the design and development of the SMPA architecture. Finally the conclusion section discusses the role and value of the SMPA approach that is supported by the application of ISO/IEC 15504.

2 Literature Review

2.1 ITSM/SPICE/ITIL

The literature associated with ITSM process assessment is rooted in the concept of service and quality. Existing work on IT service quality has looked to the service marketing literature and focused on adapting the SERVQUAL instrument [11] to the context of IT service. Research on IT service quality has largely focused on user satisfaction measures while there is limited research related to processes [12].

While it is a widely-agreed concept that service quality is ultimately determined by what the customer perceives, service providers should also strive to improve their processes. Organisations can conduct customer satisfaction surveys to assess the outcome of the service provision. However this is unlikely to assist service providers in improving their processes [13]. There is a need for organisations to redefine their ITSM processes to manage IT service quality [12]. Existing literature on IT service quality in terms of processes has shown a lack of research on this topic [14].

Measuring IT services is a challenging feat that requires both quantitative and qualitative metrics based on diverse service quality measures such as IT service quality, information systems quality, process quality, customer satisfaction, service value and service behaviour [12]. Few studies provide methodological guidance on an approach to determine process quality measures. A self-assessment methodology based on business excellence models and Six Sigma process improvement techniques used ITIL maturity assessments [9] for several ITIL service delivery processes. However several critical flaws in the assessment approach were reported, such as surveys with compound questions that allowed only a "yes" or "no" response [15].

Using ITIL processes and the international standard for process assessment ISO/IEC 15504, evidence of repeatable and objective improvement in IT service quality has been reported [7]. Extensive work on the combination of ITIL and ISO/IEC 15504 led to the development of a popular ITSM process assessment approach called Tudor's IT Process Assessment (TIPA) [1]. TIPA has been promoted as a commercial framework for ITSM process assessment [19].

ITSM process assessment approaches are discussed as best practice guidelines in the IT industry. Many of the solutions offered for ITSM process assessment are commercially available (for example, ITIL assessment services or Pink Elephant). These services can be considered as a black box since the rationale behind the assessment activities is not fully disclosed. Moreover, due to proprietary assessment processes, inconsistent outcomes from different assessment services hinder comparisons. Non-ITIL approaches such as CMMI for Services or eSCM for service providers have transparent models and methods but lack DSS support in order to conduct process assessments.

Based on the academic literature review and existing industry practices, the two key problems of lack of transparency and lack of efficiency in ITSM process assessments are apparent. Addressing transparency and efficiency are two major challenges of process assessments [3]. These challenges are taken into account in the design of the SMPA approach.

2.2 Evaluation in Design Science Research

Rigorous artefact evaluation primarily assesses two aspects: if the artefact causes a significant improvement; and if the artefact works in a real situation [17]. The Design Science Research (DSR) research methodology [18, 19] has the primary goal to develop and evaluate a new artefact. The IS design theories [20] or design principles [21] provide rigorous theoretical insights to evaluate the utility of DSR artefacts. A design theory can govern DSR based on several extant methods, such as the kernel theories [22, 23]; case studies [24] or systematic literature review [25]. By conducting a rigorous artefact evaluation, the design theories can be supported or critiqued. As a result better utility artefacts can be designed [26].

In their DSR methodology, Peffers, Tuunanen [27] suggested two steps for rigorous DSR evaluation: (1) Demonstration of how the artefact is implemented in a feasible manner; and (2) Evaluation to assess how well the artefact works.

A prominent DSR evaluation strategy should consider the "what, how, and when" aspects of evaluation design [28]. This led to the development of a DSR evaluation strategic framework which was later expanded by Venable, Pries-Heje [26]. This widely cited DSR evaluation strategic framework provides extensive evaluation design options for a DSR researcher to follow. The research methodology used to evaluate the online survey is discussed next.

3 Research Evaluation Methodology

The DSR methodology is the underpinning research methodology applied for the development and evaluation of the SMPA approach. DSR methodology is outcome-oriented and thereby provides guidelines for development and evaluation of research artefacts that contribute to specific bodies of knowledge. The six DSR methodology steps [29] were followed in the research: problem identification and motivation, objectives of a solution, design and development, demonstration, evaluation, and communication.

Evaluation of the SMPA approach was organised based on the evaluation strategy advocated by Pries-Heje, Baskerville [28]. The DSR guidelines proposed by Hevner et al. [18] were also followed in an ex-post, naturalistic evaluation conducted at an IT service organisation. In order to assess if the SMPA approach has utility in a real organisation, it was essential to ensure that the survey approach was usable. Therefore, usability was determined as the key evaluation factor. The concept of usability as defined in ISO/IEC 25010 software quality in use model [30] was applied to evaluate five quality factors of the online survey: effectiveness, efficiency, usefulness, trust and comfort.

4 Assessment Results

The assessment survey was trialled in October 2013 at the IT service department of an Australian local government authority, Toowoomba Regional Council (TRC). TRC relies on ICT tools to support the delivery of services 24 hours a day, all year round. TRC has identified a number of initiatives in its recently adopted ICT Strategic Plan [31] such as customer contact management; unified communications; eBusiness solutions for improved online accessibility of council information; spatial information services for improved web mapping services; and business architecture improvements including mobile works and self service solutions.

With the help and support from the assessment facilitators and assistance from the survey tracking functionality of the DSS tool, assessment data collection using surveys was completed by early November 2013. The assessment report was provided to TRC in the first week of December 2013 and the evaluation performed with focus groups and interviews of TRC staff from November 2013 to January 2014. The analysis of the evaluation data was completed mid May 2014.

Three IT service processes were assessed at TRC: Problem Management (PrM), Change Management (ChM) and Configuration Management (CoM). The assessment profile generated for the three processes selected for assessment is provided in Table 1. Each attribute received 9 or 10 survey responses.

Problem Management achieved CL1 due to its rating score of "Largely" (L) at PA1.1. The other two processes were "Partially" (P) at PA1.1 suggesting that they are at CL0. The majority of the rating scores for all processes demonstrated a weak reliability score (six "Poor", 18 "Medium" and only three "High" reliability scores). This meant that survey respondents were not consistent in their answers and responses were varied. Moreover, most of the rating scores were "Partially" (P). There were two "Largely" (L), only a single "Not" (N) and none of the rating score achieved "Fully" (F) at any of the process attributes. This demonstrates relatively meagre process capability levels for the three processes assessed.

Table 1. Assessment Profile for Processes at TRC

	Level 1	Level 2		Level 3		Level 4		Level 5	
Profile	PA1.1	PA2.1	PA2.2	PA3.1	PA3.2	PA4.1	PA4.2	PA5.1	PA5.2
PROBLEM MANAGEMENT (PrM)									
Process attribute	L	P	P	P	P	P	N	P	P
Reliability	HIGH	MED	POOR	POOR	MED	MED	MED	MED	MED
CHANGE MANAGEMENT (ChM)									
Process attribute	P	P	P	P	L	P	P	P	P
Reliability	MED	MED	MED	POOR	HIGH	MED	MED	MED	MED
CONFIGURATION MANAGEMENT (CoM)									
Process attribute	P	P	P	P	P	P	P	P	P
Reliability	POOR	MED	POOR	POOR	HIGH	MED	MED	MED	MED

5 Evaluation

A focus group was organised at TRC to evaluate the usability of the online survey phase in the SMPA approach. The discussion with nine participants was recorded and later transcribed to enable qualitative data analysis. Since all participants of the focus group discussion had completed the assessment surveys, it was interesting to note the inconsistencies and variations that existed among the participants in terms of their experiences and attitudes towards the usability of the online survey.

The standard definitions were transformed to operational definitions of usability characteristics to align their meaning to specific contexts of use for the evaluation of the survey approach as shown in Table 2.

Table 2. Operational definitions of usability characteristics for evaluation of online assessment survey

Usability Characteristics	Operational definition
Effectiveness	**Accuracy and transparency** of the online assessment survey
Efficiency	**Time, cost and resources** required for the online assessment survey
Usefulness	**Representative and understandable assessment questions to answer** by using online assessment survey
Trust	Confidence in **validity** of the online assessment survey
Comfort	**Ease** of using online assessment survey

Survey participants in different roles commented on the usability of the survey approach based on their context of use. The data were analysed by reviewing focus group discussion transcripts for themes or patterns related to the five software quality in use characteristics. Maintaining privacy of the individuals who participated in this research was an ethical consideration. To protect individual identities, survey participants are referred to by each individual's most relevant process role: process manager (PM), process performer (PP) or external process stakeholder (EPS). These process roles are standard IT service roles endorsed in the ITSM community [1].

A summary of the evaluation results based on discussions and interview responses on each software quality in use factor is provided as Table 3.

Table 3. Summary of TRC online assessment survey evaluation results

Usability characteristic	No. of key comments	Selected key comments
Effectiveness	☑ x 14 ☒ x 4 ◉ x 2	☑PrM-PM1: You've got the bigger data set – more reliable data. If you have an outliner, you don't skew your results. People may be more honest. ☑PrM-PP2: That whole subjective nature where it's one person deciding, based on what everybody has said, what the score is ... makes [manual]assessment dependent on the skills of that person. Survey overcomes this challenge. ☑PrM-EPS2: I think two different versions of the responses based on the group: e.g. managers say something and performers say something else will be very interesting – something that the software can easily do. ☒CoM-PM1: Some of those examples, I thought, were slightly irrelevant.
Efficiency	☑ x 6	☑PrM-PM1: the software system has the advantage of giving you a really wide data set. So you can survey 5 or 50 people with no added cost. Also that you don't have to have them in a room.
Usefulness	☒ x 15 ☑ x 3 ◉ x 1	☒PrM-PM1: I found some of the questions quite confusing and ambiguous. ☒CoM-PP4: Some of terminology used in there, depending on the way the question was asked, I think meant different things, to different people. ☒CoM-EPS4: Answer options didn't seem to be customised to the question; to the result of the question. The seemed to take a generic approach. ☑PrM-EPS2: the questions are structured well, there are relevant examples and so on

Evaluation of Software Mediated Process Assessments for IT Service Management

Table 3. (*Continued*)

Trust	☑ x 3	☑PrM-PM1: We could say six months after, let's do that again. The logic seems valid and reliable.
Comfort	☑ x 7 ☒ x 1	☑CoM-PM1: As far as the page layout, it sort of let you know how you were progressing, the colours, the font and the general interface ... was excellent.

☑ indicates the usability characteristic was strongly supported in a comment
⊙ indicates the usability characteristic was not clear or a neutral position was taken
☒ indicates the usability characteristic was strongly opposed in a comment

In terms of the evaluation of accuracy and transparency of the online assessment survey, there were greater positive comments (70%) in comparison to negative comments (20%) based on the feedback from survey respondents, therefore the survey is considered effective. Process stakeholders suggested that the online survey is very objective and that it deters bias from group dynamics in the assessment process and outcome. For example:

"I think it's more objective using a software tool compared to an external assessor coming in and listening to what you say and then say 'Mmmmm I think I'll probably give that one a largely or a fully score!' " (ChM-PM1)

"And to a degree, the group dynamics, where you don't just have one person dominating the conversation [in manual assessments], whereas the survey tool gives you a say." (PrM-EPS2)

The ability to easily conduct the survey in-house with a larger number of people was one of the highlights demonstrating effectiveness of the survey approach:

"I suppose the beauty of this is that you can do these things in house. You can pick these three processes and see what comes out at level 1. Few weeks later, see what to do to get these to level 2. You've got that control over it. Rather than organising for someone to come in and do it for you." (ChM-PM1)

"We have an advantage that we are all in one geographic location. Whereas, other organisations wouldn't have the luxury of getting everyone together, if they were really dispersed. I mean, that's the way you work. The software tool is the only way to do it then." (PrM-EPS2)

However a few disadvantages of the survey approach highlighted the risk of different interpretations of the same question by survey respondents if the questions were not clear. For example:

"Survey result is likely to be much skewed because of my interpretation of the questions, as the survey went on, it changed." (PrM-PM1)

In terms of efficiency, there was overwhelming support for the online survey that it takes less time, cost and staff resources to conduct in comparison with the manual assessment. There were no negative comments about the efficiency of the online survey. Process stakeholders suggested that the survey would be a better return on investment and cost effective to operate. For example:

"the survey is probably a better return on investment because you are not taking up everyone's time all at once." (PrM-EPS2)

"I would imagine it [survey] would be cheaper to do rather than have someone [assessor] across the table for that amount of time." (PrM-PM1)

The usefulness of the online survey in terms of clarity of the questions had largely negative comments (78%). There were many comments regarding repetitive, ambiguous and confusing questions and the terminologies used. Since TRC undertook the assessment up to CL5 and a single process stakeholder often had multiple surveys for different roles, it must have compounded the issue. Interestingly no one complained about the application of the standard to the survey. Process stakeholders at TRC thought it was useful that the questions were strictly aligned to the standard but they were fatigued with the number of questions. For example:

"There seemed to be a fair bit of repetition in the questions." (PrM-PP2)

"I am confused. I am supposed to be looking at this from this viewpoint, now it seems to be the other way around. How do I answer this?" (ChM-PP3)

"Lots of questions that seemed to be almost the same as the questions you did. That was where I struggled a little bit." (CoM-PM1)

In comparison with the manual assessment, the usefulness of the online survey was negative because of the lack of support to clarify the survey questions. For example:

"With a person on the other side of the table, you could ask a question ... 'do you mean this?'. An assessor would have gone across the ambiguity of the questions. You can get that interpretation that you don't get with online survey." (PrM-PM1)

"Plus it's the interaction [in manual assessment]; it's a group of people, so you're all talking about the topic. So, you fairly quickly get it right, or get it corrected." (CoM-PM1)

However a few process stakeholders suggested that the questions are indeed structured since they are aligned to a standard and once you understand the overall structure, the survey was useful. For example:

"Once you locked into what was being asked and how it was being presented, then it became a lot easier to answer the questions." (CoM-PP4)

The three comments regarding the trustworthiness of the online survey were all positive. Survey participants suggested that the survey is dependable and can encourage more truthful answers:

"They kind of think that they are not being watched. I can answer truthfully here because I'm not going to get in trouble – that kind of thing. It gives you a voice. I mean, you can be anonymous with a survey and not worry that your boss is sitting next to you." (PrM-PM1)

"If that's a repeatable process, you are going to get a clear measure as to whether you have improved. With the tool we can depend on it to survey in a consistent manner." (CoM-PM1)

Finally, the vast majority of comments were positive in terms of the ease of use of the online survey. Almost all survey respondents were happy with the interface and the sequencing of the questions. For example:

"The interface. I liked that and the presentation. We had just started using SharePoint and it felt very familiar. It felt 'sharepoint-ish'. It was very clean.

Some surveys you get, you are hunting – 'what would I do, where I was?' This one was very direct and very well laid-out." (PrM-EPS2)

There was one stand-out negative comment that the convenience of the survey may be ironically a disadvantage since completing the survey is not given priority:

"The interface and convenience though about being able to do it easily in your own time, at your own desk, it is a disadvantage because you don't have a set time that you are focussed on this. You've got distractions of people coming up, and then get side tracked on something else." (CoM-EPS4)

In summary, participants reported that they found the online survey easy to use and largely agreed that a self-assessment experience answering direct questions made the exercise more transparent and less costly to implement than a manual assessment. Moreover a tiered approach was recommended, wherein the SMPA approach could be used first to get an overall understanding of process capabilities. Afterwards, to engage in process improvement, human judgment is necessary for assessment validation and improvement based on results. Further clarification of the survey questions with relevant examples, clearer answer options and having more visible goal statements on every question page were suggested.

6 Conclusion

In terms of the immediate outcome of evaluation, participants reported that overall they found the online survey for assessment was trustworthy, comfortable and generally effective. Positive comments were also recorded regarding efficiency of conducting online surveys for assessments. However discussions led to a conclusion that a fully automated online survey that is strictly standard-based is not very useful. It was discussed that human input is critical for the facilitation of online assessment surveys in order to clarify survey questions with relevant examples when needed. It was also recommended that measures should be taken to provide assessment support through expert assessment facilitators, online discussion forums and/ or help screens. It was also noted that all questions do not apply well to the processes and there is a need to provide clearer answer options and better allocation of some questions to relevant process roles.

We have reported the assessment results and the evaluation of the SMPA online survey. The evaluation was based on the usability of the DSS tool that supports the SMPA approach. This paper has focused on the evaluation of one aspect of the SMPA project. Further work was also undertaken and will be disseminated regarding the evaluation of the process selection method, SMPA facilitator dashboard, assessment report, technical platform, design process, relevance to industry, alignment to ISO/IEC 15504 standard and alignment to DSR guidelines. With the current evolution of the ISO/IEC 15504 standard to the ISO/IEC 330xx family [32], modification of the survey engine and the knowledge base to reflect appropriate new process capability assessment models will be required; however there is no concern that the changes will be extreme. Further trials of the assessment survey for roll out and uptake of the SMPA approach in different organisations are planned.

The SMPA approach requires respondents to answer assessment questions based on the process indicators from the ISO/IEC 15504 PAM. A limitation of this approach is that some respondents might have unrealistic perceptions about their process activities. A more rigorous ITSM process assessment approach would involve the review of process input and output documents (work products) as instructed in the ISO/ IEC 15504 standard. Another limitation of this research is the ability of the DSS to assess only four ITSM processes. The case study in this research also has certain limitations. First, regarding internal validity, evaluation data were collected using qualitative research methods only. Moreover, a recognised limitation of the qualitative case study approach is the lack of ability to generalise the findings.

The SMPA approach is not intended to replace a formal conformity assessment. However organisations could use this approach when the focus is not on the precision but on a consistent approach to measure process improvements. The SMPA approach could also be used by assessors in a formal appraisal environment to collect evidence to determine process capability and maturity.

In closing, we suggest that the SMPA approach provides an opportunity for automation and transparency in the way process assessments are conducted. Beyond the discipline of service management, the SMPA approach could be applied to other domains where a process assessment model is available. Using the SMPA approach, a compliant process assessment model can be used to develop survey questions. Likewise, process improvement recommendations can be generated based on industry best practice guidelines such as ITIL® in our case. With the expanding significance and reach of the ISO/IEC 15504 standard and the recently published first batch of the ISO/IEC 330xx family, the SMPA approach can be applicable for process assessments in any discipline that comprises a compliant assessment model.

Note. ITIL® is a Registered Trade Mark of AXELOS Limited.

Acknowledgements: This work is supported by an Australian Research Council (ARC) Linkage grant. We thank Mr. Paul Collins of Assessment Portal Pty. Ltd. for his involvement and support in providing the platform to implement the DSS tool. We also appreciate the opportunity provided by staff at Toowoomba Regional Council to trial the SMPA and for their feedback.

References

1. Barafort, B., Betry, V., Cortina, S., Picard, M., St-Jean, M., Renault, A., Valdès, O.: ITSM Process Assessment Supporting ITIL. Public Research Centre Henri Tudor (ed.) Zaltbommel, Netherlands. Van Haren Publishing (2009)
2. Bernard, P.: Foundations of ITIL, Chittenden, J. (ed.) Zaltbommel, Netherlands. Van Haren Publishing (2012)
3. Lloyd, V.: ITIL Continual Service Improvement. The Stationery Office, London, UK (2011)
4. ISO/IEC, ISO/IEC 15504-2:2004 – Information Technology – Process Assessment – Part 2: Performing an Assessment. International Organization for Standardization: Geneva, Switzerland (2004)
5. Mesquida, A.L., Mas, A., Amengual, E., Calvo-Manzano, J.A.: IT Service Management Process Improvement based on ISO/IEC 15504: A Systematic Review. Information and Software Technology **54**(3), 239–247 (2012)

6. ISO/IEC, ISO/IEC TS 15504-8:2012 - Information Technology - Process Assessment - Part 8: An Exemplar Process Assessment Model for IT Service Management. International Organization for Standardization: Geneva, Switzerland (2012)
7. Shrestha, A., Cater-Steel, A., Toleman, M., Rout, T.: towards transparent and efficient process assessments for IT service Management. In: Mitasiunas, A., Rout, T., O'Connor, R.V., Dorling, A. (eds.) SPICE 2014. CCIS, vol. 477, pp. 165–176. Springer, Heidelberg (2014)
8. CMMI, Standard CMMI® Appraisal Method for Process Improvement (SCAMPISM) A, Version 1.3: Method Definition Document. Software Engineering Institute: Carnegie Mellon University, MA, USA (2011)
9. MacDonald, I.: ITIL Process Assessment Framework. The Co-operative Financial Services: Manchester, UK (2010)
10. Deutskens, E., de Ruyter, K., Wetzels, M.: An Assessment of Equivalence Between Online and Mail Surveys in Service Research. Journal of Service Research **8**(4), 346–355 (2006)
11. Parasuraman, A., Zeithaml, V.A., Berry, L.L.: A Conceptual Model of Service Quality and its Implications for Future Research. Journal of Marketing **49**(4), 41–50 (1985)
12. Lepmets, M., Cater-Steel, A., Gacenga, F., Ras, E.: Extending the IT Service Quality Measurement Framework through a Systematic Literature Review. Journal of Service Science Research **4**(1), 7–47 (2012)
13. Jia, R., Reich, B.H.: IT Service Climate—An Essential Managerial Tool to Improve Client Satisfaction with IT Service Quality. Information Systems Management **28**(2), 174–179 (2011)
14. Spath, D., Bauer, W., Praeg, C.-P.: IT Service Quality Management: Assumptions, Frameworks and Effects on Business Performance. In: Quality Management for IT Services-Perspectives on Business and Process Performance. IGI Global, PA, pp. 1–21 (2011)
15. Edgeman, R.L., Bigio, D., Ferleman, T.: Six Sigma and Business Excellence: Strategic and Tactical Examination of IT Service Level Management at the Office of the Chief Technology Officer of Washington, DC. Quality and Reliability Engineering International **21**(3), 257–273 (2005)
16. Barafort, B., Di Renzo, B., Merlan, O.: Benefits resulting from the combined use of ISO/IEC 15504 with the information technology infrastructure library (ITIL). In: Oivo, M., Komi-Sirviö, M. (eds.) 4th International Conference on Product Focussed Software Development and Process Improvement (PROFES). Lecture Notes in Computer Science, vol. 2559, pp. 314–325. Springer, Heidelberg (2002)
17. Checkland, P., Scholes, J.: Soft Systems Methodology in Practice, 1st edn. J Wiley, Chichester (1990)
18. Hevner, A.R., March, S.T., Park, J., Ram, S.: Design Science in Information Systems Research. MIS Quarterly **28**(1), 75–106 (2004)
19. Gregor, S., Jones, D.: The Anatomy of a Design Theory. Journal of the Association for Information Systems **8**(5), 312–335 (2007)
20. Pries-Heje, J., Baskerville, R.: The Design Theory Nexus. MIS Quarterly **32**(4), 731–755 (2008)
21. Sein, M.K., Henfridsson, O., Purao, S., Rossi, M., Lindgren, R.: Action Design Research. MIS Quarterly **35**(1), 37–56 (2011)
22. Iivari, J.: A Paradigmatic Analysis of Information Systems As a Design Science. Scandinavian Journal of Information Systems **19**(2) Article 5 (2007)
23. Walls, J.G., Widmeyer, G.R., El Sawy, O.A.: Building an Information System Design Theory for Vigilant EIS. Information Systems Research **3**(1), 36–59 (1992)

24. Van Aken, J.E.: The Nature of Organizing Design: Both Like and Unlike Material Object Design. Eindhoven Center for Innovation Studies (ECIS) (2006)
25. Carlsson, S.A., Henningsson, S., Hrastinski, S., Keller, C.: Socio-technical IS Design Science Research: Developing Design Theory for IS Integration Management. Information Systems and e-Business Management **9**(1), 109–131 (2011)
26. Venable, J., Pries-Heje, J., Baskerville, R.: A comprehensive framework for evaluation in design science research. In: Peffers, K., Rothenberger, M., Kuechler, B. (eds.) DESRIST 2012. LNCS, vol. 7286, pp. 423–438. Springer, Heidelberg (2012)
27. Peffers, K., Tuunanen, T., Rothenberger, M.A., Chatterjee, S.: A Design Science Research Methodology for Information Systems Research. Journal of Management Information Systems **24**(3), 45–77 (2007)
28. Pries-Heje, J., Baskerville, R., Venable, J.R.: Strategies for Design Science Research Evaluation. In: 16th European Conference on Information Systems. Galway, Ireland (2008)
29. Peffers, K., Tuunanen, T., Rothenberger, M.A., Chatterjee, S.: A Design Science Research Methodology for Information Systems Research. Journal of Management Information Systems **24**(3), 45–77 (2008)
30. ISO/IEC, ISO/IEC 25010:2011 – Systems and software engineering – Systems and software Quality Requirements and Evaluation (SQuaRE) - System and software quality models. International Organisation for Standardisation: Geneva, Switzerland (2011)
31. TRC, TRC Annual Report 2012/13. Toowoomba Regional Council: Toowoomba (2013)
32. ISO/IEC, ISO/IEC 33001:2015 – Information technology – Process assessment – Concepts and terminology. International Organisation for Standardisation: Geneva, Switzerland (2015)

Process Improvement

Emphasis on Personal Attributes/Skills to Produce 'Quality' Assessment Outputs that Lead to Steady Generation of SPI Effects

Takeshige Miyoshi[✉]

Miyoshi Art of Software Process Inc., Saitama, Japan
miyoshi.gunta@mirror.ocn.ne.jp

Abstract. The SPICE frameworks (ISO/IEC 15504 series and ISO/IEC 33000 series) and their conformant process models including CMMI® as well as assessment/appraisal methods have greatly evolved in the past two decades, and benefits of using them have been reported. On the other hand, however, the effects of using those frameworks or models are not necessarily easily obtained, especially in novice model user organizations. One of the reasons for this can be qualitatively traceable to the fact that the assessment/appraisal outputs are not as useful as they could be. Based on the early experience of SPICE assessments as well as a number of opportunities of CMMI-based appraisals, this paper describes the critical success factors including personal attributes/skills, and considerations for producing useful assessment/appraisal outputs. Thereby, the importance of paying more attention to personal attributes/skills is proposed from the process practitioner's viewpoint.

Keywords: ISO/IEC 15504 series · ISO/IEC 33000 series · CMMI® · SCAMPI^{SM} · Useful assessment/appraisal outputs · Critical personal attributes

1 Introduction

Since the "Software Process" came into the limelight in the 1980's, many efforts have been made in the world "Software Process" communities. The SPICE frameworks (ISO/IEC 15504 series [1-11] and ISO/IEC 33000 series [12-17]) and their conformant process models including CMM(I) [18-20] as well as assessment/appraisal methods [21, 22] have greatly evolved in the past two decades, and benefits of using them have been reported [23, 24]. Accordingly, users of those frameworks and models have increased year by year. However, the effects of using those frameworks or models are not necessarily easily obtained, especially in those organizations that are inexperienced model users. Even under the disadvantageous research conditions, where corporate confidentiality is very strict and thus it is difficult to gain access to quantitative business data to substantiate business effects, one of the reasons for the difficulty of producing business effects can be qualitatively traceable to the fact that the assessment/appraisal outputs are not necessarily used effectively, in the successive SPI (Software Process Improvement) steps.

Since 1994, the author has been heavily involved in SPICE assessments for over a decade [25], and CMM(I) assessments/appraisals until the present [26], at many companies in Japan. Through experience, one has become convinced that there are some important factors for producing useful assessment/appraisal outputs and for connecting them to produce specific business effects out of the organizations' SPI activities. At the same time, the motto of "Get Back to Basics" is strongly recognized: "Having pragmatic ... viewpoints of the process frameworks and models." Actually, Watts S. Humphrey emphasizes the importance of the characteristics of "software process" which must be pragmatic and adjustable. He also stresses the necessity of avoiding fruitless usage of CMM by mentioning the danger of following a 'checklist strategy.' In the Foreword of the classic CMM book [18], he advocates:

> "The CMM is an explicit framework software engineers can use, debate, and augment. The CMM documents must be reasonably stable, but they also must change. Producing a document like this also entails a risk. Some individuals will always seek fixed formulas or checklists for evaluating organizations. When organizations follow this checklist strategy, they often produce piles of documents and mountains of paper to "prove" that their process is at some prescribed level. Unfortunately, this approach invariably overlooks the critical point: what the people actually do. The software process concerns people and their work and thus must be pragmatic and adjustable, or it will not be used. This is why the CMM and this book are guidelines, not rules. Their objective is to set goals for each maturity level and key process area, and to provide examples for each practice. No organization, however, should attempt to do everything in this book. Doing so would solve some problems several ways and miss others completely. That could get very expensive."
> ibid., Foreword

Accordingly, in this paper, Critical Success Factors (CSFs) for producing useful assessment/appraisal outputs, including critical personal attributes/skills, are explained in Section 2. Section 3 describes experience-based considerations in CMMI-based appraisal situations. Then the impact of personal attributes on assessment/appraisal is analyzed in Section 4. Finally, conclusions and future steps are provided in Section 5. Since the author's experience of 15504-based assessment is limited to the early days, only Section 2 is explained in both of the 15504-based assessment and CMMI-based appraisal settings. The remaining sections are described for only the CMMI-based appraisal setting. The relationship among primary sections is shown in Figure 1.

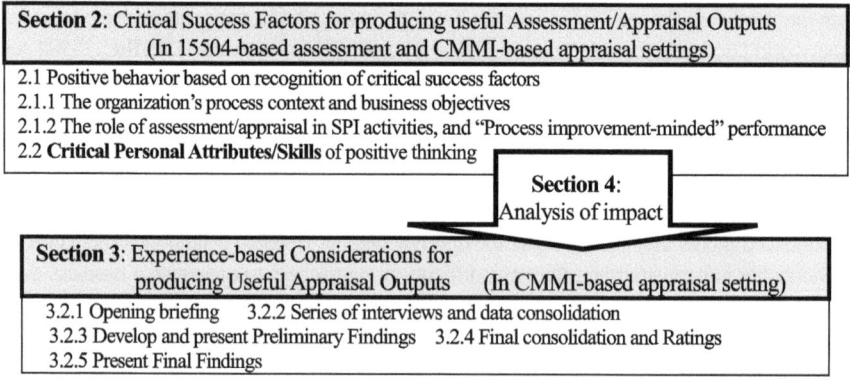

Fig. 1. Relationship among primary Sections

2 Critical Success Factors for Producing Useful Assessment/Appraisal Outputs

As shown in Table 1, five critical success factors for producing useful assessment/appraisal outputs are explained. These factors are further explained in the following subsections.

Table 1. Critical success factors for producing useful assessment/appraisal outputs

In SPICE context	In CMM(I) context
1. Understanding the organization's process context *See 2.1.1*	
process context: the set of factors, documented in the assessment input, that influence the judgment, comprehension and comparability of process attribute ratings [12] An understanding of the **context** within which a process operates within an OU (Organizational Unit) is critical to accurately assessing whether a practice that has been implemented fulfills its purpose [27] (P125).	The software process concerns people and their work and thus must be pragmatic and adjustable, or it will not be used. This is why the CMM and this book are guidelines, not rules [18] (Foreword). Interpreting the practices requires the organization or project to consider the **overall context** in which they are used [18] (P77). **process context:** The set of factors documented in the appraisal input that influences the judgment and comparability of appraisal ratings. These include, but are not limited to, (a) the size of the organizational unit to be appraised, (b) the demographics of the organizational unit, (c) the application domain of the products or services, (d) the size, criticality, and complexity of the products or services, and (e) the quality characteristics of the products or services. [22]
2. Understanding business objectives *See 2.1.1*	
Step 1 of the improvement cycle ("Examine organization's needs") starts with a recognition of the organization's needs and **business goals**, usually based on one of the main drivers for process improvement [27] (P183).	**organization's business objectives:** Senior-management-developed objectives designed to ensure an organization's continued existence and enhance its profitability, market share, and other factors influencing the organization's success [20]. The first rule of an assessment is that an organization should make its real **business objectives** clear and understandable to everyone in the organization and to the assessment team [28] (P54).
3. Recognizing the role of assessment/appraisal in SPI activities *See 2.1.2*	
5.2 Steps of process improvement 5.2.3 Step 3–Assess current capability [17] **Assessment** is performed for improvement purposes in Step 3 of 8 SPI steps [27] (P184).	**Assessments** fall into the Diagnosing phase of the IDEAL approach, which concerns identifying current processes, developing recommendations, and emphasizing follow-on activities [28] (Preface).
4. Demonstrating "Process improvement-minded" performance *See 2.1.2*	
5. Possessing **critical personal attributes/skills** *See 2.2*	

2.1 Positive Behavior Based on Recognition Of Critical Success Factors

2.1.1 The Organization's Process Context and Business Objectives

First of all, considering the "organization's process context and business objectives" is very important when performing assessment/appraisal. In real-life SPI situations, however, it is not always easy to consider them, clearly and accurately. The reasons for this will broadly range from a simple reason, such as a lack of the "SPI frame of mind" among senior management to a complicated situation, caused by the organizational structure and problems at the human level.

Table 1 shows how these key words, the "organization's process context" and "business objectives," are emphasized in SPICE and CMM(I) contexts.

In the SPICE context, "process context" is defined as "the set of factors, documented in the assessment input, that influence the judgment, comprehension and comparability of process attribute ratings" in *ISO/IEC-33001:2015, Information technology - Process assessment - Concepts and terminology* [12]. In addition, the criticality of understanding the "process context" is cited in *SPICE - The Theory and Practice of Software Process Improvement and Capability Determination -* [27], Chapter 6, Subsection, "Process context."

On the other hand, in the CMM(I) context, the importance of recognizing the "organization's process context and business objectives" is implied in Watts S. Humphrey's foreword of *The Capability Maturity Model: Guidelines for Improving the Software Process* [18]. In addition, how to consider the "overall context" is explained in Section 4.7 "Applying Professional Judgment" of the above-mentioned book [18]. In the current version of SCAMPI MDD, *Standard CMMI® Appraisal Method for Process Improvement (SCAMPI^{SM}) A, Version 1.3: Method Definition Document* [22], "process context" is defined as "The set of factors documented in the appraisal input that influences the judgment and comparability of appraisal ratings. These include, but are not limited to, (a) the size of the organizational unit to be appraised, (b) the demographics of the organizational unit, (c) the application domain of the products or services, (d) the size, criticality, and complexity of the products or services, and (e) the quality characteristics of the products or services."

Next, concerning the "business objectives," the importance of recognizing the "business goals" is also cited in Chapter 8, the Subsection titled; "Guidelines for software process improvement" of the SPICE book [27]. In the CMMI context, "organization's business objectives" is defined as "Senior-management-developed objectives designed to ensure an organization's continued existence and enhance its profitability, market share, and other factors influencing the organization's success." [20] Also, the importance of making real "business objectives" clear and understandable is emphasized in *CMMI Assessments - Motivating Positive Change -* [28], Chapter 3, Subsection 3.1.3, "Establishing (with the Lead Assessor) the Business Goals and the Scope of the Assessment."

In the actual SPI activities, making the "organization's process context and business objectives" clearly recognized from top management to the project members is very important. In a variety of real-world SPI environments, however, it is "Easier said than done." One of the solutions is to disseminate the principle of the "Field-oriented" policy throughout the organization. Years ago, it was sometimes heard from those involved in SPI activities that it's difficult to promote such activities. The reason for this was that the SPI didn't lead to actual business effects, such as increased customer satisfaction and improved product quality. In most of these cases, the process context and business objectives were not clearly disseminated within the organizations. Besides, what was really going on in real-life projects within the organizations was not clearly understood by everyone. If SPI stakeholders correctly understand their organizations' process context and business objectives, many important hints can be obtained from within their own companies, especially from project managers and engineers. In order to share useful information necessary to improve the organization's processes, the "process assets sharing" framework is very helpful and is to be explained in the next subsection 2.1.2.

2.1.2 The Role of Assessment/Appraisal in SPI and "Process Improvement-Minded" Performance

Next, clearly recognizing the "role of assessment/appraisal in SPI activities" is also very important. The assessment/appraisal is a meaningful event, performed at one of the series of SPI steps. Therefore, the quality of the assessment/appraisal outputs has much influence on the successive SPI steps. Table 1 shows how the literature describes where in the SPI steps the assessment/appraisal is conducted.

In the SPICE context, referring to the current Technical Report, *ISO/IEC TR 33014:2013, Information technology — Process assessment — Guide for process improvement* [17], the process assessment is conducted at "5.2.3 Step 3 – Assess current capability" of subsection "5.2 Steps of process improvement." Also, as cited in *SPICE - The Theory and Practice of Software Process Improvement and Capability Determination* - [27], Chapter 8, Subsection "Guidelines for software process improvement," the assessment is performed in Step 3 ("Prepare for and conduct a process assessment") of eight Software Process Improvement steps.

Similarly, in the CMM(I) context, the assessment falls into the Diagnosing phase of the IDEAL^{SM} approach, as cited in *CMMI Assessments - Motivating Positive Change* - [28], Preface, Subsection "Assessments Are Part of the Larger Subject of Process Improvement."

Years ago, a number of companies were thought to have experienced the 'Compliance-driven Improvement' for quickly achieving a Maturity Level, because the management expected quick results. Times have changed now. When considering the severe economic situation of recent years, we must promote 'Performance-driven Improvement' by thinking over how to make good use of the "process assets," which have accumulated data and experience within the organization. In this sense, the CMM(I)'s traditional "Conceptual software process framework" depicted in Figure 4.1 of the classic CMM book, *The Capability Maturity Model: Guidelines for Improving the Software Process* [18] could be considered to be the most useful "process assets sharing" framework in the real-life SPI environment.

Considering the importance of recognizing the role of assessment/appraisal in SPI activities, it is also critical for the assessment team leader to carefully demonstrate a "process improvement-minded" performance in every situation of assessment/appraisal. A few examples are listed in Table 2.

Table 2. Examples of "process improvement-minded" performance

	Examples of "process improvement-minded" performance
1	Clearly understanding the mapping of the process model's practices and terminology to those of the organization.
2	Asking practical questions and eliciting prioritized 'Weaknesses' during interview sessions, which are called 'Improvement Opportunities' in a positive way.
3	When developing the Findings statements, using concrete or specific expressions and the organization's terminology, and not using the same wording or terminology as the process models.

2.2 Critical Personal Attributes/Skills of Positive Thinking

Originally, the "Assessor personal attributes" was defined in *ISO/IEC TR 15504-6:1998, Information Technology – Software Process Assessment - Parts 6:Guide to competency of assessors* [29]. According to it, the assessor should have the personal attributes and skills which are listed in Table 3, in addition to the technical knowledge and experience required.

Through experience of 15504-based assessments during the early days and CMMI-based appraisals until the present, these personal attributes and skills are recognized as being important and helpful for performing assessment/appraisal successfully, as well as promoting successful SPI activities.

Table 3. Assessor personal attributes

Assessor personal attributes/skills
1. Effective written and verbal communication,
2. Diplomacy,　　　　　　3. Discretion,
4. Persistence and resistance-handling ability,
5. Judgment and leadership,　6. Integrity,　　7. Rapport.

On the other hand, the critical personal attributes/skills shown in Table 4 are uniquely defined from the author's experience.

First, one of the lessons learned is an understanding that the traditional virtues of "Bushido" [30] such as 'rectitude,' 'courage,' and 'benevolence' can be helpful in strengthening the basic attitudes necessary for producing useful assessment/appraisal outputs. In other words, having a sense of justice, showing consideration for other people, and being a person of action toward achieving useful and quality outcomes are important attitudes for performing successful assessment/appraisal.

Second, the 'communicative competence with composure (i.e., keeping presence of mind) and perseverance' is also helpful to smoothly conducting every session on the Onsite period, especially when a discussion becomes an argument, for example, during data consolidation time.

Third, the 'Capability to organize complicated issues in real-world situations, and to clearly explain them to the point' is one of the most useful and powerful skills of the SPI activities. It is very important in the assessment/appraisal, especially when developing the Preliminary/Final Findings, determining Ratings, and when explaining them clearly to the participants. If key persons do not possess this capability, the assessment team will waste much time in arguing over unclear draft statements and also in determining Ratings based on ambiguous rationales. Needless to say, this is one of the important skills of systems engineers in software development projects. Even in the SPI activities, when key persons, such as SPI group members and lead appraisers possess this capability, it is possible to increase the efficiency of overly long meetings and thus, the saved time can be allotted to other productive activities.

Table 4. Experience-based critical personal attributes/skills

	Personal attributes/skills
1	Rectitude, courage, and benevolence
2	Communicative competence with composure and perseverance
3	Capability to organize complicated issues in real-world situations, and to clearly explain them to the point

The personal attributes/skills listed in Tables 3 and 4 push the performance of the assessment/appraisal team. In order to produce useful assessment/appraisal outputs, it's important to elicit honest opinions from interviewees by creating a natural and relaxed atmosphere based on the assessment/appraisal team's positive attitude. This means to have lively and interactive dialogues by showing consideration for people's feelings when conducting interviews. This makes it possible for the organization to progressively accept their Weaknesses (i.e., Improvement Opportunities), and to move forward to the next steps of their SPI activities, toward achieving their business objectives.

3 Experience-Based Considerations for Producing Useful Appraisal Outputs

Having considered the positive behavior explained in the previous section, the experience-based considerations for producing useful appraisal outputs are presented in this section, using the flow of CMMI-based appraisal method: SCAMPI℠ (Standard CMMI® Appraisal Method for Process Improvement) Class A. [22]

3.1 Steps of Appraisal

The SCAMPI appraisal is composed of "Pre-onsite" and "Onsite" phases, as depicted in Figure 2. The first event of the Onsite phase is the **opening briefing**. After this, a series of **interviews** is conducted. The interview data, together with document review data usually collected in the Pre-onsite phase, are organized and consolidated. Based on these data, the "**Preliminary Findings**," i.e., 'Strength/Weakness' statements, are developed. The Preliminary Findings are presented to the interviewees, and their feedback comments are collected. After examining those comments, the Preliminary Findings are refined into the "Final Findings" statements. Then, the Process Area goals, Process Areas and Maturity Level are **rated** and determined. Finally, the **Final Findings** are presented to the sponsor and the other participants.

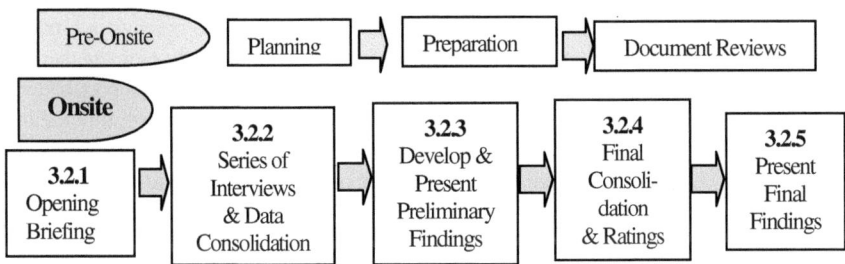

Fig. 2. Summarized flow of SCAMPI Class A appraisal

3.2 Considerations in Each Situation

In order to produce useful appraisal outputs, collecting as many real opinions as possible is critically important. For this purpose, paying careful attention, especially in the following situations, is needed. In this subsection, consideration points in each situation are explained along the flow of the Onsite period: Opening briefing, Interview sessions, Preliminary Findings presentation, Ratings and Final Findings presentation.

3.2.1 Opening Briefing

This is the first important session in the Onsite period, especially for establishing and inspiring a spirit of 'buy-in' and an ownership of appraisal outputs by the organization's participants. The spirit of 'buy-in' causes the mindset of active participation to their SPI activities. Generating an open atmosphere, the appraisal team leader should provide a natural and friendly presentation, in which the "role of appraisal in SPI activities" should be emphasized.

3.2.2 Series of Interviews and Data Consolidation

By generating an open and natural atmosphere, the interview sessions should be lively and interactive dialogues between the ATMs (Appraisal Team Members) and the interviewees. By doing so, real and honest points-of-view from the practitioners and managers can be elicited. Considering the business objectives, the team leader should also ask practical questions in order to elicit the organization's prioritized Improvement Opportunities.

Actually, during the interactive dialogues, the ATMs must see through what is hidden behind the interviewees' words, which could be very important Improvement Opportunity for the organization. This would be possible by using a sound understanding of the intent of the model practices and also based on the sufficient experience of software development projects. During the interview sessions, the ATMs should carefully listen to what each interviewee says and steadily take as many notes as possible. Interview notes are the primary data for the appraisal team's judgments which generate accurate results, leading to obtaining credibility for the appraisal team.

3.2.3 Develop and Present Preliminary Findings

As much time as needed should be allotted to develop and refine the Process Areas' Findings, i.e., Strength and Weakness statements, because they are the primary sources for the successive SPI activities. One of the important points when generating those statements is to use concrete expressions including the organization's specific terminology, thus bridging the model practices to the organization's actual tasks.

When developing those Findings statements, paying careful attention, especially to the Weakness statements (i.e., Improvement Opportunities), is most important. They should be polished as much as possible so that the interviewees who provided the opinions are not treated coldly after the appraisal. This thoughtfulness is very important to soundly promote the SPI program. It is also critical to include Strength Findings in as many Process Areas as possible, in order to make the organization positively accept the Weakness statements. Of course, this means that the ATMs should make their best efforts to discover Strength Findings. Sometimes, specific, unique 'good practice' is overlooked due to lack of correct and operational knowledge of the model practices.

3.2.4 Final Consolidation and Ratings

After the Preliminary Findings are presented, the participants' comments are carefully examined. Then the appraisal team moves on to the Rating session, where Process Area goals, Process Areas, and the Maturity Level are rated and determined. When rating goals of each Process Area, if a discussion escalated into an argument, the team leader should lead to a reasonable consensus in a timely manner. Here the team leader's opinions should be shared, based on an operational knowledge of the model practices, the organization's context, interview notes and his or her management and engineering experience of real-life projects.

3.2.5 Present Final Findings

The Final Findings statements and the style of writing should be carefully reviewed and cautiously brought to consensus by all ATMs, especially in terms of its accuracy and usefulness for the successive SPI activities. When presenting Final Findings, the team leader should clearly read them aloud page by page, emphasizing the important pages which are relevant to the successive SPI activities. After reading the Final Findings statements, it would also be helpful to present "ATM comments" in order to bridge the formal statements of Strengths and Weaknesses to the organization's real-life environment. This "ATM comments" could include encouraging statements for promoting their continuous SPI activities that will lead toward achieving the organization's business objectives.

4 Analysis of the Impact of Personal Attributes on Assessment/Appraisal

From a comprehensive viewpoint, it could be said that the successful performance of human behavior, intended to draw real and pragmatic opinions from people for a specific purpose, (i.e., 'software process improvement,') depends on the critical success factors described in Section 2, listed in Table 1:

      1. Understanding the organization's process context;
      2. Understanding business objectives;
      3. Recognizing the role of assessment/appraisal in SPI activities;
      4. Demonstrating "Process improvement-minded" performance; and
      5. Possessing **critical personal attributes/skills**.

The above-mentioned fifth factor, '**critical personal attributes/skills**,' was explained using Tables 3 and 4 in subsection 2.2. In this section, Table 5 shows the relationships between the personal attributes/skills and appraisal Onsite sessions.

Table 5. Impact of personal attributes/skills on Onsite sessions

'O' : Attributes/skills usually helpful in corresponding session
'◎' : Attributes/skills especially helpful in corresponding session

No	Personal attributes/skills	Appraisal Onsite sessions				
		3.2.1	3.2.2	3.2.3	3.2.4	3.2.5
<Assessor personal attributes/skills> *cited from Table 3*						
1	Effective written and verbal communication	O	◎	◎	O	◎
2	Diplomacy	O	O	O	O	O
3	Discretion	O	O	◎	O	◎
4	Persistence and resistance-handling ability			◎	◎	
5	Judgment and leadership		O	O	O	O
6	Integrity	◎	◎	◎	O	◎
7	Rapport	◎	O	O	O	O
<Experience-based critical personal attributes/skills> *cited from Table 4*						
8	Rectitude, courage, and benevolence	◎	◎	◎	O	◎
9	Communicative competence with composure and perseverance	◎	O	◎	◎	O
10	Capability to organize complicated issues in real-world situations, and to clearly explain them to the point		◎	◎	◎	◎

3.2.1 Opening briefing   3.2.2 Series of interviews and data consolidation 3.2.3 Develop and present Preliminary Findings   3.2.4 Final consolidation and Ratings   3.2.5 Present Final Findings

In light of the descriptions of Sections 2 and 3, all of the aforementioned personal attributes/skills, including 'Diplomacy' (2) and 'Judgment and leadership' (5), can be said to be helpful in almost every session for behaving positively during the Onsite period, as shown in Table 5.

Furthermore, based on the experience of performing hard but worthwhile and fruitful assessments/appraisals in a variety of real world situations, personal attributes or skills especially helpful in corresponding Onsite sessions were observed, as shown with '◎' in Table 5.

Reviewing each of the Personal attributes/skills in Table 5, the 'Effective written and verbal communication' capability (1) is particularly important in conducting interviews and developing Preliminary Findings. The 'Discretion,' (3) *i.e., carefulness and good judgment*, is required when developing Preliminary Findings statements, especially Weakness statements (i.e., Improvement Opportunities). Those statements should be polished as much as possible, to prevent interviewees who provided opinions being disadvantaged or ostracized. Having the 'Discretion,' it is also critical to include as many Strength Findings as possible, in order to make the organization positively accept the Weakness statements.

The 'Persistence and resistance-handling ability' (4) is especially required in developing and presenting the Preliminary Findings and in the Rating session. If a discussion within the appraisal team escalated into an argument, the team leader should lead to a reasonable consensus in a timely manner, using this ability as well as the 'Communicative competence with composure and perseverance' (9). These attributes, (4) and (9), are necessary capabilities in effectively conducting every onsite session where a number of discussions occurs. The 'composure (i.e., Keeping presence of mind)' and 'perseverance' will greatly promote the smooth operation of each session.

The 'Integrity,' (6) *i.e., honesty, sincerity, reliability*, and the 'Rectitude, courage, and benevolence' (8) are, of course, very important and helpful in getting the trust of the organization's people, especially in the Opening meeting, interview sessions, and Preliminary/Final Findings presentations.

The 'Rapport,' (7) *i.e., an ability to have close relationship and understanding with each other*, is also important in every Onsite session, but in particular when establishing a spirit of 'buy-in' and an ownership of appraisal outputs by the organization's participants at the opening meeting.

Finally, the 'Capability to organize complicated issues in real-world situations, and to clearly explain them to the point' (10) is the most important and powerful skill for effectively and efficiently operating every kind of session, especially when a large amount of data from document reviews and interviews is collected. Possessing this skill is also very important when developing the Preliminary Findings and Final Findings, because the usefulness of assessment/appraisal outputs [primarily the Weakness (i.e., Improvement Opportunity) and Strength Statements] greatly depends on this critical skill. Thereby, meaningful outcomes of the appraisal will be obtained.

5 Conclusions and Future Steps

The "process improvement" has been talked about in many books and papers [31-38]. In addition, many process improvement efforts have been made in many organizations. However, the circumstance of the "process context" which is peculiar to each organization, becomes the factor that the "process improvement" doesn't go smoothly according to plan. Based on the early experience of SPICE assessments and CMM(I)-based assessments/appraisals until the present, this paper describes the critical success factors including personal attributes/skills, and experience-based considerations for producing useful assessment/appraisal outputs. Thereby, the importance of paying more attention to human resources as human beings in addition to the processes and assessment methods is proposed from the process practitioner's viewpoint.

For this purpose, some critical success factors, including personal attributes/skills, were explained in Section 2. In addition, it was also mentioned that practical use of the "process assets sharing" framework could be the key for steadily generating business-driven SPI effects. The key point for using this concept effectively in the real world is to collect "usable" best practices, "beneficial" lessons learned, and "useful" process data, which are specific to individual organizations. At the same time, it's also critical to effectively disseminate and share them throughout the organization, in a way that functions most appropriately in the organization's business environment. When implementing this framework, the critical personal attributes/skills are very important for those who promote the organization's SPI activities. Based on the 'Capability to organize complicated issues in real-world situations, and to clearly explain them to the point,' members of SPI group can flexibly promote the complicated steps of implementing the organization's unique "process assets sharing" framework. Then, in the descriptions of the considerations for the Onsite sessions in Section 3, the critical success factors were observed to be helpful for producing useful appraisal outputs.

Furthermore, in Section 4, the result of analysis of the impact of personal attributes/skills on assessment/appraisal gives a clear roadmap to the future steps: In parallel with the continuous SPI activities, if "People" could improve their "Capability," it could be a steady way of bringing about a business effect for the organization. The "People" means those involved in an organization's SPI, including senior management as well as those involved in the assessment/appraisal, including the lead appraiser. In addition, the "Capability" is an ability which can be improved *a posteriori*, and it includes the personal attributes/skills shown in Tables 3 and 4.

Being based in a country where corporate confidentiality is very strict, it is difficult to gain access to quantitative business data. Therefore, this paper was described in an experience-based qualitative style, and it will need to be improved by considering the related external research in this field. This kind of effort by a process practitioner, however, could be one of the ideas leading to disseminating a positive culture of business-driven SPI programs, so that this will contribute to the promising further development of the process frameworks and models.

References

1. ISO/IEC 15504-1:2004, Information technology- Process assessment - Part 1: Conceptsand vocabulary
2. ISO/IEC 15504-2:2003, Information technology - Process assessment - Part 2: Performing an assessment
3. ISO/IEC 15504-3:2004, Information technology - Process assessment - Part 3: Guidance on performing an assessment
4. ISO/IEC 15504-4:2004, Information technology - Process assessment - Part 4: Guidance on use for process improvement and process capability determination
5. ISO/IEC 15504-5:2012, Information technology - Process Assessment - Part 5: An exemplar Process Assessment Model
6. ISO/IEC 15504-6:2013, Information technology - Process assessment - Part 6: An exemplar system life cycle process assessment model
7. ISO/IEC TR 15504-7:2008, Information technology - Process assessment - Part 7: Assessment of organizational maturity
8. ISO/IEC TS 15504-8:2012, Information technology - Process assessment - Part 8: An exemplar process assessment model for IT service management
9. ISO/IEC TS 15504-9:2011, Information technology - Process assessment - Part 9: Target process profiles
10. ISO/IEC TS 15504-10:2011, Information technology - Process assessment - Part 10: Safety extension

11. Rout, T.: ISO/IEC 15504 –Evolution to an International Standard, SOFTWARE PROCESS –Improvement and Practice, vol. 8, no. 1. John Wiley & Sons Ltd. (2003)
12. ISO/IEC-33001:2015, Information technology - Process assessment - Concepts and terminology
13. ISO/IEC-33002:2015, Information technology - Process assessment - Requirements for performing process assessment
14. ISO/IEC-33003:2015, Information technology - Process assessment - Requirements for process measurement frameworks
15. ISO/IEC-33004:2015, Information technology - Process assessment - Requirements for process reference, process assessment and maturity models
16. ISO/IEC-33020:2015, Information technology - Process assessment - Process measurement framework for assessment of process capability
17. ISO/IEC TR 33014:2013, Information technology — Process assessment — Guide for process improvement
18. Paulk, M.C., et al.: The Capability Maturity Model – Guidelines for Improving the Software Process. Addison Wesley (1997)
19. CMMI Product Team, CMMI for Software Engineering, Version 1.1, Staged Representation (CMMI-SW, V1.1, Staged), Technical Report CMU/SEI-2002-TR-029. Software Engineering Institute (2002)
20. CMMI Product Team, CMMI for Development, Version 1.3, Technical Report CMU/SEI-2010-TR-033, Software Engineering Institute (2010). http://resources.sei.cmu.edu/library/asset-view.cfm?assetID=9661
21. Software Engineering Institute, CMM-Based Appraisal for Internal Process Improvement (CBA IPI) Version 1.2 Method Description, Technical Report CMU/SEI-2001-TR-033 (2001)
22. SCAMPI Upgrade Team, Standard CMMI® Appraisal Method for Process Improvement (SCAMPI^{SM}) A, Version 1.3: Method Definition Document, HANDBOOK CMU/SEI-2011-HB-001 (2011). http://resources.sei.cmu.edu/library/asset-view.cfm?assetID=9703
23. Software Engineering Institute, Demonstrating the Impact and Benefits of CMMI: An Update and Preliminary Results, Technical Report CMU/SEI-2003-SR-009 (2003). http://resources.sei.cmu.edu/library/asset-view.cfm?assetid=6365
24. Software Engineering Institute, Performance Results of CMMI-Based Process Improvement, Technical Report CMU/SEI-2006-TR-004 (2006). http://resources.sei.cmu.edu/library/asset-view.cfm?assetid=8065
25. Miyoshi, T.: Early Experience with Software Process Assessment using SPICE Framework at Software Research Associates, Inc., SOFTWARE PROCESS – Improvement and Practice, vol. 2. Issue 3. John Wiley & Sons Ltd. (1996)
26. Miyoshi, T.: Useful SCAMPI results come from improvement-driven appraisals with a human touch–"Bushido" spirit helps SCAMPI, 1st SEPG-AP, Ohsaka, Japan (2009)
27. Emam, K.E., Drouin, J.N., Melo, W.: SPICE –The Theory and Practice of Software Process Improvement and Capability Determination. IEEE Computer Society Press (1998)
28. Bush, M., Dunaway, D.: CMMI Assessments –Motivating Positive Change. Addison Wesley (2005)
29. ISO/IEC TR 15504-6:1998, Information Technology – Software Process Assessment - Parts 6:Guide to competency of assessors
30. Nitobe, I.: Bushido - The Soul of Japan. Charles E. Tuttle Co., Inc. (1969)
31. Raynus, J.: Software Process Improvement With CMM, Artech House (1999)
32. Potter, N.S., Sakry, M.E.: Making Process Improvement Work – A Concise Action Guide for Software Managers and Practitioners. Addison-Wesley (2002)

33. Ahern, D.M., Clouse, A., Turner, R.: CMMI Distilled: A Practical Introduction to Integrated Process Improvement, 2nd edn. Addison-Wesley (2003)
34. West, M.: Real Process Improvement Using the CMMI. Auerbach Publications (2004)
35. Ahern, D.M., Armstrong, J., Clouse, A., Ferguson, J.R., Hayes, W., Nidiffer, K.E.: CMMI SCAMPI Distilled: Appraisals for Process Improvement. Addison-Wesley (2005)
36. Garcia, S., Turner, R.: CMMI Survival Guide – Just Enough Process Improvement. Addison-Wesley (2006)
37. Persse, J.: Project Management Success with CMMI – Seven CMMI Process Areas. Prentice Hall (2007)
38. Kulpa, M.K., Johnson, K.A.: Interpreting the CMMI – A Process Improvement Approach, 2nd edn. CRC Press (2008)

Proposing an ISO/IEC 15504 Based Process Improvement Method for the Government Domain

Ebru Gökalp[✉] and Onur Demirörs

Informatics Institute, Middle East Technical University, Ankara, Turkey
{egokalp,demirors}@metu.edu.tr

Abstract. Model based process improvement has been successfully applied for software organizations. After observing this success, customizing it to specific domains/sectors becomes one of the most critical challenges. On the other side, there are some quality problems in government domain as: low efficiency and process performance, employee and citizen dissatisfaction, high cost and defect rates. Assuming that successful processes will be reflected in higher quality, the government processes have to be improved. However known capability/maturity models don't deal with particularities of government domain. Therefore, it's necessary to design and evaluate a domain-specific capability model. Towards this goal, we develop Government Process Capability Determination Model based on ISO/IEC 15504. Moreover, we propose a method which is a disciplined guidance for governmental organizations to perform process capability assessment systematically. The method is described in detail in the study.

Keywords: Government · ISO/IEC 15504 · Capability models

1 Introduction

Increasing quality becomes one of the major aims of government administration to align government actions with the desires of the government institution's customers. Assuming that successful processes will be reflected in higher government administration success, the government processes have to be improved. In this regard, an increasingly important contribution to government administration transformation is to be made by applying private sector business process improvement approaches. Nonetheless, known maturity models do not take the specialties of government domain into consideration. Therefore, it is necessary to design and evaluate a domain-specific maturity model before applying it in the area of government [1].

There are various well-accepted generic Software Process Capability/Maturity Models (SPCMMs), such as ISO/IEC TR 15504 [2]-[5] which is part of a series providing the requirements to conduct a process assessment and to design process models: guidelines for process improvement or capability determination: and exemplar process models. The ISO/IEC TR 15504 standard has recently entered a revision cycle. It will be replaced by a new series of standards: the ISO/IEC 33000 series [6].

These assessment standards are not limited to a specific field of activity: there can be applied to various industry sectors. Customizing ISO/IEC TR 15504 [2]-[5] to different sector is subject of growing interest in the literature. Since ISO/IEC TR 15504 [2]-[5] is not limited to software development processes, many initiatives proposed for various domains such as automotive sector [7], enterprise processes [8], IT security [9], IT service management [10], knowledge management [11], internal financial control [12], industrial processes [13], regulation compliance [14], medical devices [15] and space [16].

We intend to utilize the same approach for the government domain by developing the Government Process Capability Determination Model (Gov-PCDM) based on ISO/IEC TR 15504 standard [2]-[5]. The aim of Gov-PCDM is to provide the base for improving the processes of governmental organizations. It pursues a structured and standardized approach by assessing relevant processes in order to perform quality improvement initiatives in a consistent, repeatable manner, assessed by adequate metrics with guidance on what to do to increase quality in government institutions. Gov-PCDM focuses to provide improvement in governmental business processes to provide benefits of generic process improvement models (i.e:CMMI, ISO 15504 etc.) as increasing in service quality, in customer and employee satisfaction, as well as decreasing in operating cost.

We propose a method to implement Gov-PCDM in an organization to achieve its benefits and to be useful by providing a disciplined guidance to perform process capability assessment systematically for governmental organizations. The method becomes a roadmap that shows the next steps to take when determining capability level of the process. The proposed method can be executed as a process in governmental organizations. Thus, it can be performed throughout the life of the organization to assess its processes.

The remainder of the paper includes motivation of the study, description of the proposed Gov-PCDM and the details of the method description, and finally the conclusion of the study.

2 Motivation

Government organizations are not profit-oriented, have no competition, are often historically grown and often result from considerable political influences while their processes are frequently unstructured, and depend on employee judgment. Accordingly, there are quality problems as low efficiency, employee and citizen dissatisfaction, high cost and defect rates. Assuming that successful processes will be reflected in lower quality problems: the government processes have to be improved. Nevertheless, known maturity/capability models do not consider the specialty of government domain. There are different characteristics of the organizations operating in public sector comparing to private sector.

The main difference between the public and private sectors are the bureaucratic principles of administrative actions [17] which directly affect governmental processes. Table 1 partially developed based on [17] shows a selection of those principles and several further characteristics of the public sector in comparison to the private sector.

The principles and characteristics which are valid for the public sector constitute special conditions for task fulfillment in public authorities in comparison to private sector organizations [18]. The government processes are defined by binding of actions to specific intents, laws, and welfare.

Table 1. Differences between Organizations Operating in Private Sector and Public Sector

	Private Sector	**Public Sector**
Aim	Profit maximization	Public task fulfillment
Lawfulness of actions	Actions are primarily unbounded but aligned to the organization's visions and objectives	Actions are primarily bound to laws and regulations (principle of lawfulness)
Control	Economical market organization	-Political legitimization -Changing 'Board of Directors' every 3-4 years has a dramatic impact
Market position	Competitive environment	No competition (monopoly character)
Organization structure	No established structure: individual to the organization	-Strict hierarchical structure possessing clear line of authority -High level of division of work and specialization -Horizontal and vertical structure of administration (de-central task fulfillment)
Documentation requirements	No explicit documentation requirements	All decisions and occurrences have to be documented for control purposes
Processes	-Economic efficiency principle -Homogeneity in provided services	-Multitude of weakly structured processes -High concentration of decisions and manual processes -Heterogeneity and amount of public services -Multiple stakeholders for many processes

As seen in Table 1, public sector differs from private sector in many aspects. Customization of known process capability/maturity approaches in private sector to public sector makes an important contribution [17]. Besides the contribution to the improvement of efficiency and effectiveness of public administration, these approaches also enable the improvement of service orientation.

We investigated quality improvement models developed for public sector, including the Total Quality Management approach, Enterprise Architecture Models, and E-Government Maturity Models, it is published in [19]. There are studies in the literature for improving quality in public domain, they provide benefits from different aspects. For instance, e-government initiatives have the potential to improve the quality of governmental services, however, existing processes should be improved beforehand. Automation practices in governmental institutions have not provided the expected efficiency improvements in Turkey, since the automation of processes are carried out with existing process defects. Studies in the literature don't aim to improve process quality directly to guarantee the consistency of services with each other through the use of standard processes where the capability level can be assessed and improved with guidance. The aim of developing Gov-PCDM is to address this aspect.

We performed an exploratory case study in [19] to explore applicability of using process assessment in the government domain. As a result of the study, although initial findings indicated the usefulness and adequacy of the proposed approach: the necessity of a methodology incorporating guidelines for application was determined. Government Process Capability Determination Method, proposed in this study, is developed to address this aspect.

3 Government Process Capability Determination Model

Gov-PCDM is developed for capability determination of processes performed in government institutions. Gov-PCDM is based on the assumption that business service quality can be achieved by the means of process quality – process capability.

The aim of Gov-PCDM is providing the base for improving the processes of governmental organizations. It pursues a structured and standardized approach by assessing relevant processes in order to perform quality improvement initiatives in a consistent, repeatable manner, assessed by adequate metrics with guidance on what to do to increase quality in government institutions. It aims to provide improvement in governmental business processes to provide benefits of ISO/IEC TR 15504 [2]-[5] as increasing in service quality, in customer and employee satisfaction, as well as decreasing in operation cost. Structure of the Gov-PCDM, shown in Figure 1 below, is made up of two dimensions.

The process dimension consists of governmental business processes. This dimension is characterized by process purpose statements which are the essential measurable objectives of a process: process outcomes, base practices, and work products which are constructed based on the standard of ISO/IEC TR 15504- part 2 [2].

The capability dimension, which is characterized by a series of process attributes, is applicable to any process, which represents measurable characteristics necessary to manage a process and improve its capability to perform. Capability levels and process attributes are adapted from ISO/IEC TR 15504-part 5 [5].

3.1 Government Process Reference Model (Gov-PRM)

Gov-PRM constitutes process dimension of Gov-PCDM. We classified Governmental business processes into 2 main groups. One of them is Agency-Specific Process which is performed specifically for one institute, such as: birth, death and marriage registration process is performed just in civil registry office. A *generic process definition* is developed for being used level 1 assessment of agency-specific processes.

The second one is Management of Government Resources and Support Processes (MGRSPs), common processes across the governmental agencies, refer to the support activities that enable the government to operate efficiently, There are 7 main classes for management of government resources processes as human resource management, information resource management, financial& physical resource management, external relationship management, inspection& auditing, regulatory development and management, strategy& policy development. Gov-PRM includes definitions of these processes.

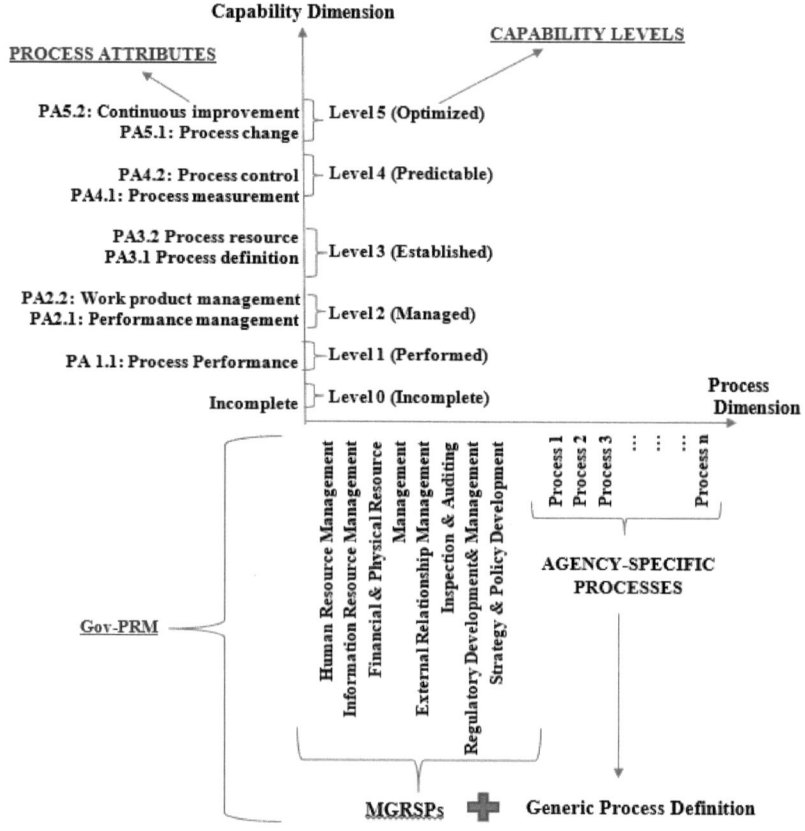

Fig. 1. Gov-PCDM Structure

Process Definitions of MGRSPs are developed by harmonizing existing quality improvement models and standards as FEAF (Federal Enterprise Architecture Framework) [20], APQC [21], ISO 15504 [2]-[5], CMMI [22], CMMI-SVC [23], People-CMM [24], ITIL [25], FAA-iCMM [26]. The definitions are established by one of the authors and validated by process owners working in three different governmental organizations of Turkish government.

The *generic process definition* is established by one of the authors on the basis of process modeling diagrams of 40 agency-specific processes performed in five different public agencies. Developed generic process definition is reviewed by 30 process owners working in 10 different departments in three different organizations.

All process definitions in Gov-PRM are formally approved by the management with executive responsibility within two different organizational units and one of the authors who has both professional and academic experience in using ISO/IEC TR 15504 [2]-[5] after reviewing respective process definitions.

3.2 Government Process Assessment Model

Government Process Assessment Model constitutes capability dimension of the Gov-PCDM. Assessment procedures related to details of activities such as planning, briefing of the participants, data collection and validation and reporting are based on ISO/IEC 15504- part 3 [3]. Process capability is classified into six levels in ISO/IEC 15504-part 2 [2]: as Level 0: Incomplete: Level 1: Performed: Level 2: Managed: Level 3: Established: Level 4: Predictable: Level 5: Optimizing.

The measure of capability is based upon a set of process attributes (PA). Process capability indicators are the means of achieving the capabilities addressed by the considered process attributes. Process Attribute of Level 1 is Process Performance attribute which is a measure of the extent to which the process purpose is achieved. Developed Process definitions are used for Level 1 assessment. For the assessments of levels 2 to 5, we use exactly the same 'generic practices indicators', 'generic resources indicators' and 'generic work products indicators' as the exemplar PAM provided by the ISO/IEC 15504- part 5 [5].

The capability level of each process instance is determined by rating process attributes. For example, to determine whether a process has achieved capability level 1 or not, it is necessary to determine the rating achieved by PA1.1 (Process performance attribute). A process that fails to achieve capability level 1 is at capability level 0. Each process attribute is measured by an ordinal rating F (Fully), L (Largely), P (Partially), or N (Not) achieved that represents the extent of achievement of the attribute. A process instance is defined to be at capability level k if all process attributes below level k satisfy the rating F and the level k attribute(s) are rated as F or L, as defined in ISO/IEC TR 15504-2 [2].

4 Government Process Capability Determination Method

It is essential to provide a systematic way to implement an approach in an organization to achieve its benefits and to be useful. We propose Government Process Capability Determination Method which is a disciplined guidance for governmental organizations to perform process capability assessment systematically. The method becomes a roadmap that shows the next steps to take when determining capability level of the process. The proposed method can be executed as a process in governmental organizations. Thus, it can be performed throughout the life of the organization to assess its processes. This process consisting of 4 phases as seen in the Figure 2 below.

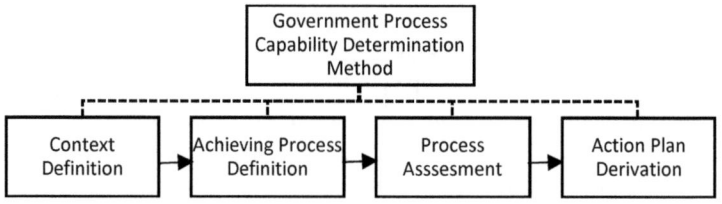

Fig. 2. Phases of Government Process Capability Determination Method

In the *Context Definition Phase*: all process owners, top management, stakeholders meet in a kick-off meeting. They collectively define the aim and scope of the government process capability determination project. Project execution plan is produced at the end of the meeting.

In the *Achieving Process Definition Phase*: process definition is performed if the process selected for capability determination is an agency-specific process. Since for the level 1 assessment, process definition is needed to check if the process is performed. Gov-PRM is used to achieve process definition.

In the *Process Assessment Phase*, process is assessed based on ISO/IEC 15504-part 3 [3] and part 5 [5] and as a result of this phase, assessment report is produced.

In the *Action Plan Derivation Phase*, action plan to improve the capability level of the assessed process is derived for the assessment report based on ISO/IEC 15504-4 [4].

As a result of successful implementation of this process;

- A target capability appropriate to the particular specified requirement is identified
- Reviews of the governmental processes are carried out to determine their suitability for the particular specified requirement in the light of process assessment results
- Strengths and weaknesses within the assessed processes are identified
- An action plan for process improvement is achieved

The proposed method is described and its phases in detail in the sub-sections.

4.1 Context Definition

This phase sets up the organization for government process improvement initiative. The primary goal is to determine processes to be improved. Thus, a structural frame of the organization in terms of a high level process, and their relationship are achieved in this phase. Figure 3 illustrates the process diagram for the context definition phase. First, the participants determine and state the aim and objectives for process improvement. The processes that will be determined and the roles that participate in those processes are depicted on scope diagram. The assessment and review teams are established. Roles are mapped to the stakeholders, the execution plan is documented, and approved by all participants.

Roles participating in this phase are as follows:

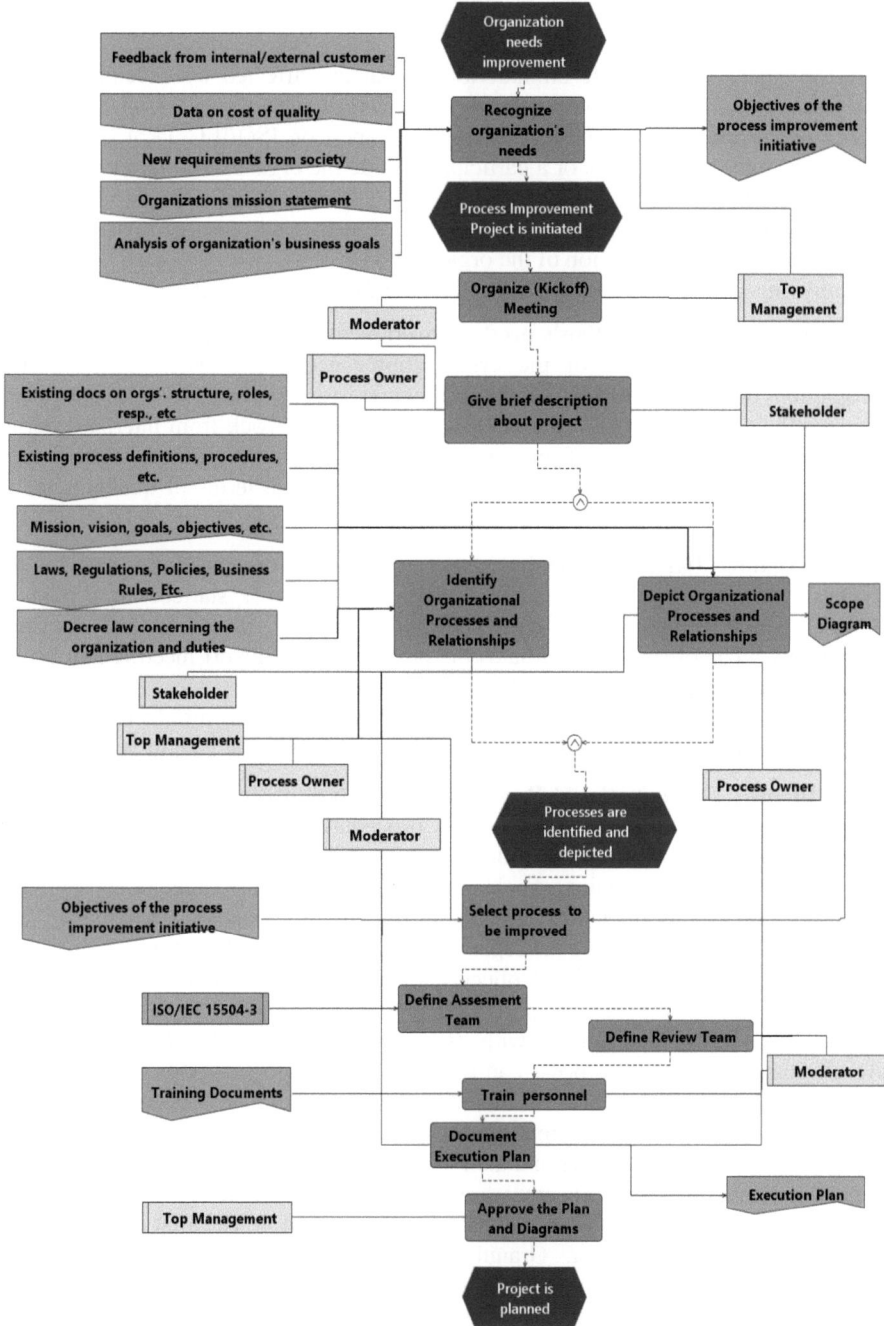

Fig. 3. Context Definition Phase

Process owners include the individuals that participate in the execution of the processes.

Stakeholders may include all individuals that are affected by execution of the processes.

The moderator who can be a consultant or expert on ISO/IEC TR 15504 [2]-[5] outside from the organization or a participant inside the organization familiar with the ISO/IEC TR 15504 [2]-[5].

Top Management supports process improvement and ensures that processes promote the vision and mission of the organization.

Following subsections describe the activities of this phase in detail.

i.   Recognize organization's needs: Government process improvement initiatives start with the recognition of the organization's needs and business goals. The recognition derives from any of the following: organizations mission statement: organization's business goals: data on cost of quality: feedback from internal/external customer: new requirements from society. Objectives of the process improvement initiatives are defined based on analysis of these inputs in terms of quality, time to market, cost, employee and customer satisfaction.

ii.   Organize (Kickoff) Meeting: After recognizing organizations need for the process improvement, the process improvement program is started. It should be considered as a project in its own right, and planned, resourced and managed accordingly. The organization initiates the project with a kickoff meeting that brings all related process owners, stakeholders and top management together.

iii.   Give Brief Description about Project: The moderator introduces the aim of the project and Gov-PCDM and presents a brief overview of the path to be followed.

iv.   Identify Organizational Processes and Relationships: Variety of resources including existing process definitions and procedures; documents representing the organizational structure, roles and responsibilities; resources representing organization's mission, vision, goals and objectives; laws, regulations, policies, business rules; or any related documents such as quality standards, handbooks, and etc. can be used for identifying the organizational processes and relationship.

Business process is defined as 'collection of related, structured activities or tasks to serve particular goal(s) for a particular customer(s)'. Goals are derived from organization's vision and aligned with its mission: the reason for its existence. The overall goal of a business process can be decomposed into sub-goals. A goal-driven and a collaborative approach in identifying and judging processes is generally necessary. This is because different groups of people in the organization are likely to identify and judge the processes and their salience differently.

Governmental business processes are classified into 2 main groups as Agency-Specific Process and MGRSP as described in Gov-PRM. The first one should be defined by the organization. Granularity level of the agency-specific process identification and the level of formality applied must be nearly same. In order to provide this, moderator has some responsibilities as follows:

- Envisaging the top view of processes as a whole, explaining and analyzing it
- Facilitating and monitoring the definition process
- Providing guidance to the agency-specific process definers

- Facilitating the maintenance of individual agency-specific process definitions
- Validating that the resulting of an agency-specific process definition is all that should be performed to serve the goal of that project.

v.   Depict Organizational Processes and Relationships: The coverage on a scope diagram represents the processes and their relationships as well as the roles that participate in these processes. Variety of resources including existing process definitions and procedures: documents representing the organizational structure, roles and responsibilities: resources representing organization's mission, vision, goals and objectives: or any related documents such as quality standards, handbooks, and etc. are used by identifying and depicting the processes.

vi.   Select Processes to Be Improved: The participants in the meeting set the priorities of the process improvement objectives. The processes and their relationships should be analyzed in order to evaluate which processes have direct impact on the improvement objectives identified.

vii.   Define Assessment Team: Assessment team consists of competent assessor who can lead or be part of, and staffs from quality management department of the organization if there is.

viii. Define Review Team: Review team is responsible for reviewing agency-specific process definitions. The team can consist of moderator, staff from quality management department, and executive members who manage the respective process.

ix.   Train Personnel: The moderator, or if possible trainer from outside the organization who has knowledge about ISO 15504 train related staff about process definition, process assessment, and analyzing assessment results. Agency-specific process definers, and assessors attend this training. Training documents are used.

x.   Documenting Project Execution Plan: The moderator (project leader) document project execution plan includes work assignments, time, risk and configuration management plans. The scope, role assignments for moderator, agency-specific process definers, and assessors, the schedule and other concerns such as, risk and configuration management are documented on an Execution Plan. The plan is approved by all participants and base-lined before description phase commence and the consequent changes are communicated to all parties.

xi.   Approve the Plan and Diagrams: As the final step of context definition phase, generated project execution plan is approved by the top manager.

Depending on the scope, once the aim is determined, roles and responsibilities are assigned, execution plan and process diagrams are approved, and the kickoff meeting is closed. Subsequent meetings will be arranged to perform succeeding activities.

4.2   Achieving Process Definition

Users need process definition for perform Level 1 assessment to check whether the process is performed. We follow the ISO/IEC TR 15504-2 [2] standard to determine what the process definition should contain. It includes followings: *Title* conveying the concept of the process as a whole, purpose formulating the aim, the usefulness of the process; *Purpose* high level, overall goal for performing the process; *Outcome* expressing the objectives expected from the successful performance of the process; *Base Practices (BPs)* decomposing the process to state what the process does to obtain the outcomes; *Information Items* separately identifiable bodies of information produced and stored for human use.

Developed Gov-PRM includes process definitions for MGRSPs. Additionally it includes Generic Process Definition to guide process owners for agency-specific process definition including title, purpose, outcomes, BPs, information items. Achieving Process Definition for agency-specific processes includes following steps;

i. **Define Process Title:** The title identifies the principle concern of the process and distinguishes the process from other processes in the model. Some examples for process title as follows: Strategy and Policy Management, Law Development.

ii. **Define Process Purpose:** The purpose of the process describes the goal of performing the process. In cases where processes might be thought to overlap, the purpose should be used to characterize the scope or bounds of the process. Goal-driven approach is used in this definition. Once the process identified, main goal of the process will be defined. It is candidate of purpose of the process. Since governmental process are established based on the laws, procedures, etc. The purpose of the process is written in the related laws or legislation like Decree Law Concerning the Organization and Duties in Turkish government.

iii. **Define Process Outcomes:** An outcome is an observable and assessable result of the successful achievement of the process purpose. In order to define outcomes of governmental process, related laws, regulations, and policies are used as resource. Generic outcomes defined in Generic Process Description for agency-specific processes are as follows:

1. Politics/strategy is defined
2. Policies and guidelines are published
3. Requirements are derived and allocated
4. Interactions with involved parties is managed
5. Technical effort is performed to obtain the result
6. Approval of the result is achieved
7. Results are made available to all related parties

iv. **Define Base Practices (Activities):** The base practices are a list of actions that may be used to achieve the outcomes. Rather than describing the results of executing a process, activities describe a set of actions that might be undertaken to execute the process. Generic Base Practices defined in Generic Process Definition for agency-specific processes are as follows:

BP1. Develop a strategy for the process: Produce Strategy document by higher level management of government. i.e: law, decree law, etc. [Outcome: 1]
BP2. Publish policies and guidelines: Establish Policies and guidelines which include how work gets done. i.e: Regulations, legislation etc. [Outcome: 1, 2]

BP3. Define requirements for the process: Obtain requirements for performing the process from higher level management. These requirements can be amount of budget, maximum number of people, or maximum amount of resource, etc. [Outcome: 2, 3, 4]

BP4. Establish interactive communication methodologies and structures with involved parties: A communication mechanism for receiving/storing/sending information or documents (if there is) with involved parties is established. [Outcome:4]

BP5. Perform Technical Effort: Receive/collect, analyze, distribute information and generate documents if necessary, and also support service and solutions to perform technical work. [Outcome: 4, 5]

BP6: Achieve approval for the result: Establish and maintain and approval mechanism from inside the agency and the institutions the agency is dependent on (if necessary) [Outcome: 2, 4, 6]

BP7: Share results with involved parties: Establish and maintain an informing mechanism for sharing results with all involved parties. Publishing results on the web page of the agency, publishing in the official gazette, sending e-mail to involved parties can be some alternatives for sharing results. [Outcome: 2, 4, 7]

v.   Define Information Items: Information items are process products that are identifiable bodies of information produced and stored for human use. Laws, decree laws, regulations, legislations, guidelines, application documents, generated reports, approved documents, communication records [e-mails, minutes of meetings, etc] can be information items of the agency- specific governmental processes.

4.3   Process Assessment

Assessment is conducted by an assessment team whose member(s) are from the Organizational Unit. Assessment team consists of competent assessor who can lead or be part of, and staffs from quality management department of the organization if there is. The competent assessor can be from inside the organization, but assessor drawn from outside the organizational unit may appear to be more credible on account of a more independent viewpoint. The assessment team follows the ISO/IEC 15504-part 3 [3] as the documented procedural approach for conducting the assessment. Details of the assessment activities such as planning, documenting assessment plan, briefing of the participants, data collection and validation are put together into an assessment plan and an assessment report. Assessment is conducted based on ISO/IEC 15504-part 5 [5].

4.4   Action Plan Derivation

Based on assessment findings, improvement plan to shift to next capability level is generated taking ISO/IEC 15504-Part 4: Guidance on use for Process Improvement and Process Capability Determination as a reference [4]. Defined steps are as follows:

   i. Analyze assessment strengths and weaknesses
  ii. Identify process-related risks
 iii. Identify opportunities for improvement
  iv. Review organizational improvement goals

  v. Analyze effectiveness measurements
  vi. List improvement areas
  vii. Define detailed improvement objectives
  viii. Set targets for objectives
  ix. Document action plan

As a result of this phase; strengths and weaknesses of the processes are identified based on assessment findings. Process related risks are assessed from the probability of a particular problem occurring, and its potential consequence are identified. Opportunities for improvement are derived based on the identified weaknesses of the processes. Processes and their relationships are analyzed in order to evaluate which processes have direct impact on the organizational objectives identified in the Execution plan. A prioritized list of improvement areas is compiled from all of the factors listed above. Targets for improvement are set with regard to the organization's business goals which can be objectively measured, and which can reasonably be achieve. Finally the action plan is derived, it includes activities, tasks, responsible, resources, schedule, cost, and risk.

5 Conclusion

We proposed a methodology incorporating guidelines for governmental process improvement. As a result of the study, it is observed that:

- There are some characteristics in government domain and there is a need to develop a government-specific process improvement model.
- Governmental process can be defined using requirements in ISO/IEC TR 15504.
- ISO/IEC TR 15504-5 [5] is of great help in identifying indicators for levels 2 to 5.
- ISO/IEC TR 15504-3 [3] can be used by assessor to perform a conformance assessment.
- ISO/IEC TR 15504-4 [4] is used as the main guideline for developing the proposed roadmap for process capability improvement.
- Governmental processes are more repetitive and stable comparing to software processes. This difference is a positive variance to ensure a systematic performance.

In parallel with ISO/IEC TR 15504 [2]-[5], our approach aims to provide a variety of benefits for government organizations, including the followings: cost savings; more involved employees; improved and predictable quality as well as productivity; generating a consistency of process capture and use.

 Future studies include validating the proposed approach by performing different case studies in various government agencies.

References

1. OMG Business Process Maturity Model (BPMM) Version 1.0 (2008)
2. ISO, ISO/IEC 15504-2: Information technology - Process assessment - Part 2: Performing an assessment (2003)

3. ISO, ISO/IEC 15504-3: Information technology – Process assessment – Part 3: Guidance on performing an assessment (2004)
4. ISO, ISO/IEC 15504-4: Information technology – Process assessment – Part 4: Guidance on use for process improvement and process capability determination (2004)
5. ISO, ISO/IEC 15504-5: Information technology - Process assessment - Part 5: An exemplar Process Assessment Model (2012)
6. ISO/IEC 33000 – Information Technology – Process Assessment, International Organization for Standardization (2014)
7. ISO, AutomotiveSPICE. http://www.automotivespice.com/
8. ISO, EnterpriseSPICE. http://www.enterprisespice.com
9. Barafort, B., Humbert, J.P., Poggi, S.: Information security management and ISO/IEC 15504: the link opportunity between security and quality. In: SPICE Conference, Luxembourg (2006)
10. Malzahn, D.: A service extension for spice? SPICE Conference, Seoul, South Korea (2007)
11. Barafort, B., Renault, A., Picard, M., Cortina, S.: A transformation process for building PRMs and PAMs based on a collection of requirements – example with ISO/IEC 20000. In: SPICE Conference, Nuremberg, Germany (2008)
12. Ivanyos, J.: Implementing process assessment model of internal financial control. In: The International SPICE Days, Frankfurt/Main, Germany (2007)
13. Coletta, A.: An industrial experience in assessing the capability of non-software processes using ISO/IEC 15504. Software Process: Improvement and Practice **12**(4), 315–319 (2007)
14. Rifaut, A., Dubois, E.: Using goal-oriented requirements engineering for improving the quality of ISO/IEC 15504 based compliance assessment frameworks. In: 16th IEEE International Requirements Engineering Conference, Barcelona, vol. 16, pp. 33–42 (2008)
15. McCaffery, F., Dorling, A.: Medi SPICE Development, Software Process Maintenance and Evolution: Improvement and Practice Journal **22**(4) (2010)
16. Cass, A., et al.: SPICE for SPACE trials, risk analysis, and process improvement. Software Process: Improvement and Practice **9**(1), 13–21 (2004)
17. Zwicker, J., Fettke, P., Loos, P.: Business process maturity in public administrations. In: Handbook on Business Process Management 2, pp. 369–396. Springer (2010)
18. Lenk K, Traunmüller R, Wimmer M.A.: The significance of law and knowledge for electronic Government. Electronic government: design, application & management, pp 61–77 (2002)
19. Gökalp, E., Demirörs, O.: Government process capability model: an exploratory case study. In: Mitasiunas, A., Rout, T., O'Connor, R.V., Dorling, A. (eds.) SPICE 2014. CCIS, vol. 477, pp. 94–105. Springer, Heidelberg (2014)
20. Council, C.I.O.: Federal Enterprise Architecture Consolidated Reference Model (2007)
21. American Productivity & Quality Center (APQC)., Process Classification Framework, APQC (2012). http://www.apqc.org/free/framework.htm
22. Software Engineering Institute (SEI): CMMI Product Team, CMMI® for Development, Version 1.3, Improving processes for developing better products and services (2010)
23. C. P. Team. CMMI for Service, Version 1.3, CMMI-SVC v1.3, SEI (2010)
24. Curtis, B., Hefley, B., Miller, S.: People Capability Maturity Model (P-CMM) (2009)
25. Office of Government Commerce, ITIL Service Strategy, TSO, London (2007)
26. Ibrahim, L.: The Federal Aviation Administration Integrated Capability Maturity Model, Version 1.0. Federal Aviation Administration (1997)

Evaluating VSEs Viewpoint and Sentiment Towards the ISO/IEC 29110 Standard: A Two Country Grounded Theory Study

Mary-Luz Sanchez-Gordon[1], Rory V. O'Connor[2,3(✉)], and Ricardo Colomo-Palacios[4]

[1] Universidad Carlos III de Madrid, Madrid, Spain
mary_sanchezg@hotmail.com
[2] Lero, the Irish Software Research Centre, Dublin, Ireland
[3] Dublin City University, Dublin, Ireland
Rory.OConnor@computing.dcu.ie
[4] Ostfold University College, Halden, Norway
Ricardo.colomo-palacios@hiof.no

Abstract. The ISO/IEC 29110 standard has at its core a Management and Engineering Guide [1] which are targeted at very small entities (enterprises, organizations, departments or projects) having up to 25 people [2], to assist them unlock the potential benefits of using standards which are specifically designed to address their needs. This paper is concerned with understanding the issues that affect the adoption of software process standards by Very Small Entities (VSEs), their needs from process standards and their willingness to engage with the new ISO/IEC 29110 standard in particular. This paper bring together two complimentary studies undertaken in Ireland and Ecuador which pose questions to VSE management regarding opinions, attitude and sentiment towards the adoption of the VSE designed standard ISO/IEC 29110. A series of interviews were untaken in both countries counties with qualitative data analysis utilizing the grounded theory coding mechanisms, to produce a picture of the current situation. This paper serves as a roadmap for both researchers wishing to understand the issues of process standards adoption by very small companies and also for the software process standards community.

Keywords: VSE · ISO/IEC 29110 · ISO · Standards · Process improvement

1 Introduction

There are multiple approaches to organizing the software development process and multiple factors influencing the software development process [3], with two major ones being the traditional (or plan based), which rely primarily on managing explicit knowledge, and agile methods, which primarily rely on managing tacit knowledge and recognizes the importance of human interaction in the software process [4, 5]. Due to the rich variety of software development settings (for example: the nature of the application being developed, team size, requirements volatility), the implementation of a set of practices for software development may be quite different from one setting to another [6].

Projects are the cornerstone of all business activities in small and very small companies. Firms must complete various projects to achieve their financial goals and obtain information. Business owners and managers have only one attempt executing a project successfully. Hence, the process must be carefully thought out and planned. In their study into why software projects fail [7] have shown that software specialists spend about 40 to 50 percent of their time on avoidable rework rather than on what they call value-added work, which is basically work that's done right the first time

Administering software development is usually achieved through the introduction of a software project management process. However, implementing software project management controls in very small software companies is a major challenge. This paper introduces the project management practices in the newly published ISO/IEC 29110 [1] standard Software Process Lifecycles for Very Small Entities. The following sections discuss the role of project management in general, the structure of ISO/IEC standard and its project management practices.

1.1 Research Problem

In the current economic environment software quality is increasingly being seen as a subject of concern for growth and evolution of software companies in general, no matter what the size. Further quality orientated process approaches and standards are maturing and gaining acceptance in many companies. However, the use of ISO/IEC systems and software engineering standards remains limited to a few of the most popular ones. VSE specific standards such as *ISO/IEC 29110 Software Process Lifecycles for Very Small Entities* has been developed to assist and encourage very small software organization in assessing and improving their software.

This paper is concerned with understanding VSEs issues regarding adoption of standards, their needs from process standards and their willingness to engage with the new ISO 29110 standards' in particular. Accordingly the research question addressed by this study is *"What is the opinion, attitude, sentiment and feeling towards the potential benefits of adopting a VSE specific standard such as ISO/IEC 29110 by VSE management and staff?"*. In order to investigate this research question, the authors have conducted two complimentary studies, one in Ireland and the other in Ecuador, which pose questions to VSE management and staff regarding opinions, attitude and sentiment towards the adoption of the ISO/IEC 29110 standard.

This paper is divided into 5 sections. Section 2 presents the background study of the study and outlines ISO/IEC 2910 in detail. Section 3 explains the overall research processes that have been applied in this study. A section 4 discusses all the findings and results of the study. Section 5 presents some concluding remarks and discusses future work.

2   ISO/IEC 29110 Standard

The ISO/IEC 29110 standard "Lifecycle profiles for Very Small Entities" [1] is aimed at addressing the issues identified above and addresses the specific needs of VSEs

[8–10] and to tackle the issues of poor standards adoption by small companies [11–13]. The approach [14, 15] used to develop ISO/IEC 29110 started with the pre-existing international standard ISO/IEC 12207 dedicated to software process life-cycles. The overall approach consisted of three steps: (1) Selecting ISO/IEC 12207 [16] process subset applicable to VSEs of up to 25 employees; (2) Tailor the subset to fit VSE needs; and (3) Develop guidelines for VSEs.

The basic requirements of a software development process are that it should fit the needs of the project and aid project success [10]. And this need should be informed by the situational context where in the project must operate and therefore, the most suitable software development process is contingent on the context [5, 17]. The core situational characteristic of the entities targeted by ISO/IEC 29110 is size, however there are other aspects and characteristics of VSEs that may affect profile preparation or selection, such as: Business Models (commercial, contracting, in-house development, etc.); Situational factors (such as criticality, uncertainty environment, etc.); and Risk Levels. Creating one profile for each possible combination of values of the various dimensions introduced above would result in an unmanageable set of profiles. Accordingly VSE's profiles are grouped in such a way as to be applicable to more than one category.

Profile Groups are a collection of profiles which are related either by composition of processes (i.e. activities, tasks), or by capability level, or both. The "Generic" profile group has been defined [10] as applicable to a vast majority of VSEs that do not develop critical software and have typical situational factors. This profile group does not imply any specific application domain, however, it is envisaged that in the future new domain-specific sub-profiles may be developed in the future. To date the Basic Profile [1] has been published, the purpose of which is to define a software development and project management guide for performing one project at a time.

Finally, the results obtained from systematic literature review of the ISO/IEC 29110 standard [18] show that there is an increasing interest on it.

2.1 Engineering and Management Guide

At the core of this standard is a Management and Engineering Guide (ISO/IEC 29110-5) [1] focusing on *Project Management* and *Software Implementation*. The purpose of the *Project Management* process is to establish and carry out in a systematic way the tasks of a software implementation project, which complies with the project's objectives in terms of quality, time and cost. *Project Management* generates a *Project Plan* to direct the software project. During the execution of the project *Change Requests* may cause revisions to the *Project Plan*. The project is the subject of *Project Assessment and Control* during the lifetimes of the project until the *Software Implementation* is complete and *Project Closure* occurs.

Software Implementation (SI) produces a specified software system implemented as a software product or service. This process starts with the establishment of *Software Requirements*, after which *Architectural and Detailed Design* are produced. Software is the *Constructed* and verified using *Integration and Test* procedures. The final staged being *product delivery* to the customer.

Within ISO/IEC 29110, the purpose of the Project Management process is to establish and carry out in a systematic way the Tasks of the software implementation project, which allows complying with the project's Objectives in the expected quality, time and costs. It is intended to be used by the VSE to establish processes to implement any development approach or methodology including, e.g., agile, evolutionary, incremental, test driven development, etc. based on the VSE organization or project needs.

2.2 Deployment and Implementation Assistance

In order to assist with the deployment of ISO/IEC 29110 and to provide guidance on the actual implementation of ISO/IEC 29110-5 in VSEs a series of *Deployment Packages* and *Implementation Guides* have been developed to define guidelines and explain in more detail the processes defined in the ISO/IEC 29110 profiles [19].

A set of *Deployment Packages* (DP) (which are freely available from [20]) are a set of artifacts developed to facilitate the implementation of a set of practices, of the selected framework, in a VSE. A DP is not a process reference model (i.e. it is not prescriptive). The elements of a typical DP are: description of processes, activities, tasks, roles and products, template, checklist, example, reference and mapping to standards and models, and a list of tools. Packages are designed such that a VSE can implement its content, without having to implement the complete framework at the same time.

To date a series of pilot projects have been completed in several countries utilizing some of the deployment packages developed [21]. For example in France, a pilot study [22] was conducted with a 14-people VSE that builds and sells counting systems about the frequenting of natural spaces and public sites. Furthermore a series of studies have been conducted to understand the perceptions [23] and potential commitment [24] of VSE management towards ISO/IEC 29110 [25].

3 The Research Process

The investigation of stakeholder perception in VSEs towards the adoption of process standards and ISO/IEC 29110 in particular relies heavily on eliciting and understanding the views of those who manage and deploy the software processes in situ and the interpretation of these experiences and the reality of the situation under study. The study therefore, naturally lends itself to the application of qualitative research methods, as they are orientated towards how individuals and groups view and understand the world and construct meaning out of their experiences. Therefore, the need for a deep understanding of the issues in VSEs calls for a qualitative research approach. The objective of the present study is more focused on creating a detailed description rather than creating a theory, accordingly a pure Grounded Theory (GT) method is not applicable but only GT coding process will be used in order to assist researcher in analyzing present study data [26, 27]. As depicted in Fig. 1, this study has four main phases. In the first two phases, the data collection processes in two countries are completed utilizing individual and focus group interviews. In the third phase, GT coding process was used in analysis data. Finally the data is interpreted and presented in this paper.

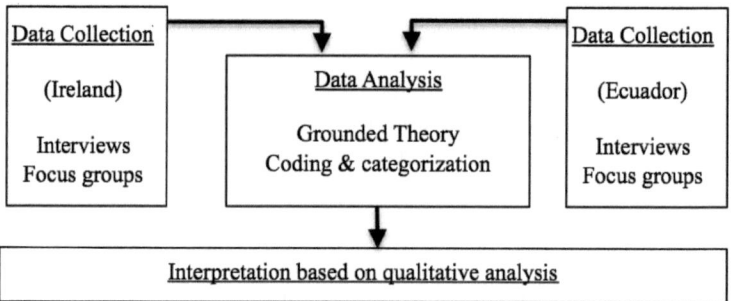

Fig. 1. Research Process

3.1 Data Collection Methods

For quantitative data collection two complimentary data collection methods individual and focus group interviews. Interviews and Focus Groups are a resource-demanding data collection method; activities such as planning, conducting and analyzing are time-consuming by nature. However, interviewing people provides insight into their world; their opinions, thoughts and feelings and therefore we propose these as suitable data collections mechanisms. In particular focus groups explicitly use dynamic group interaction as part of the method to achieve enhanced data gathering, as it can for example activate details of forgotten experiences and also generate better data through wide range of responses. This means that instead of the researcher asking each person to respond to a question in turn, people are encouraged to talk to one another: asking questions, exchanging anecdotes and commenting on each other's experiences and points of view [28]. Both methods should be used properly and the sessions should be planned and executed well and with appropriate rigor in order to avoid potential sources for unwanted bias. Interviews and focus group were also recorded in order to prevent loss of information. Thus, the interviewer was able to pay more attention to the subject.

The individual interview approach was used in this study in order to discuss the topics in depth, to get respondents' candid discussion on the topic and to be able to get the depth of information of the study situation for the research context [28]. This process followed by semi-structured interviews approach which includes the open-ended and specific questions. This approach allowed us to gather not only the information foreseen, but also unexpected type of information. The respondents for the individual interview session are the managers from the identified Irish Software VSEs and went around 20 to 30 minutes in duration. Although, the approach carried out in Ecuador was tailored due to the language, cultural differences and actual development of the Ecuadorian software industry, the duration of the sessions is described in section 3.4. The use of semi-structured interviews is very frequent in the software engineering literature e.g. [29–31].

The second interview method is the focus group interview. It was used in this study because team members develop the software and the existence team interactions helped to release inhibitions amongst the team members and are from the same company as the individual interviews participants. Focus group interviews were also chosen because it was the most appropriate method to study attitudes and experiences; to explore how opinion were constructed and to understand behaviors, values and feelings [28]. Focus groups have been used in the past in software engineering scenarios as valid qualitative methods, e.g. [32, 33].

3.2 Data Analysis Methods

We followed the qualitative contents analysis method and adopted the Grounded Theory (GT) [34] data coding process to analyze all collected data and have a systematic data coding activities. This study has essentially employed the Strauss and Corbin [34] approach because the researchers have personal and professional experience on software development. It is supportive of theory building and contributes to "theoretical sensitivity", the ability to understand the data's important elements and how they contribute to theory. According to Strauss and Corbin [34], the theory that is derived from the data is more likely to resemble what is actually going on than if it were assembled from putting together a series of concepts based on experience or through speculation.

Data analysis may begin informally during interviews and continue during transcription, when recurring themes, patterns, and categories become evident. Coding is the key process in GT. It is the first step of data analysis and begins in the early stages after the first interviews for data collection. They assert that the coding procedures in GT are neither automatic nor algorithmic - *"we do not at all wish to imply rigid adherence to them"*. Therefore, flexibility may be necessary in certain circumstances. There are two types of codes produced as a result of data analysis or coding. This process involves the development of the codes, code-categories and inter-relationship of categories which is based on the GT process and coding strategy. Three coding techniques proposed by GT methodology: open coding, axial coding and selective coding have been applied in order to assist researchers in analyzing qualitative data and are explained below in the context of this study. In this part all qualitative data gathered from individual interviews and focus group interviews were analyzed and coded. This process involves the development of the codes, code-categories and inter-relationship of categories based on the GT process and coding strategy [34].

3.3 Study Participants

Recruiting participants is a significant challenge for any research project as they have to spend time on what are often seen as a "non-productive" activity. As two of the authors has firsthand knowledge of their local software industry (ie. Ireland and Ecuador), potential candidates from commercial software VSEs were been identified through prior working relationships. In addition, in Ecuador an e-mail invitation was distributed to 30 enterprises of Ecuadorian Association of Software (AESOFT). Despite this effort, the organizations were selected based on availability therefore it was a crucial factor for their selection, which is a common practice [35].

To ensure participants were fully informed about the implications of their involvement in the research and to comply with the issue ethics, each potential VSE was provided with a research profile. In addition, each person who agreed to participate in the research project as an interviewee was asked to notify via e-mail that confirmed that they had understood the implications of their involvement and that they were willing to participate.

Within the Ecuadorian software community 3 VSEs, representing 3 interviews and 3 focus groups, took part in the fieldwork the semi-structured interview and focus group were performed. Within Ireland 6 Irish-based VSEs, representing 6 interviews and 6 focus groups, took part in the fieldwork the semi-structured interview and focus group were performed. In Ecuador the data collection process took 3 months and in Ireland 6 months, which included identifying suitable companies, contacting and confirming potential respondents' process, conducting individual and focus group interviews process.

3.4 Conducting the Interview and Focus Group Sessions

All of the interview and focus group sessions were conducted in a similar manner with one exception. In Ireland all interviews and focus groups were conducted in person at the VSE office location. However, in Ecuador on-line meetings were selected because the geographical location of the researchers (at the time of the study was conducted) and associated difficulties. Although these online forms provide many advantages over traditionally conducted meetings (e.g., savings in travelling and venue costs, participants feel more comfortable giving negative or controversial feedback), they also have distinct drawbacks, too, such as the task of the moderator can be much more demanding in online than in face-to-face settings [36].

The data was collected by conducting semi-structured interviews with Software Project Managers. Two interviews lasted approximately two hours and a half and one three hours. Conducting Semi-structured interviews instead of completely structured ones help with emergence of the real concerns of participants rather than forcing a topic that may be viewed as trivial by the participants. As the nature of the interviews had been open, when the conversation moved towards new and interesting areas relevant to the subject, the interviewer pursued and explored the new directions. Keeping this in mind, the focus group was performed with software developers, lasting from one hour and a half to two hours. Again, this approach was helpful to understanding of respondents based on data collected previously.

Every meeting was voice recorded and then transcribed. A complete transcription is very time consuming, but it avoids the loss of data. In this way, it was easier to recall the content clearly and to gain a thorough insight into the all the data material. The transcriptions were used for the coding of data in the subsequent analysis phase.

4 Study Findings and Discussion

From the qualitative data analysis process, which adopted the GT coding approach, we categorise the issues into several identified categories as shown in table 1. The details of the main categories are presented below, which grouped and listed out in detail the important variable that was gathered from the analysis of understanding the actual software process development in very small companies.

Table 1. GT Themes, core categories and categories

Sub Category	Category	Main Category
High Awareness on Standard	Level of Interest and Awareness	Quality Standard Acceptance Level
Standard Benefit Awareness		
Low Acceptable	Level of Acceptance	
Less Priority		
Perceived Need	Barriers Towards Adoption	
Resource Demand		

4.1 Level of Interest and Awareness

This category explains VSEs level of interest and awareness regarding software quality standards in general and of ISO/IEC 29110 in particular. Our analysis has shown that there is an interest and awareness about software process standards and the potential benefits from having a quality standard especially the ISO standards. Leading to a quality product, create consistency, improve company image, create consistency in development work, improve work process and good for business are the main points that the interviewees gave, which indicates VSEs high awareness and interest about the benefit of having software quality standard. One company explicitly expressed that the company had planned to adopt the ISO 9000 but due to several constraints as have been discussed above made the plans to be put on hold. This situation shows that VSEs have an interest and are aware about the benefit adopting software quality standard. This level of interest and awareness is illustrated in the following interview extracts: *"Yes we do plan too, but since we started we have growth so quickly... we spend time learning how we want to do... we started to put those processes in place so when we grow we have a good platform."* and *"They [software quality standard] are nice. It would be great to have them in order to have a consistence software process up and running."*

The analysis has also shown that there is an indicator that small companies are interested and are aware about software process and quality standards. The interviewed companies believe that the potential benefits from having a quality standard, and in particular ISO/IEC 29110, could be a quality product, improving company image, improving work process, creating consistency in development work, making the business more profitable because less time is spent on non-productive work. As one interview subject explained *"I think it [standard] is necessary, let us not beat around the bush, but you have to adapt it to the reality of the company. As I told you, each reality is different ... so I have assumed few things and implemented few things because it is necessary. You cannot live without it*". This concept was backed up by another who explained "*If you could achieve the standard ... eventually you could decrease the costs because you would have a defined process*". Finally a further participant remarked, "*The great benefit is a more controlled software development process so take less time to finish ...*"

4.2 Level of Acceptance

Based on the analysis of the data the researchers found that none of the VSEs are or have plans to adopt or accredited any particular standard in their software development process. Interview data analysis identified several reasons that have been divided to 2 main subcategories (*Low Acceptable* and *Less Priority*) in order to understand the problem in adopting standards. The first subcategory is on the low standard acceptable issues, which is due to the perception that process standards are overly involved / complicated and lacking in detailed implementation guidance.

The Level of Acceptance is low because none of the companies are accredited to or have plans to adopt any particular lightweight software quality standard. They argue that the software quality standards are not tailored with the current development process so it is a big challenge. The following three interview extracts describe this situation: "*There is still a lot to do, to document*"; "*Many companies do not adopt the standards as they are cumbersome and will not have a return on investment*"; and "*I think the first step is to have our well-defined process, we probably need to have our own product, and I think the next step is to address the quality issues*".

The second subcategory in this part is on the low priority issues. The interviews analysis also indicates that a software quality standard is a low priority task in software development process and activities in VSEs. The interviewees have explained several reasons, which indicate this situation. Not compulsory or low demand of the accreditation to standards from their client is the main reasons given by all the interviewees. Higher quality of code and delivery time are seen as more important that the evaluation of the development process. Software quality standards were seen as 'sale tool' only. They also responded that current software quality standard objective such as encapsulated in standards such as ISO 9000 are more toward on the management and services of the software development process rather than a software technical issues and product. They also believed that the software quality standards are built for the big companies rather than for VSEs. This is illustrated in these interview extracts: "*If you want to get done quickly then what you need is focusing to the output not the process*"; "*A lot of process in quality standard is nonsense. Some ISO standards tell you to do XYZ steps but they may be not being beneficial to our business*"; "*We do informal research if we found something cool article I will try to followed to improve our process. But seriously standards quality is not on my list*" and "*Standard is just a sale tool.*"

4.3 Barriers to Adoption

This category explains the barriers to adoption in particular die to a lack of *Perceived Needs* and a high level of perceived *Resource needs*.

The data analysis indicates that VSE believe that they do not need it because they are small and have limited resources in the company. They were not interested in adopting any quality standard due to the cost, time and effort involved. In addition, there are perceived difficulties in implementing a new process that everyone can understand and follow clearly. One company in relation to CMMI explained such barriers as *"These methodologies [such as CMMI] are still very large for our size. There are still a gap between our human resource and our financial resources"*. Another remarked on the effect of people related perceptions as barriers by stating that *"I just tell you the people. People should be involved ... there is always resistance to change"*.

On a related point one participant highlighted the need for integration to counteract barriers by stating *"You have to do it along with the daily work ... paper can withstand all but you have to put it into practice, too"*. Another company explained that *"We made up our own methodology, it was adapted to our reality and it works, we need agility, unfortunately we also need to have formal documentation otherwise the customer relationships are complicated but I cannot overburden"*.

In addition, the adoption of standards would require additional resources which would have an additional cost to the company. Participants also believed that the processes as described in software standards are not easy to actually tailor and implement in these organizations. For example, the view was consistently expressed that current software quality standards such as ISO9000 cannot be adapted and followed. In relation to that, all the interviewees believed that involving or adapting software quality standard in their process will increase the project cost and delay the project delivery. Meanwhile, they argue that the process involved software quality standards are not tailored with the current development process, which are more brief, informal and very light in process. The following interview extracts describe this situation: *"In a company of our size they [standards] would not necessarily add value... we would need more sophisticated process if we were a larger company"*; and *"Too much documentation and you need somebody to just work on the software process alone. Because our developers are busy with coding, documentation is the last thing they do."*

Furthermore, the analysis also indicates that the lack of requirement from the market in general and their customer in particular has contributed to low acceptance of such standards. During the interviews it was also shown that accreditation against software quality standards is only important when companies involved or plan to work with the government bodies or state agencies that have such a requirement. Contributing to this is the fact that most VSEs clients are private, small or individual companies which do not have a standards accreditation requirement. The following interview extracts best describe this situation: *"We had never had a problem selling our stuff or not selling our stuff because of an ISO standard. Microsoft Windows standard are sometimes important, but ISO who cares!"* and *"I never heard anything from sales that we couldn't sell anything because of lack of ISO standard."*

4.4 Requirements of a Standard

In order to understand more about software quality standards in VSEs, we asked the interviewees the criteria they considered important in a software quality standard. The purpose here is to understand in detail the criteria that VSEs consider is important in order to encourage among small companies the adoption of a software quality standard such as ISO/IEC 29110. The respondents indicated that it requires a number of issues to be addressed such as:

- Minimum overhead of resources (time, people and financial)
- More information about the standards such as guidelines, deployment packages and certification process scheme.
- Papers about case studies of its adoption in terms of time required, workload and lessons learned.
- Expert Assistance and detailed guidelines
- Provide clear templates
- Provide workshop and/or training on how to actually apply it

Although not all participants were knowledgeable in software quality standards, all of them agreed that ISO/IEC 29110 could be helpful. As a project manager in one of the companies, which is EFQM certified company, said: "*I think and I am increasingly convinced that many past years with adequate knowledge could be compressed into a tablet ... we have done things differently*".

5 Conclusions

The issues identified can be as: the level of acceptance, level of awareness and new standard criteria. The first category has prevailed that the acceptance level of any type or model of software quality standard in VSEs is very low and less priority. The reasons are mainly related to the low level of customer or market requirement, lack of resources and, lengthy and difficult procedures. However, the analysis also showed that the level of awareness of software quality standards and its advantage are high and there are some initiatives or plans to adopt in the not near future. The third category indicates the criteria needed or proposed by the VSEs, which include the detail guideline and assistance, less overhead and resources and aligned with VSEs current process, that must be aware in order to encourage or to attract VSEs seriously involved in software quality standards.

As ISO/IEC 29110 is an emerging standard there is much work yet to be completed. The main remaining work item is to finalize the development of the remaining profiles and the development of additional Profile Groups for other domains such as critical software, game industry [37], scientific software development are being studied. In addition, recently, the ISO working group was mandated to develop a standard for VSEs developing systems engineering [38, 39] and is investigating ITSM [40] and agile development approaches [41].

The relationship between the success of a software company and the software process it utilized has been investigated [42–44] showing the need for all organizations, not just VSEs to pay attention to software process practices such as ISO standards [45]. Here fore ultimately it is the position of the authors that standards such as ISO/IEC 29110 have a potential important impact on the software industry.

Acknowledgments: The Irish elements of this study were supported, in part, by Science Foundation Ireland grant 03/CE2/I303_1 to Lero, the Irish Software Engineering Research Centre (www.lero.ie).

References

1. International Organization for Standardization (ISO): ISO/IEC TR 29110-5-1-2 Software engineering - Lifecycle profiles for Very Small Entities (VSEs) Part 5-1-2: Management and engineering guide: Generic profile group: Basic profile, Geneva (2011)
2. Laporte, C.Y., Alexandre, S., O'Connor, R.V.: A software engineering lifecycle standard for very small enterprises. In: O'Connor, R., Baddoo, N., Smolander, K., Messnarz, R. (eds.) Proceedings of EuroSPI, pp. 129–141. Springer, Heidelberg (2008)
3. Ryan, S., O'Connor, R.V.: Acquiring and sharing tacit knowledge in software development teams: An empirical study. Information and Software Technology **55**, 1614–1624 (2013)
4. Ryan, S., O'Connor, R.V.: Development of a team measure for tacit knowledge in software development teams. Journal of Systems and Software **82**, 229–240 (2009)
5. Clarke, P., O'Connor, R.V.: The situational factors that affect the software development process: Towards a comprehensive reference framework. Journal of Information and Software Technology **54**, 433–447 (2012)
6. Jeners, S., Clarke, P., O'Connor, R.V., Buglione, L., Lepmets, M.: Harmonizing software development processes with software development settings – a systematic approach. In: McCaffery, F., O'Connor, R.V., Messnarz, R. (eds.) EuroSPI 2013. CCIS, vol. 364, pp. 167–178. Springer, Heidelberg (2013)
7. Charette, R.N.: Why Software Fails. IEEE Spectrum **42**, 42–49 (2005)
8. O'Connor, R.V., Laporte, C.Y.: Deploying lifecycle profiles for very small entities: an early stage industry view. In: O'Connor, R.V., Rout, T., McCaffery, F., Dorling, A. (eds.) SPICE 2011. CCIS, vol. 155, pp. 227–230. Springer, Heidelberg (2011)
9. O'Connor, R.V., Laporte, C.Y.: Using ISO/IEC 29110 to harness process improvement in very small entities. In: O'Connor, R.V., Pries-Heje, J., Messnarz, R. (eds.) EuroSPI 2011. CCIS, vol. 172, pp. 225–235. Springer, Heidelberg (2011)
10. O'Connor, R., Laporte, C.Y.: Towards the provision of assistance for very small entities in deploying software lifecycle standards. In: Proceedings of the 11th International Conference on Product Focused Software (PROFES 2010), pp. 4–7. ACM (2010)
11. Coleman, G., O'Connor, R.: Investigating software process in practice: A grounded theory perspective. Journal of Systems and Software **81**, 772–784 (2008)
12. O'Connor, R., Coleman, G.: Ignoring "Best Practice": Why Irish Software SMEs are Rejecting CMMI and ISO 9000. Australasian Journal of Information Systems **16** (2009)
13. O'Connor, R.V.: Evaluating management sentiment towards ISO/IEC 29110 in very small software development companies. In: Mas, A., Mesquida, A., Rout, T., O'Connor, R.V., Dorling, A. (eds.) SPICE 2012. CCIS, vol. 290, pp. 277–281. Springer, Heidelberg (2012)
14. O'Connor, R.V., Laporte, C.Y.: An Innovative Approach to the Development of an International Software Process Lifecycle Standard for Very Small Entities. International Journal of Information Technology Systems Approach **7**, 1–22 (2014)

15. Laporte, C.Y., O'Connor, R., Fanmuy, G.: International Systems and Software Engineering Standards for Very Small Entities. CrossTalk - The Journal of Defense Software Engineering **26**, 28–33 (2013)
16. Clarke, P., O'Connor, R.: Harnessing ISO/IEC 12207 to examine the extent of SPI activity in an organisation. In: Riel, A., O'Connor, R., Tichkiewitch, S., Messnarz, R. (eds.) EuroSPI 2010. CCIS, vol. 99, pp. 25–36. Springer, Heidelberg (2010)
17. Jeners, S., O'Connor, R.V., Clarke, P., Lichter, H., Lepmets, M., Buglione, L.: Harnessing software development contexts to inform software process selection decisions. Software Quality Professional **16**, 35–36 (2013)
18. Moreno-Campos, E., Sanchez-Gordón, M.-L., Colomo-Palacios, R., de Amescua Seco, A.: Towards measuring the impact of the ISO/IEC 29110 standard: a systematic review. In: Barafort, B., O'Connor, R.V., Poth, A., Messnarz, R. (eds.) EuroSPI 2014. CCIS, vol. 425, pp. 1–12. Springer, Heidelberg (2014)
19. Laporte, C.Y.: Contributions to Software Engineering and the Development and Deployment of International Software Engineering Standards for Very Small Entities (Ph.D thesis of the Université de Bretagne Occidentale) (2009)
20. ISO/IEC JCT1/SC7 Working Group 24 Deployment Packages repository. http://profs.logti.etsmtl.ca/claporte/English/VSE/index.html
21. O'Connor, R.V., Sanders, M.: Lessons from a pilot implementation of ISO/IEC 29110 in a group of very small irish companies. In: Woronowicz, T., Rout, T., O'Connor, R.V., Dorling, A. (eds.) SPICE 2013. CCIS, vol. 349, pp. 243–246. Springer, Heidelberg (2013)
22. Ribaud, V., Saliou, P., O'Connor, R.V., Laporte, C.Y.: Software engineering support activities for very small entities. In: Riel, A., O'Connor, R., Tichkiewitch, S., Messnarz, R. (eds.) EuroSPI 2010. CCIS, vol. 99, pp. 165–176. Springer, Heidelberg (2010)
23. Basri, S., O'Connor, R.V.: Understanding the perception of very small software companies towards the adoption of process standards. In: Riel, A., O'Connor, R., Tichkiewitch, S., Messnarz, R. (eds.) EuroSPI 2010. CCIS, vol. 99, pp. 153–164. Springer, Heidelberg (2010)
24. O'Connor, R.V., Basri, S., Coleman, G.: Exploring managerial commitment towards SPI in small and very small enterprises. In: Riel, A., O'Connor, R., Tichkiewitch, S., Messnarz, R. (eds.) EuroSPI 2010. CCIS, vol. 99, pp. 268–279. Springer, Heidelberg (2010)
25. Basri, S., O'Connor, R.: Organizational commitment towards software process improvement an irish software VSEs case study. In: Proceedings of 4th International Symposium on Information Technology 2010 (ITSim 2010), pp. 1456–1461. IEEE, Malaysia (2010)
26. Hoda, R., Noble, J., Marshall, S.: Developing a grounded theory to explain the practices of self-organizing Agile teams. Empirical Software Engineering **17**, 609–639 (2012)
27. O'Connor, R.: Using grounded theory coding mechanisms to analyze case study and focus group data in the context of software process research. In: Mora, M., et al. (eds.) Research Methodologies, Innovations and Philosophies in Software Systems Engineering and Information Systems, pp. 256–270. IGI Global (2012)
28. Patton, M.Q.: Qualitative Evaluation and Research Methods. Sage Publications Inc., Newbury Park (2002)
29. Colomo-Palacios, R., Casado-Lumbreras, C., Soto-Acosta, P., García-Peñalvo, F.J., Tovar, E.: Project managers in global software development teams: a study of the effects on productivity and performance. Software Quality Journal **22**, 3–19 (2014)
30. Casado-Lumbreras, C., Colomo-Palacios, R., Ogwueleka, F.N., Sanjay, M.: Software development outsourcing: challenges and opportunities in Nigeria. Journal of Global Information Technology Management **17**, 267–282 (2014)

31. Herranz Sánchez, E., Colomo-Palacios, R., de Amescua Seco, A., Yilmaz, M.: Gamification as a disruptive factor in software process improvement initiatives. Journal of Universal Computer Science **20**, 885–906 (2014)
32. Colomo-Palacios, R., Soto-Acosta, P., García-Peñalvo, F.J., García-Crespo, Á.: A study of the impact of global software development in packaged software release planning. Journal of Universal Computer Science **18**, 2646–2668 (2012)
33. Colomo-Palacios, R., Casado-Lumbreras, C., Soto-Acosta, P., Misra, S., García-Peñalvo, F.J.: Analyzing human resource management practices within the GSD context. Journal of Universal Computer Science **15**, 30–54 (2012)
34. Strauss, A., Corbin, J.M.: Basics of Qualitative Research: Techniques and Procedures for Developing Grounded Theory. SAGE Publications Inc., Thousand Oaks, CA (1998)
35. Benbasat, I., Goldstein, D., Mea, M.: The Case Research Strategy in Studies of Information Systems. MIS Quarterly **11**, 369–386 (1987)
36. Kontio, J., Lehtola, L., Bragge, J.: Using the focus group method in software engineering: obtaining practitioner and user experiences. In: Proceedings of the 2004 International Symposium on Empirical Software Engineering, ISESE 2004, pp. 271–280. IEEE (2004)
37. Osborne O'Hagan, A., Coleman, G., O'Connor, R.V.: Software development processes for games: a systematic literature review. In: Barafort, B., O'Connor, R.V., Poth, A., Messnarz, R. (eds.) EuroSPI 2014. CCIS, vol. 425, pp. 182–193. Springer, Heidelberg (2014)
38. Laporte, C.Y., O'Connor, R.V.: A systems process lifecycle standard for very small entities: development and pilot trials. In: Barafort, B., O'Connor, R.V., Poth, A., Messnarz, R. (eds.) EuroSPI 2014. CCIS, vol. 425, pp. 13–24. Springer, Heidelberg (2014)
39. Laporte, C.Y., O'Connor, R.V.: Systems and software engineering standards for very small entities: implementation and initial results. In: Proceedings of the 9th International Conference on the Quality of Information and Communications Technology (QUATIC), Portugal, pp. 38–47 (2014)
40. Mora, M., Raisinghani, M., O'Connor, R.V., Gomez, J., Gelman, O.: An Extensive Review of IT Service Design in Seven International ITSM Processes Frameworks: Part I. International Journal of Information Technologies and Systems Approach **7**(2) (2014)
41. Galván-Cruz, S., Mora, M., Connor, R., Acosta-Escalante, F., Alvarez, F.: On project management process in agile systems development methodologies and the ISO/IEC 29110 standard (entry profile). International Conference on Informatics and Computing (CNCIIC-ANIEI), Mexico (2014)
42. Clarke, P., O'Connor, R.V.: The influence of SPI on business success in software SMEs: An empirical study. Journal of Systems and Software **85**, 2356–2367 (2012)
43. Clarke, P., O'Connor, R.V.: Business success in software SMEs: recommendations for future SPI studies. In: Winkler, D., O'Connor, R.V., Messnarz, R. (eds.) EuroSPI 2012. CCIS, vol. 301, pp. 1–12. Springer, Heidelberg (2012)
44. O'Connor, R.V., Basri, S.: Understanding the role of knowledge management in software development: a case study in very small companies. International Journal of Systems and Service-Oriented Engineering **4**, 39–52 (2014)
45. O'Connor, R.V., Laporte, C.Y.: Software project management in very small entities with ISO/IEC 29110. In: Winkler, D., O'Connor, R.V., Messnarz, R. (eds.) EuroSPI 2012. CCIS, vol. 301, pp. 330–341. Springer, Heidelberg (2012)

Agile Processes

LAPIS – LOGO Agile Process Improvement System

Tuğrul Tekbulut, Ayhan İnal, and Betül Doğanay(✉)

LOGO Yazılım, Kocaeli, Türkiye
{tugrul.tekbulut,ayhan.inal,betul.doganay}@logo.com.tr

Abstract. We propose a new approach to agile methodologies leading us to a new agile implementation that is formed as the result of works and studies conducted to make risks in development process predictable and manageable owing to analytical data.

In this paper, the time parameter is taken as the most crucial independent variable to manage and secure efficiency and productivity for Software Intensive Organizations. Our work elaborates on the unique methodology obtained by adapting Agile Software Development methods, which are of late years being used in the industry in software development processes.

We demonstrate a new approach to the concept of Story Point, which is defined in agile methods, and Business Value [3] - a topic of Lean-Agile Software Development and a performance index OTEQ which embodies measures related to efficiency and quality.

Keywords: Software engineering · Agile software methodologies · Statistical process management

1 Introduction

Approximately 80 percent of the costs incurred by Software Intensive Organizations of which main activity field is software development; meaning that even the slightest improvement in development processes makes a major contribution.

LAPIS is an agile implementation influenced by lean management philosophy; it is contributed by all members of LOGO product development teams. LAPIS like all agile approaches start by accepting from the beginning that the scope of project may change continuously during the process. Therefore, it does not see possible changes as an exception. It manages complexity through short-cycle outputs and continuous feedback loops in order to minimize the risks encountered due to unexpected changes.

Logo was founded in the early eighties to develop business applications for small and medium size enterprises. Over the decades, several methods were developed in house, modelling from earlier engineering disciplines, or were adopted from outside for product, project and quality management. Logo is one of the early adopters of SPICE in 1996, and later of CMMI. The attempt to reach the aggressive target of CMMI-4 failed, and the project was abandoned in 2005. For a company selling software packages, under severe time pressure, the documentation process of these methodologies looked excessive and not feasible.

Since the problems of timely delivery, resource estimation and high quality have not disappeared to anywhere, a need to develop a new software process was reconsidered in 2008. Due to the previous failures, and to overcome the resistance of the developers to outside methodologies, the new process was not developed and introduced at once, but let it be evolved in time. First, the timely delivery problem was handled and a company wise system clock was introduced which was based on LogoWeek with inspiration from Toyota Manufacturing System[2]. Release plans are subdivided into weekly cycles, each of which is called as LOGOWeek. Release cycle consists of 7 weeks and each cycle has a planning of its own.

After completing several cycles successfully, every operation primarily related to product development, and, then sales & marketing and customer support is synchronized to this system clock. Thus the company was operated synchronously around in a corporate rhythm. This synchronous operation had helped the software development department to gain the confidence of the management, the partners and the customers by timely deliveries.

Relying on the success of the method, the chance of introducing a more rigorous and complete system had increased and the work towards a more comprehensive system started. By adopting roles and concepts like Product Owner, Story Point from Scrum [7] and Business Value from Lean-Agile Software development [3], a custom methodology which is suitable for a mature business software company developed. As the system is evolved and matured, measurement experience coming from CMMI-4 was easily introduced. Again with inspiration of OEE from Toyota Manufacturing System, an new index OTEQ was developed to monitor the performance of the development system. And, thus, the system which helped the phenomenal growth and profitability of the company, LAPIS (Logo Agile Process Development System) had been developed.

2 LAPIS Components

2.1 Roles in LAPIS

LAPIS integrated 3 fundamental roles used by Scrum methodology into its model.

Product Owner [4][6]: Responsible of maximizing the Return of Investment (ROI) by compiling and managing all features and functions needs to be developed in product backlog. Prioritizes the items of product backlog and negotiates over the required developments with Development Team in sprint planning meeting where sprint backlog is determined by considering development capacity. Development teams negotiate these concerns with their Product Owner during the whole process.

Agile Coach [5]: Conducts process adaptation and is responsible of managing the process properly.

Development Team: Responsible of developing the sprint backlog which is determined after the negotiations took place in sprint planning meeting with the Product Owner. Development team has the right to decline candidate items during the planning meeting. However, the team is responsible of delivering all accepted items at the end of the sprint.

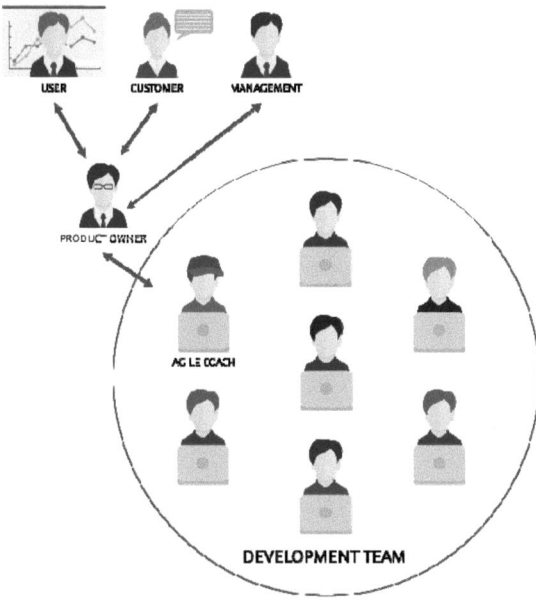

Fig. 1. Roles in LAPIS and their communication channels

Unlike agile methodologies, LAPIS has more than one development team for the same product, and these teams are managed by team leaders. The members of development team are not cross-functional. Testing is performed by testing team separateely.

2.2 Process in LAPIS

The details of processes managed in the time-scale of LAPIS are shown in Figure 2. The followings are explanations of the operations numbered in this picture.

- Product Backlog is created and managed to maximize the ROI. *(Figure2-(1))*

- The Product Owner prioritizes the product backlog before the sprint starts, and negotiates with the Development Teams in sprint planning meeting to determine which of the prioritized items will be included in the upcoming sprint. Development Team accepts to assume a number of items depending on their capacity, referring to how much effort (Story Point value of items) it will take to complete each item. The items accepted in the meeting are announced as the sprint backlog. *(Figure2-(2))*

- During the process of Sprint, sprint backlog items are developed and tested. The date of completion is fixed (5+2 weeks) and this date cannot be changed during the sprint process (time-boxed). *(Figure2-(3))*

- At the end of the Sprint, Development Team delivers a product including all development items in sprint backlog. Team presents a demo showing all developments in Spring Review Meeting. Prospective improvements within the

scope of continuous improvement works are evaluated in Sprint Retrospective Meeting and are put into practice for the upcoming Sprint.
- Development teams perform bug-fix requests of the testing team within +2 week in which integration tests are conducted. By this means, team begins the developments of the next version. *(Figure2-(4))*

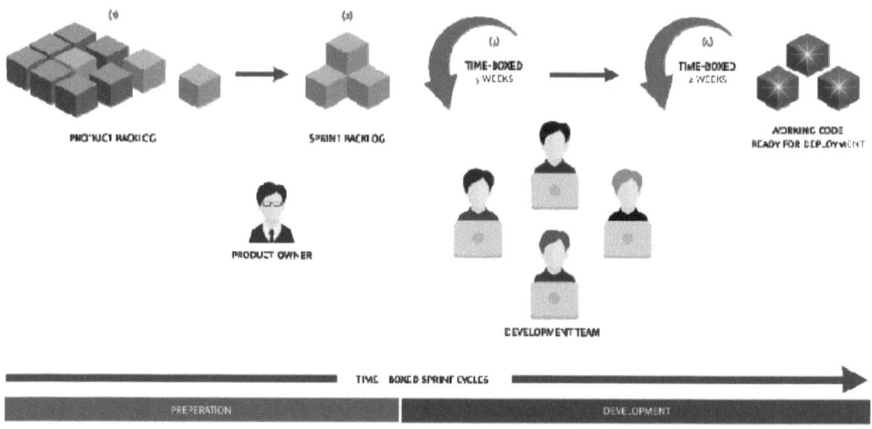

Fig. 2. LAPIS process

A detailed process calendar of Preparation period works (in Figure 2) are shown in Figure 3.

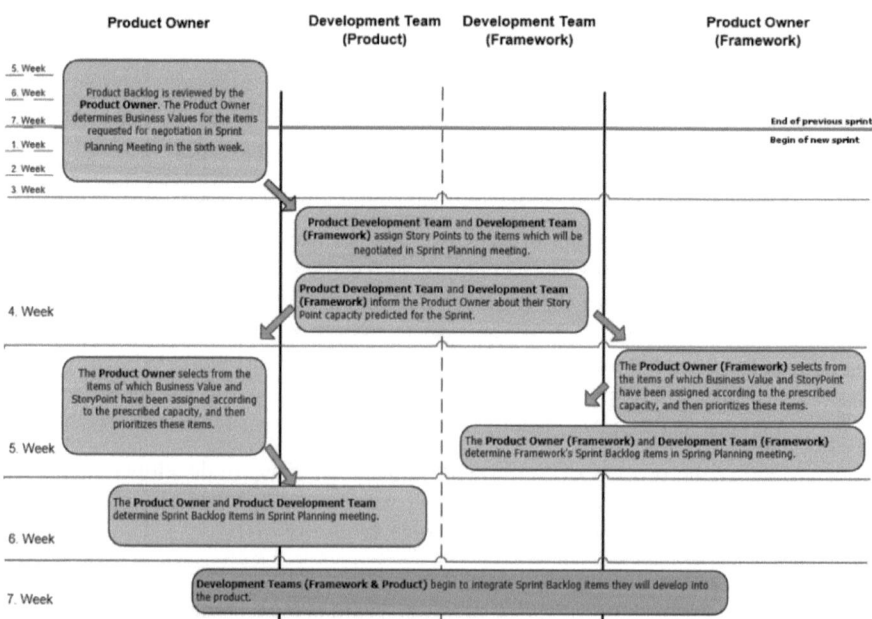

Fig. 3. Process calendar of determining Sprint backlog

Feedbacks considering the efforts made in development process are provided with the help of BurnDown [7] Charts shown on the screens, which were placed in the environment of Development Teams. Thanks to the BurnDown Charts, continuous feedback has contributed positively to the project follow-up and motivation. BurnDown Charts shown in Figure 5 and Figure 6 prove such improvement over the years.

2.3 Time Management in LAPIS

All software development projects are complex systems. Long-term / big waterfall projects imply risks that are hard to manage. LOGO produces mission critical products. All products are being used in customer environments and have iterative and incremental development of new functionalities. Therefore, risk management is crucial. Software development projects, dissimilarly from various engineering projects (e.g. aircraft project) allow for evolution to occur continuously. Therefore, it can be redesigned and developed after short-term development processes in case of not being able to achieve target results. Managing the risk that incur due to incorrect designs is almost impossible in big Waterfall projects. LOGOWeek envisages the division of planning the sprint backlog items in weekly cycles to ensure the full realization of short-term plans within the sprint cycle again to minimize the risk of failure or faulty completion. At the beginning of each week, development team gathers to make a weekly plan. After deciding on the weekly plan, unlike other agile applications, no other daily evaluation or meeting is conducted until the last day of the week when the weekly build is done[1]. It is aimed to adapt time-management notion into corporate culture and create an understanding of a common system-time for company's ecosystem. LOGOWeek can be seen as a short-term Waterfall approach.

2.4 Story Point in LAPIS

Story point as a measure of the effort that is required to implement a story is integrated from other agile methodologies into LAPIS.

Story Point is a numerical value which represents the effort to develop a function/feature or a bug-fix. Agile methodologies like Scrum try to estimate the efforts of implementations using limited and fixed numerical sequences (Fibonacci sequence)."Scrum Poker" is commonly used as a consensus-based technique for estimating development effort and the assignment of Story Points values. This method makes it harder to carry out measurement in the long run and evaluate development teams working on different platforms by the same unit of measure in SIO companies. Therefore LAPIS uses a table of Story Points allowing to determine the work load of each item depending on analytical and continuous data. "LAPIS Story Point" table keeps software development activities in a table. Development teams split the backlog items into smaller work items in this table, and then add up Story Point values of each activity to determine the required Story Point value to perform an item. This method provides convenience in measuring and evaluating analytically the sub-sets of the relevant development and units of work for each development. It also provides the details of the "Definition of Done" criterion.

2.4.1 Story Point Calculation Method
In order to calculate Story Points, we use a table of Story Point developed within the scope of LAPIS. This table has a comprehensive software development activity set.

The table presents a base point (difficulty level: easy) for each activity and coefficient assigned to each difficulty level.

The base point of the activity which will take the shortest time and is easiest to implement among all activities in Story Point table is determined as "1". After that, a base point is given to all other activities with reference to the aforementioned activity. The first activity is determined by common consent based on the experiences of software specialists.

All activities are defined in terms of activity type, difficulty and quantity, and activities' total Story Point related to the software development activity is calculated.

Example: Let's assume that our development activity has two new reports of *Degree 1* difficulty level. The activity type we need to select, according to the table below, is *Report - Development of New Report*. The difficulty level would be Difficult (Degree 1) and the quantity should be 2.

Total Story Point : 35x4x2 = <u>280</u>

Table 1. Story Point calculation table

Story Point table for coding		Difficulty					
		Easy	Normal	Difficult (Degree 1)	Difficult (Degree 2)	Difficult (Degree 3)	Difficult (Degree 4)
	Coefficient	*1*	*2*	*4*	*8*	*12*	*16*
Activity type	*Base value*						
Report - Development of new report	*35*			2			
Report – Modify existing report	*5*						
Report – Performance improvement of existing report	*8*						
						Total Coding SP	**280**

2.5 Business Value in LAPIS

The purpose of Business Value (BV) as one of the topics of Lean-Agile Software Development is to ensure that shipped implementations are customer driven and meet customer requirements. LAPIS bases BV value on a specific calculation to be between 0-500 values. There are 5 questions which must be answered to calculate BV value for all items in Sprint Backlog of the product. There is a numerical value and a coefficient corresponding to the answer given for each question/criterion. The total of all values gathered from these answers is accepted as the Business Value of item. Business Value is assigned by the Product Owner.

The 5 questions are;

- What is the priority of this item
- What is the severity of this item
- How frequently is this item encountered by customers
- Is this functionality available in rival products
- What will it cost if it is not implemented

2.5.1 BV Calculation Method

The Product Owner must assign BV for all defects/new features that are requested in Sprint scope.

In order to assign Business Value, the Product Owner answers five questions given above. The Product Owner's answer to each question is a criterion that will represent a numerical value, and the total of these numerical values is accepted as Business Value of the relevant defect/new feature.

For example, the options, which are available for the Severity criterion and their numerical values, are as below. (Since the contribution of Severity criterion to the

Table 2. Effect of Severity criterion on BV

Severity	Condition	Effect to Business Value
New Feature - Mandatory	Function related to customers' critical activities.	125
New Feature - Useful	Without this function, customer activities are not blocked but it causes some difficulties. Performance and usability will increase if implemented.	62,5
New Feature - Nice to have	Not a function of product's core functionalities but user experience and usability will improve if implemented.	12,5
New Feature - Unnecessary	Unnecessary function for the product.	0
Defect – Critical	System fails, data loss or data corruption occurs, critical function fails due to this defect.	125
Defect – Major	An important function does not work as expected, there is no possible workaround for this problem in some cases system restart is needed.	93,75
Defect – Minor	Function failure can be tolerated. Workaround or usage	43,75

	difficulties exist.	
Defect – Insignificant	Visual problems or defects that do not affect product functions.	12,5

Business Value is determined by a coefficient, there are fractional numbers.) The options are selected and are classified according to the description given in Condition field. For instance, in order to accept a defect as "critical", it should comply with "System fails, data loss or data corruption occurs, critical function fails due to this defect" description.

3 OTEQ (Overall Team Efficiency, Quality) formula:

The OEE (Overall Equipment Effectiveness) formula that is used in Lean Production has inspired the OTEQ (Overall Team Efficiency, Quality) formula by which we aim to define a new performance metric that will take quality factor into account.

OEE formula is defined as below.

$$OEE = Availability \times Performance \times Quality$$

OTEQ formula is defined by adjusting the components of this formula within the scope of LAPIS.

(i) *"Availability" parameter:*

According to the original OEE, *Availability* parameter is defined as below.

Availability = Operation Time / Planned Production Time

Assuming that the performance of man can be infinite owing to flexible working hours, *Availability* is accepted as *"1"*.

(ii) *"Performance" parameter:*

According to the original OEE, *Performance* parameter is defined as below.

Performance = (Total Pieces/Operating Time)/Ideal Run Rate)

By adjusting the Performance parameter, the following formula is defined to calculate how much Story Point is spent in *t* number of days by *n* number of coders.

$$(\sum Story\ Point / (\sum \#\ of\ Coders)(\#\ of\ Days))$$

(iii) *"Quality" parameter :*

According to the original OEE, Quality parameter is defined as below.

Quality= Good Pieces/Total Pieces

The total of damage points belonging to the defects reported by customers is included in quality formula as denominator. The damage value of a defect is the numerical value assigned to the damage caused by the defect. A damage point can have values between 1 and 13.

Below is the adjustment of OEE formula into OTEQ formula:

(OTEQ=(1)($\sum$ Story Point /($\sum$ #Coders)(#Days)(1+$\sum$ Damage Value of Defects))

Figure 4 is a chart showing OTEQ values calculated by data which is gathered from a product line of LOGO Software. The chart demonstrates a period between 2012 and 2014.

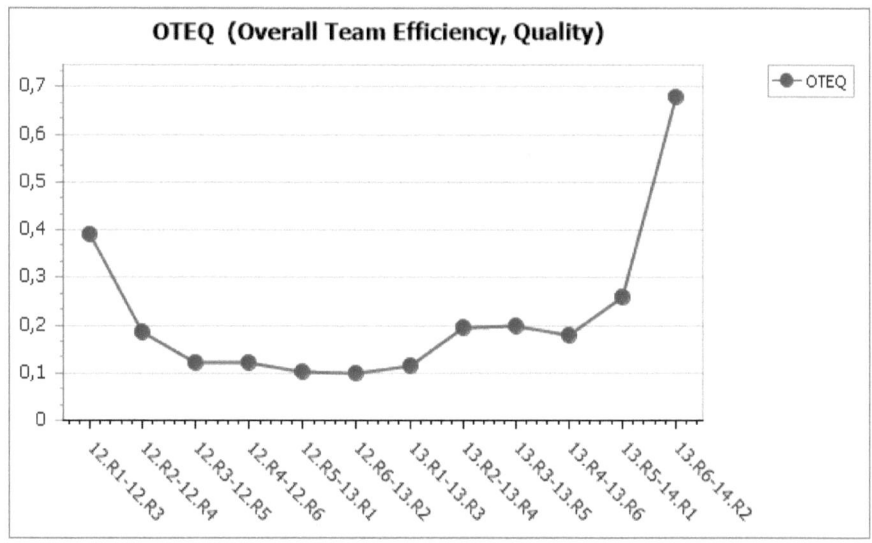

Fig. 4. OTEQ chart

Figure 4 shows that the performance criterion that is represented by OTEQ formula built upon the quality criterion has positively increased during the application of LAPIS. After examining our data, we concluded that the increase from 13.R4 until 14.R2 in the above chart resulted from the decrease in $\sum$ Damage Value. This information points out to the decrease in the number of errors and / or in the severity of these errors, which are reported by the customers directly.

3.1 Damage Value Calculation Method

All defects reported by customers are classified as "new" or "old" according to their report date. If the reported defect exists in the version that is released a year ago as of the report date, it is classified as "old". If it does not exist in a-year-old version, it is classified as "new".

Only the new defects are included in damage value calculation. By considering the Severity value given in BV assignment, Product Owners assign a numeric value according to the table below.

Table 3. Damage Value table

Business Value - Severity	Damage Value
Defect-Critical	13
Defect-Major	8
Defect-Minor	3
Defect-Insignificant	1
New Feature-Mandatory	5
New Feature-Useful	0.0001
New Feature-Nice to have	0.0001
New Feature-Unnecessary	0.0001

The Product Owner assigns BV only for the defects/new features which are requested in the new version. The defects, which are not included in version and thus have no Damage Value, are assigned the average of DV calculated in the relevant period, and they are included in OTEQ calculation.

4 Results of LAPIS Applications to Development Process

There is hard data for certain main topics and processes to which this system has contributed. Evaluating the results of measurements and using them as system inputs have significant effects on continuous improvement. Some of the main topics and examples of such improvements achieved by LAPIS are as below.

(i) Providing continuous feedback to all product development team increased performance and reduced potential delays in release dates.

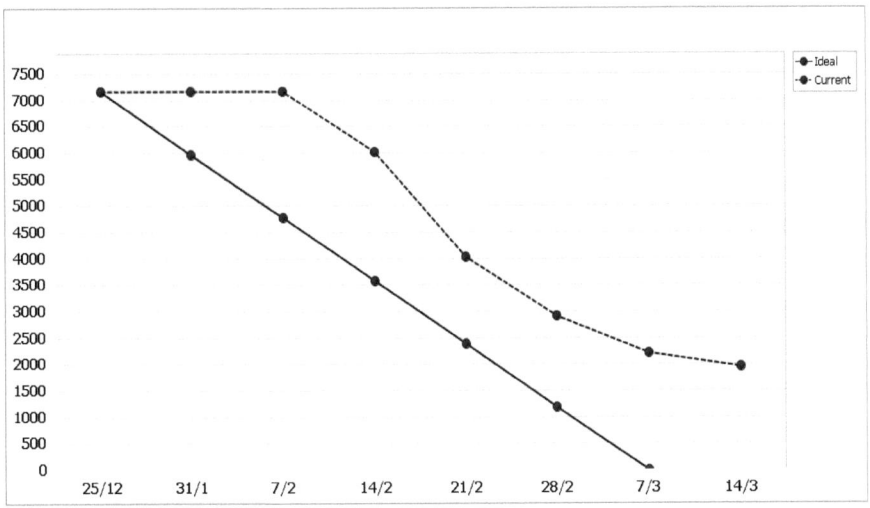

Fig. 5. Burndown chart of second release in 2011 (2011. R2)

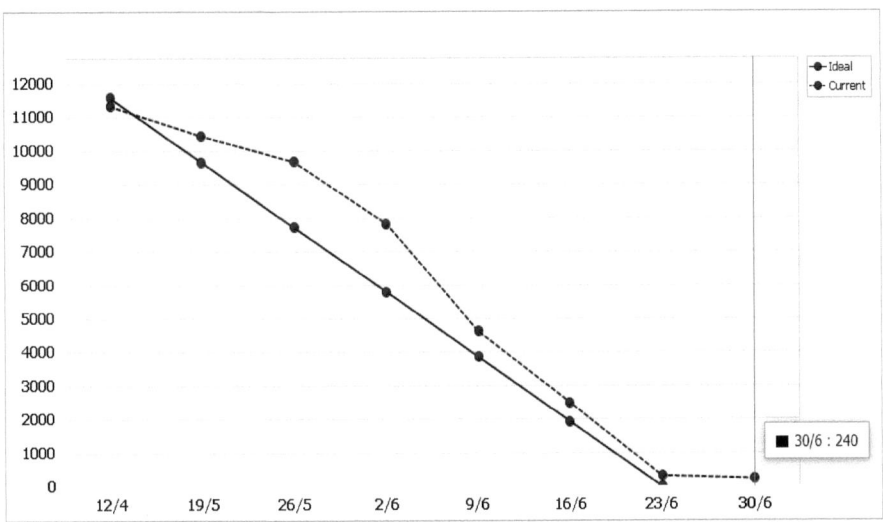

Fig. 6. Burndown chart of fourth release in 2014 (2014. R4)

In Burndown chart shown in Figure 5 and Figure 6, dotted line represents actual use of storypoints while the solid line shows the expected use of storypoints. In the burndown chart of 2014.R4, it is clearly observed that actual consumption has improved.

Actual burndown values converge target burndown line in Figure 6, indicating process improvement and equal distribution of workload density during the Sprint.

(ii) Improving the quality of software development by minimizing content changes during the sprint. Increasing the concentration by reducing the divided jobs during development.

Figure 7 shows the average number of failed tests returned to testing team by coders and the number of items returned to coders. It is observed that return count has decreased. 10 out of 100 items sent by coders to the testing team to be tested need bug-fix. This ratio was 32 items out of 100 at the beginning.

Return count decrease shown in Figure 7 is attributed to the fact that coders' concentration has increased in comparison to the previous period; they were rarely interrupted due to external works and their to-do items were described more clearly by the use of Storypoint table.

(iii) Estimating staff needs by evaluating the average storypoint consumption data.

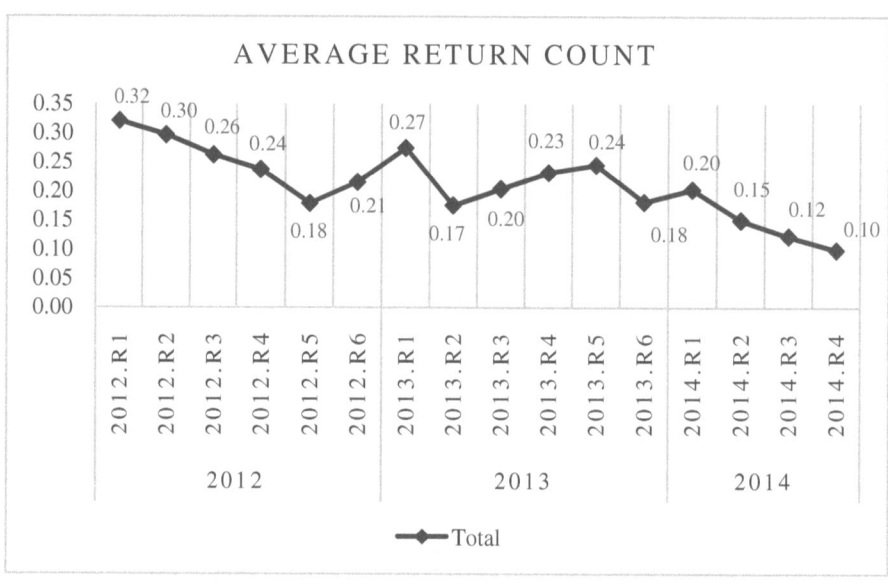

Fig. 7. Average of Return Count on Version Basis

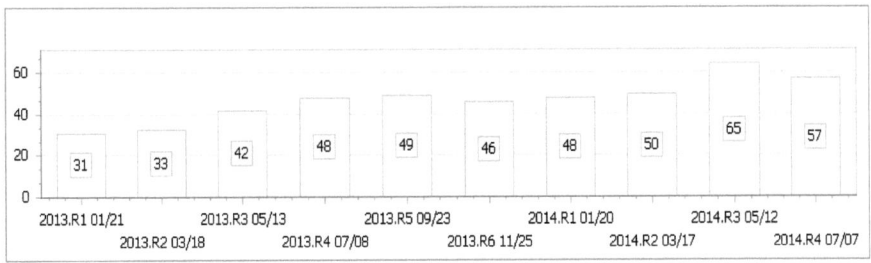

Fig. 8. Daily average coder/storypoint consumption

Daily storypoint consumptions per coder is an important input parameter that triggers annual recruitment plans and strategic development plans. Before LAPIS, such estimations were attempted without numeric values.

(iv) Early on LAPIS, spring planning meetings lasted a day on the average while it now turned into 2-3 hour meetings.

5 Survey Results

A survey was conducted on the purpose of measuring the changes LAPIS has brought into the lives of product development team members. 39 people participated in total, and the results are as below:

Table 4. LAPIS Survey Results

	Definitely	Agree	Not Sure	Do not agree	Definitely disagree
Motivation has increased	2%	52%	30%	13%	3%
LAPIS is useful	25%	60%	5%	5%	5%
Friction between teams has decreased	20%	40%	37%	0%	3%
Interruptions has decreased	8%	56%	15%	18%	3%
Overall efficiency has increased	15%	50%	15%	17%	3%
Product quality has increased	12%	52%	18%	13%	5%
Realistic project planning opportunities were obtained	7%	65%	18%	5%	5%
Due to LAPIS I'm able to plan my time better	10%	62%	13%	10%	5%
Knowing that my personal performance is followed has a positive impact on my performance.	7%	58%	20%	10%	5%

6 Conclusion

Thanks to LAPIS, product development activity processes have been grounded on systems that are measurable, predictable and through which teams can reach a consensus. The improvements have affected the whole ecosystem and increased confidence in company outputs. Now we announce annual release dates to the company ecosystem at the beginning of the year. Delays in project due dates - which are almost accepted as default - are now prevented. This system provided an average of 0.3 days deviation in the standard sprint cycle of 35 workdays in the last 3 years.

By developing a standard software work unit (Story Point), potentially problematic issues in software sector such as capacity planning, cost calculation, delivery date assignment etc have been rendered measurable and traceable analytically. It is observed that customer satisfaction has increased owing to company's response time. Working systematically has been proven to affect competitive power positively through our business partners and then customers.

References

1. Cusumano, M.A., Selby, R.W.: Microsoft Secrets
2. Morgan, J.M., Liker, J.K.: The Toyota Product Development System
3. Shaloway, A., Beaver, G., Trott, J.R.: Lean – Agile Software Development Achieving Enterprise Agility
4. Pichler, R.: Agile Product Management with Scrum – Creating Products that Customers Love
5. Adkins, L.: Coaching Agile Teams – A Companion for Scrum Masters, Agile Coachers, and Project Managers in Transition
6. Cooper, R.G.: Winning at new Products – Creating Value through Innovation
7. https://www.scrumalliance.org

A Reference Model for Software Agility Assessment: AgilityMod

Ozden Ozcan-Top[✉] and Onur Demirörs

Infomatics Institute, Middle East Technical University, 06800, Ankara, Turkey
`ozdentop@gmail.com, demirors@metu.edu.tr`

Abstract. In this paper, we present AgilityMod that we developed with the purpose of identifying agility levels of software development projects, indicating agility gaps and providing roadmaps to organizations in adopting agile principles/practices. AgilityMod shares the meta-model structure of ISO/IEC 15504, software process assessment model, however, it differentiates from ISO/IEC 15504 in terms of its process architecture, process descriptions and description of other model elements. In this paper, we focus on the structure of the Model and describe the development stages of the Model. In addition, we briefly present a multiple case study that included eight cases, which was conducted to identify applicability and suitability of the Model.

Keywords: Agility assessment · Agile software development · Agile · ISO/IEC 15504 · AgilityMod

1 Introduction and Motivation

Agile software development approaches are developed as a reaction to traditional methods that are characterized with extensive planning, heavyweight processes and bureaucracy [1]. They are characterized by delivering a working software to the customer through short, time-boxed iterations, and encouraging people to minimize bureaucracy, collaborating, self-organizing, embracing variability, balancing up-front work and just-in-time work, favoring adaptive and exploratory approaches and providing fast-feedback [2, 3]. Agile software development methods are frequently adopted in the recent years by the software community as they are seen as a complete solution for problems like missing deadlines, exceeding budgets, delivering final products that do not meet the needs of the customer [4]. In the state-of-agile survey, VersionOne presents that 52% of the projects are managed with agile techniques in software organizations [5].

On the other hand, Ambler [4] states that there are an increasing numbers of project failures associated with agile strategies. In the 2013 IT Project Success Rates Survey, 30% of the participants reported that they had experienced challenges in an agile project, and 6% of the participants reported failure [6].

These failure stories indicate that organizations do not get a full benefit from agile software development techniques. What we also observed from our personal experiences is that the organizations that are new at agile software development techniques start by selecting a few agile practices, adapt them in the way they prefer and convince themselves as doing agile software development, until they see no improvement or even get worse results than their traditional techniques. In addition "agile" is being used as an excuse for being undisciplined by some of the organizations.

Because of these reasons there is a fundamental need to assist organizations in adopting agile methods/practices and to guide them for improving their agile capability [7].

In the current state, there are about forty models related to agile maturity, including both academic publications and Internet publications [8, 9]. These models are grouped into three based on the classification by Schweigert et al.: ones that are influenced by the structure of CMMI, ones that have a specific leveling structure and ones that do not use explicit leveling structure [8]. They argue that these models do not measure the real agility and support guidance. Instead, they check for the implementation of some specific agile practices.

In one of our previous studies [10], five of the most frequently referenced agile maturity models were applied in an organization, and evaluated. The evaluation was based on six quality criteria: fitness for purpose, completeness, definition of agile levels, objectivity, correctness and consistency. The results of this study indicated that none of these models satisfies all the expected criteria, and need to be improved in terms of scope, definitions of agility levels and objectivity. The most obvious deficiency of the models is that they do not support an agile process architecture holistically. Each model focus on different parts of the software development life cycle. None of the models has a well-defined structure with process inputs, practices and outputs forms.

Among this model quagmire, there is no commonly accepted agile maturity/assessment model.

In order to cover this need, we developed a well-structured Software Agility Assessment Reference Model (AgilityMod) to be utilized for the agility assessment of software projects. AgilityMod is designed fully compatible with the agile process architecture (the structural design of the processes). The Model provides a complete guidance to organizations so that they could observe their weaknesses and problematic areas and implement the agile processes and practices correctly and in consistency with agile manifest. The model also provides means for helping project teams avoid incorrect tailoring.

In this paper, we present the structure of the Agility Assessment Reference Model_v3.0 in detail, and briefly describe the development stages of the Model. We performed a multiple case study including eight cases with the purpose of observing the applicability of AgilityMod in real projects. Although our focus in this paper is the description of the Model, we briefly present a multiple case study.

2 A Software Agility Assessment Reference Model

Software Agility Assessment Reference Model has been developed in two years time. The first version was published in July 2014. Since then, various works have been published wih the previous versions of the Model [11-13]. The version that is introduced in this paper is the latest and the third one.

2.1 Relation of AgilityMod with ISO/IEC 15504

Existing agile maturity models do not have sound structures [10]. These models provide agile level descriptions, basic key characteristics and assessment questions. They are insufficient in defining outcomes and performance indicators such as practices and work products [10].

Although there are different ways to describe a model, we selected to use ISO/IEC 15504 (SPICE) [14, 15] as a basis for the meta model structure of AgilityMod. Major reason of selecting ISO/IEC 15504 as a basis is, its well-defined and is a commonly accepted meta-model structure. On the other hand, SPICE which has been developed based on 12207 Software Life Cycle proceeses [16], has not been extended to be compatible with agile practices and processes. The current process structure of ISO/IEC 15504 does not comply with agile processes and principles.

ISO/IEC 15504 provides a structured assessment framework for software processes. It facilitates process assessment, provides a basis for use in process improvement and capability determination, and provides process rating, which represents an objective image of current state of a process. The structure of ISO/IEC 15504 allows evaluation and improvement of processes separately. This property brings a significant level of flexibility to process improvement endeavors. There is no need to classify a numbers of processes for a maturity level and define the rationale behind that classification.

On the other hand, although studies show that SPICE can be effectively used in agile contexts [17, 18], existing process structure of ISO/IEC 15504 does not comply with agile processes and principles. ISO/IEC 15504 provides a two dimentional approach for assessment: the capability dimension and the process dimension. The process dimension includes 48 processes defined in conformance to ISO/IEC 12207 Software life cycle processes AMD1 [16] and AMD2 [19]. Capability dimension defines software capability in five levels. We do not go into further details of ISO/IEC 15504 here but we need to mention that, in order to achieve compatibility with agile process architecture, we had to change its components and component descriptions.

2.2 Components of AgilityMod

AgilityMod consists of the following concepts and components:

Dimensions: AgilityMod has two dimensions: the aspect dimension, and the agility dimension. We define agility levels and aspect attributes at the agility dimension, and define aspects, aspect practices, outcomes and example work products at the aspect dimension.

Aspects: Formal process layers of traditional software development are intertwined to each other in agile software development. It is difficult to specify boundaries of agile processes. Aspects which are new modularization of agile processes and practices are integrated under meaningful and agile compatible abstract definitions. They are sets of interrelated and interacting activities. From this point of view, we defined four aspects in AgilityMod, fully covering a software development life cycle: Exploration, Construction, Transition, and Management. Aspects belong to the aspect dimension.

Aspect Practices: Aspect practices are activities or activity groups that contributes to achievement of an aspect purpose and outcomes. Aspect practices also include agile elaborations which describe how plain software development practices can be applied from an agility perspective.

Aspect Attributes: An aspect attribute is an indicator of the aspect performance. It defines the characteristic of an aspect. AgilityMod defines 5 aspect practices, all of which are applicable to all aspect practices. Aspect attributes are represented in the agility dimension, are listed below:

The Aspect Attribute of Level 1 is "Perform Aspect Practices". "Performing Aspect Practices" attribute is a measure of the extent to which purposes and goals of the aspects are achieved by implementing the related practices described in aspect dimension.

The 1st Aspect Attribute of Level 2 is "Iterative". "Iterative" attribute is a measure of the extent to which the work products are delivered in an iterative and incremental way to achieve the specific outcomes.

The 2nd Aspect Attribute of Level 2 is "Simple". This attribute is a measure of the extent to which the aspect practices are arranged and performed by focusing on delivering business value. The purposes of "simple" attribute are to support aspects to eliminate any kind of activity that does not add value and cause waste in software development process, to achieve the balance between the just-in-time works and up-front works and to manage the incoming and outgoing workflows.

The 1st Aspect Attribute of Level 3 "Technically Excellent". This attribute is a measure of the extent to which the agile engineering methods and tools are integrated into aspects to improve productivity and lower defects. Agile engineering practices such as test-driven development, continuous integration, and pair programming and integration of agile tools bring technical excellence to aspects. When technical excellence and other attributes from second level are brought together, teams gain the Agility to manage technical debt, improve team productivity and decrease defects.

The 2nd Aspect Attribute of Level 3 is "Learning". "Learning" attribute is a measure of the extent to which from a broader point of view aspects serve for the purpose of organizational learning and improvement

All these attributes are derived from the agile manifesto and twelve agile principles [20] by combining the related principles together. We cover each principle in one of the aspect attributes.

Example Work Product: Example work products are outputs that are produced at the end of the successful achievement of an aspect or agility attribute.

Fallacy: Fallacies describe the wrong implementations which are assumed to be true.

Generic Agility Practice: Generic agility practices are activities or activity groups that contributes to achievement of an aspect attribute. Descriptions given after each generic practice specify the outcomes after a successful achievement of a practice.

Generic Resource: A kind of resource that is utilized in the conduct of an aspect or agility attribute.

Outcome: Outcomes are observable results of aspects.

After the description of the components, we provide the mapping of AgilityMod components and ISO/IEC 15504 components in Table 1.

Table 1. Mapping Between AgilityMod Components and ISO/IEC 15504 Components

ISO/IEC 15504 Component	AgilityMod Component
Process	Aspect
Base Practice	Aspect Practice
Process Attribute	Aspect Attribute
Generic Practice	Generic Agility Practice
Generic Resource	Generic Resource
Work Product	Example Work Product
Purpose Statement	Purpose Statement
Outcome	Outcome

2.3 Dimensions in Detail

The Figure below shows the dimensions of the Model, the aspects, and the agility levels:

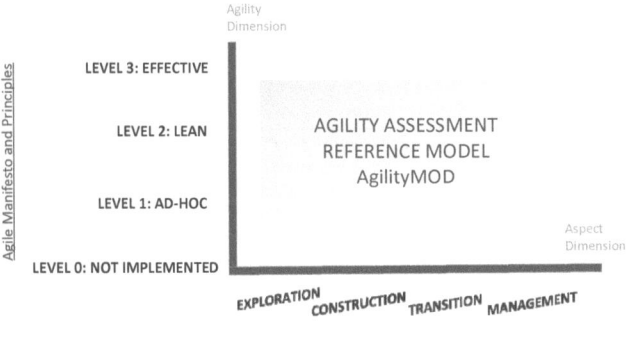

Fig. 1. Major components of AgilityMod

Agility Dimension

Each aspect might be at one of the 4 levels of agility that are "Not Implemented", "Ad-Hoc", "Lean" and "Effective". When an aspect's agility progresses from the bottom level: "Not Implemented" to the top level: "Effective", its conformance to agile values and principles increases.

At Level 0, aspect practices are either partially achieved or not achieved. At Level 1, organizations are capable of performing fundamental development processes such as requirements development, design, coding, integration, testing, and deployment consistently. There are transition attempts towards the agility by exploring best fitting agile practices or approaches. Aspect practices are implemented and aspect purposes are achieved; however agile values and principles are not fully incorporated into aspect practices. At Level 2, work products are developed iteratively and incrementally, non-value added activities are eliminated from the aspect practices, balance is achieved between adaptive and predictive works. At Level 3, each aspect is performed to achieve delivering value with high productivity and low defects by employing agile engineering practices and using agile tools to support a continuously improving environment.

In Table 2, we provide aspect attributes and generic agility practices related to each agility level.

Table 2. Generic Agility Practices and Aspect Attributes of Agility Levels

Agility Level	Aspect Attribute	Generic Agility Practices
Level 1: Ad-Hoc	1.1 Performing Aspect Practices	GP 1.1.1 Perform aspect practices
Level 2: Lean	2.1 Iterative	GP 2.1.1 Develop work products in an iterative and incremental way
		GP 2.1.2 Communicate effectively
	2.2 Simple	GP 2.2.1 Balance the predictive work and adaptive work
		GP 2.2.2 Employ minimally sufficient ceremony
Level 3: Effective	3.1 Technically Excellent	GP 3.1.1 Incorporate agile engineering methods/practices to the aspect practices
		GP 3.1.2 Integrate tools to aspects to improve the productivity
	3.2 Learning	GP 3.2.1 Support collaborative work and shared responsibility
		GP 3.2.2 Adopt agile leadership styles and adjust the behaviors towards mistakes of people
		GP 3.2.3 Encourage people in the organization to participate in learning, teaching and improvement
		GP 3.2.4 Collect measures to support learning and improvement

Aspect Dimension

Aspect dimension is characterized with 4 aspects: Exploration, Construction, Transition and Management. In this dimension, we describe the aspect purposes, the outcomes, the aspect practices, the relation of the aspect practices with outcomes, the example work products and the fallacies which needs to be avoided. We provide the aspect practices of each aspect in Table 3.

Table 3. Aspect Practices based on each Aspect

Aspects	Aspect Practices
Exploration Aspect	E.AP1: Capture the customer and user needs
	E.AP2: Elaborate requirements artifacts
	E.AP3: Detect and resolve conflicts of requirements arti-
	E.AP4: Specify dependencies among requirements arti-
	E.AP5: Manage the requirement artifacts
	E.AP6: Make the artifacts visible to everyone
Construction Aspect	CN.AP1: Elaborate the work items
	CN.AP2: Explore the design
	CN.AP3: Develop the solution
	CN.AP4: Ensure the correctness of software at developer
Transition Aspect	T.AP1: Create and Manage the Workspace
	T.AP2: Integrate the Code
	T.AP3: Deploy the solution
	T.AP4: Test the integrated solution
	T.AP5: Make the progress visible
	T.AP6: Create the supporting documentation
Management Aspect	M.AP1: Initiate the project
	M. AP2: Form the team
	M.AP3: Align and adopt the environment
	M. AP4: Establish the physical work space
	M.AP5: Plan the progress
	M.AP6: Estimate the work items
	M.AP7: Monitor the progress
	M.AP8: Manage and mitigate the risks

3   Development Stages of AgilityMod

In this sub-section, we describe the progress of development of AgilityMod in time. All of the development stages, the findings and the actions that was taken to improve the model, worth further explanation. However, because of the page limitation, we just mention them here and leave the detailed discusions to further studies.

We developed the first version of the Model after the research on agile software development, agile adoption and agile transition concepts. We also evaluated existing agile maturity models through a multiple case study [10]. By exploring agile models [21-25], we understood the agile values in practice and the reasoning behind the practices, and developed *the aspect dimension* of the model. By exploring how organizations mature in agile environments [26-30], we developed *the agility dimension* of the model. Following that, we performed an exploratory case study to observe the applicability of AgilityMod in a real case and to discover improvement opportunities related the Model. The details of the case study can be found at [11]. We updated and published the second version of the Model based on our observations, and the case study findings [13].

The second version of the Model were reviewed by three agile software development and process improvement experts. Three experts reviewed the Model. Expert A has 10 year-experience in software process improvement consultancy. He is an internal and external process assessor since 2001. He has knowledge on agile processes. Expert B: a SEI (Software Engineering Institute) authorized CMMI lead appraiser who has 4 years hands on practices on Scrum and ISO/IEC 15504. He is from India. Expert C is a hands on agile practitioner and trainer. She is a scrum master since 2006. She is a consultant in agile adoption and co- author of a book in French on Agile. The book was awarded "Best French Informatics Book of 2012 by the Association Française d'Ingénierie de Systèmes d'Information (AFISI), whose members are voting the best book annually for over 20 years. She is also a CMMI consultant. She is from Canada.

We asked experts to review the model based on a set of criteria (fitness for purpose, completeness, definitions of agile levels, objectivity, correctness and consistency) that were set in one of our previous studies [10]. Two of the experts mentioned that the component descriptions are clear enough to perform agility assessment and the model is capable of providing directions for improvement on agility and can be used as a roadmap by organizations for getting better at agility. Expert A expressed his ideas in these topics as follows:

"The model aims to bring a maturity view on the agile principles, and I believe it is a successful model. Using ISO 15504 as a reference model supports the validity of the model and increases the possibility of usage among organizations. The model perfectly fits the need of providing roadmap by organizations for getting better at agility"

In the Model, we described the agility in an abstract way to cover various agile methods and approaches. Therefore it is very important the Model components' and component descriptions' both cover all agile principles in an abstract way and be independent of any agile method. Experts evaluated the Model from these perspectives and rated as fully and largely achieved ratings. Expert A found the level of abstraction appropriate when the audience of the model is considered as daily agile practitioners. The more you keep the abstraction at a reasonable level, the more the experience and knowledge of the assessor becomes important. The target group that is expected to use AgilityMod for assessment are experts who have specific knowledge and experience in the agile domain.

Expert C gave specified the descriptions of components that is too specific or valid for a particular agile method. The Model is updated considering the expert comments and 3rd version of it is published.

In terms of "consistency", experts specified minor inconsistencies and concluded that the Model is internally consistent and does not include any logical conflicts.

All experts thought that the Model is "correct" such that all component descriptions are compatible with agile values and principles.

One of the requirements of an assessment model is to achieve a required level of "objectivity" in order to guarantee the repeatability of the assessment results. AgilityMod aims to achieve "the objectivity" through clear description of aspect purpose and outcomes, and aspect and agility practices. AgilityMod uses a common rating scale with ISO/IEC 15504 [15] that clearly specifies the ranges for rating. In terms of objectivity, Experts A mentions that clarifying the normative and informative features of the Model would increase the objectivity. Expert C calls attention to the need for a rating scheme for assessing multiple agile projects and specifying agility of an organization rather than project basis. We are going to define the rules for assessing agility of organizations, however, this improvement is not in the scope of this study. Therefore we consider that these comments of experts do not violate "objectivity" characteristic of AgilityMod.

We performed required changes on the Model based on experts' feedback and published the third version [31].

4 Case Studies

Following the second update of the Model, we performed a multiple case study including eight software companies. The domains of companies ranges from technical media to home appliances, from ERP solutions to multimedia solutions and e-governance solutions. The team sizes of the assessed eight projects change between 6 employees to 45 employees.

The purpose of this case study is to answer the following research questions:

RQ1: How suitable is the third version of Software Assessment Agility Reference Model to be used with the purpose of identifying aspects' agility, identifying the agility gaps and providing roadmaps for improving agility in a software project?

RQ2: What are the strengths and weaknesses of the third version of AgilityMod?

For assessment performance, we met groups of people who belong to project teams, asked them to answer a set of questions and evaluated the projects' direct evidences. Following the assessment process, we prepared detailed assessment reports and discussed the findings with assessment team members, or in some cases with all project team members, managers and CEOs. We obtained feedback from them about the following issues:

— if there is a misunderstood concept or practice presented in the report or presentation
— if the report or presentation covers all the improvement areas that are noticed about project's agile processes
— if the findings presented to them are beneficial for getting better at agility
— if they follow the same improvement path suggested in the report and presentation
— which of the suggested practices are new to them or noticed previously
— and to what extent the presented findings and improvement opportunities in their projects overlap with reality

We used a four-level scale to express the achievement of the aspect attributes: "not achieved (0-red), partially achieved (1-yellow), largely achieved (2-orange) and fully achieved (3-green) and not applicable (NA)". For an agility level to be reached, all practices should be largely or fully achieved. Below, we provide the colored schemas of the assessment ratings for Case #1 and Case #2 as samples which enable capturing detailed results at a glance. For the other assessment results, the technical report [32] can be requested.

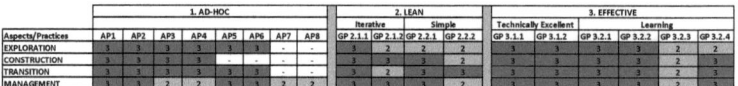

Fig. 2. Rating of Each Practice of Case 1

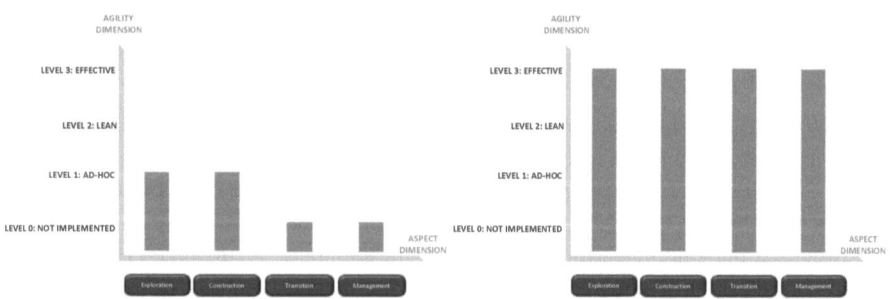

Fig. 3. Rating of Each Practice of Case 2

Figure 4 below shows the achieved agility levels of Case 1 and Case 2 in a bar chart view.

Fig. 4. Achieved Agility Levels of Aspects for Case 1 and Case 2

Figure 5 below, shows the gap between the ideal case (outer trapezoid) and the current situation of Case 2 (trapezoid in the middle) and Case 1 (inner trapezoid). The data to draw this radar chart is obtained by adding the rating values of each aspect given on Fig. 2 and Fig. 3. Here, we can see from radar chart display that, even if Case 2 reached Level 3 agility levels for all of the aspects, there are still some space for improvement for Case 2, especially for the exploration aspect.

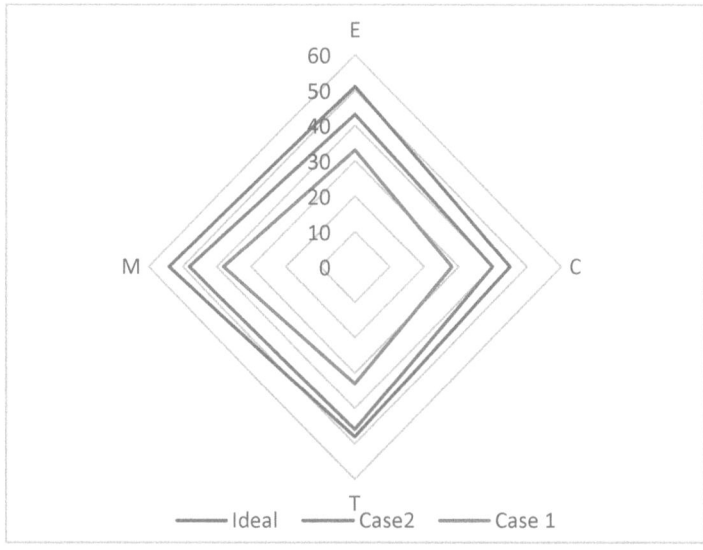

Fig. 5. Display of the Gap among Ideal Case, Case 1 and Case 2

Because of the page limitation, we will not go into the details of the case study discussion part. Interested readers may request the resources in [32, 33] for further information. The feedback that we obtained from people about the findings and the model are provided in [33] in detail. In Table 4, we present the feedback results. Each person, who evaluated the accuracy of our findings about the aspects, gave a rating in a range from "Not Achieved (NA)" to "Fully Achieved (FA)".

In order to construct the table, we calculated the median of the ratings if the assessment findings were rated more than one person. In the overall, 84.4 % percent of the evaluation indicated that the findings and improvement suggestions fully overlap with current problems in the projects. The remaining 15.6 % thinks that aspect findings largely overlaps with current problems. Achieving such high ratios for finding the gaps in the projects is an indicator of how successful the Model in revealing agility improvement opportunities and the potential of the Model for the usage of agility assessment.

Table 4. Rating of the Findings' Accuracy by Aspect Owners

Aspects	C1	C2	C3	C4	C5	C6	C7	C8
Exploration	FA	FA	LA	FA	FA	FA	FA	FA
Construction	FA	FA	FA	FA	FA	FA	LA	FA
Transition	FA	LA	FA	FA	FA	FA	LA	FA
Management	FA	FA	FA	LA	FA	FA	FA	FA

5 Conclusion

In this study, we presented the structure of Agility Assessment Reference Model in detail. We briefly described the development stages that had continued until the Model reached a maturity level to be published. AgilityMod's meta-structure relies on the meta-structure of ISO/IEC 15504. Therefore, we explained the reasons of this choice and the relation between the components of two models.

AgilityMod presents dimensions, aspects, aspect attributes, aspect practices and generic agility practices, which are very specific to agile software development phenomenon. On the other hand, the Model has been developed independent of any specific agile software development method. Its holistic structure allows the assessment of software projects developed with different type of agile software development approaches.

Considering the multiple case study results, the opinions of the interviewees on the results and the feedbacks of experts, we conclude that we could use AgilityMod to identify the agility gaps in projects, to specify agility levels of aspects and to provide roadmaps to projects for agility improvement.

The Model allows agility assessment of projects in terms of four aspects instead of checking compatibility of processes to some agile practices. In AgilityMod, we do not only evaluate the existence of some specific agile practices such as performing daily stand-up meetings or pair programming or collective code ownership. Instead, we evaluate the aspects from a holistic approach and understand if the teams are capable of keeping the design structure sound while responding to the changes quickly, are disciplined, and serving for organizational learning or not.

The level of abstraction used in the Model, objectivity, accuracy, completeness and consistency issues were evaluated and approved by the experts. The multiple case study that we conducted with the 3rd version of the Model including eight cases, indicated that the Model can be applied with a reasonable effort in software companies by agile experts. Improvement suggestions given based on the Model can be utilized as a roadmap for improving organizations' agility.

AgilityMod is a model that was developed to assess software projects' agility. We consider updates to extend the Model's coverage for organizational agility assessment. In addition, more case studies will be valuable that is to be conducted by other researchers to observe the applicability of the Model.

Acknowledgement. This study was supported by Turkish Scientific and Technological Research Council of Turkey (TUBITAK), Project 113E528.

References

1. Dingsøyr, T., Dybå, T., Moe, N.B.: Agile Software Development: Current Research and Future Directions, vol. 1. Springer, Heidelberg (2010). ISBN 978-3-642-12574-4
2. Rubin, K.S.: Essential Scrum: A Practical Guide to the Most Popular Agile Process. Addison-Wesley Professional (2012)
3. Cockburn, A.: Agile software development: the cooperative game (agile software development series). Addison-Wesley Professional (2006)

4. Ambler, S.W., Lines, M.: Disciplined Agile Delivery: A Practitioner's Guide to Agile Software Delivery in the Enterprise. IBM Press (2012)
5. VersionOne, 8th Annual State of Agile. http://stateofagile.com/8th-annual-state-of-agile-form/2013
6. Ambler, S.: IT Project Success Rates Survey Results (2013). http://www.ambysoft.com/surveys/success2013.html
7. Sidky, A.: A structured approach to adopting agile practices: The agile adoption framework. Virginia Polytechnic Institute and State University (2007)
8. Schweigert, T., Vohwinkel, D., Korsaa, M., Nevalainen, R., Biro, M.: Agile maturity model: a synopsis as a first step to synthesis. In: McCaffery, F., O'Connor, R.V., Messnarz, R. (eds.) EuroSPI 2013. CCIS, vol. 364, pp. 214–227. Springer, Heidelberg (2013)
9. Schweigert, T., Vohwinkel, D., Korsaa, M., Nevalainen, R., Biro, M.: Agile maturity model: analysing agile maturity characteristics from the SPICE perspective. Journal Of Software: Evolution And Process (2013)
10. Özcan-Top, Ö., Demirörs, O.: Assessment of Agile Maturity Models: A Multiple Case Study. In: Woronowicz, T., Rout, T., O'Connor, R.V., Dorling, A. (eds.) SPICE 2013. CCIS, vol. 349, pp. 130–141. Springer, Heidelberg (2013)
11. Özcan-Top, Ö., Demirörs, O.: Assessing Software Agility: An Exploratory Case Study. In: Mitasiunas, A., Rout, T., O'Connor, R.V., Dorling, A. (eds.) SPICE 2014. CCIS, vol. 477, pp. 202–213. Springer, Heidelberg (2014)
12. Özcan-Top, Ö.: AgilityMod: Agility Assessment Model v1.0, Informatics Institute, METU/II-TR-2014-37
13. Özcan-Top, Ö.: AgilityMod: Agility Assessment Model v2.0, Informatics Institute METU/II-TR-2014-38
14. I. O. f. Standardization and I. E. Commission, ISO/IEC 15504-2:2003 Information technology – Process assessment – Part 2: Performing an assessment, ed (2003)
15. ISO/IEC 15504-5:2012 Information technology – Process assessment – Part 5: An exemplar software life cycle process assessment model, ed (2012)
16. ISO/IEC 12207:1995/Amd.1:2002, Information technology — Software life cycle processes, ed (2002)
17. Lami, G., Falcini, F.: Is ISO/IEC 15504 applicable to agile methods? In: Abrahamsson, P., Marchesi, M., Maurer, F. (eds.) Agile Processes in Software Engineering and Extreme Programming. LNBIP, vol. 31, pp. 130–135. Springer, Heidelberg (2009)
18. Bianco, C.: Agile and SPICE capability levels. In: O'Connor, R.V., Rout, T., McCaffery, F., Dorling, A. (eds.) SPICE 2011. CCIS, vol. 155, pp. 181–185. Springer, Heidelberg (2011)
19. ISO/IEC 12207:1995/Amd.2:2004, ed (2004)
20. Agile Manifesto (2001) www.agilemanifesto.org
21. Schwaber, K., Beedle, M.: Agile Software Development with Scrum. Prentice-Hall (2002)
22. Beck, K.: Embracing change with extreme programming. Computer **32**, 70–77 (1999)
23. Poppendieck, M., Poppendieck, T.: Lean software development: An agile toolkit. Addison-Wesley Professional (2003)
24. Middleton, P., Joyce, D.: Lean Software Management: BBC Worldwide Case Study. IEEE Transactions on Engineering Management, **59**, 20–32 (2012)
25. Ambler, S.: Agile modeling: effective practices for extreme programming and the unified process. John Wiley & Sons (2002)
26. Elssamadisy, A.: Agile adoption patterns: a roadmap to organizational success. Addison-Wesley Professional (2008)

27. Tomasini, A., Kearns, M.: Agile Transition: What you need to know before starting. InfoQueue Enterprise Software Development Series (2012)
28. Adkins, L.: Coaching agile teams: a companion for ScrumMasters, agile coaches, and project managers in transition. Addison-Wesley Professional (2010)
29. Williams, L., Brown, G., Meltzer, A., Nagappan, N.: Scrum+ engineering practices: experiences of three microsoft teams. In: 2011 International Symposium on Empirical Software Engineering and Measurement (ESEM), pp. 463-471 (2011)
30. Benefield, G.: Rolling out agile in a large enterprise. In: Proceedings of the 41st Annual Hawaii International Conference on System Sciences, p. 461 (2008)
31. Özcan-Top, Ö.: AgilityMod: Software Agility Assessment Reference Model v3.0, Informatics Institute, METU/II-TR-2014-392014
32. Özcan-Top, Ö.: AgilityMod: Software Agility Assessment Reference Model v3.0 Application: Case Study Results, Informatics Institute, METU/II-TR-2014-40 (2014)
33. Özcan-Top, Ö.: Agilitymod: A Software Agility Reference Model for Agility Assessment, PhD, Information Systems. Middle East Technical University, Ankara (2014)

Observations on Utilising Usability Maturity Model-Human Centredness Scale in Integrating Agile Development Processes and User Centred Design

Dina Salah[1(✉)], Richard Paige[2], and Paul Cairns[2]

[1] Sadat Academy for Management Science, Cairo, Egypt
dina.salah.nasr@gmail.com
[2] University of York, York, UK
{richard.paige,paul.cairns}@york.ac.uk

Abstract. The aim of this paper is to investigate usability maturity models' role in integrating agile processes and user centred design. Usability maturity models can be used as a diagnostic tool to assess the consistent, systematic and effective implementation of user centred design in agile projects. The researcher investigated the suitability of two usability maturity models in assessing user centred design capability in agile projects. This paper reports on utilising one of those models: Usability Maturity Model-Human Centredness Scale (UMM-HCS). It reports on applying UMM-HCS in five case studies that integrated agile and user centred design and using the model in assessing the usability maturity level of those five case studies. The paper reflects on and scrutinises the suitability of UMM-HCS for utilisation in the context of agile projects.

Keywords: Agile Software Development Processes · User centred design · Agile User Centred Design Integration · Usability maturity models

1 Introduction

Agile methods are lightweight methods that attempts to balance excessive process and process absence to deal with plan-driven methods limitations [11].

User Centred Design (UCD) is a set of methods, techniques, procedures and processes and a philosophy that places the user at the centre of the development process [5,13]. UCD goal is to satisfy users via producing usable products that meet their needs, goals, abilities, context of use, and limitations [5].

Maturity models are normative reference models based on the assumption of predictable patterns of evolution [14]. They aim to evaluate the weaknesses and strengths and prioritize and plan for improvement [14]. Improvement occurs via evolutionary stages that denote step-by-step patterns of evolution designating the current or desirable capabilities against a class of entities [12,20,23].

Usability Maturity Models (UMMs) aim to assist organisations in conducting a systematic analysis in order to evaluate UCD strengths and weaknesses and accordingly plan for improvement actions [16]. Usability capability is defined as "A characteristic of a development organisation that determines its ability to consistently develop products with high and competitive level of usability [16]".

The researcher investigated Agile and User Centred Design Integration (AUCDI) challenges via an empirical study [24] and a Systematic Literature Review (SLR) [25], then investigated UMMs suitability for resolving some AUCDI challenges. A comparative study of UMMs was conducted and resulted in using two UMMs: Nielsen Model and UMM-HCS, the results of utilising Nielsen Model were reported in [26] whereas the results of utilising UMM-HCS are reported here.

The rest of this paper is organised as follows: section 2 provides a background on AUCDI. Section 3 discusses the research approach. Section 4 reports on applying UMM-HCS on five case studies that integrated agile and UCD and utilising the model in assessing their usability maturity level. Section 5 discusses the results and section 6 discusses the conclusion.

2 Agile and User Centred Design Integration (AUCDI)

The main stream of AUCDI research is focused on improving the usability and user satisfaction of software. This occurs via applying UCD methods, techniques, procedures and processes so as developers can understand the potential users' needs and how to achieve their goals and activities. Nevertheless, none of the major agile methods provides explicit guidance on the methods to develop usable software [18]. Moreover, the interaction design role, usability, and user interface design in an agile team is vague and largely overlooked [1,3]. Additionally, practices and principles for comprehending and eliciting usability and user requirements and evaluating the software produced via agile methods for usability and User eXperience (UX) are deficient [18]. Third, there exists differences between agile methods and UCD in focus, evaluation methods, culture and documentation that makes their integration challenging [24].

The researcher conducted a SLR [25] that included 71 AUCDI papers and classified the integration approaches proposed by them. This SLR revealed 8 different categories, non of which focused on UMMs utilization [25]. UMMs can be used in the agile development projects as a diagnostic tool; they can assist in assessing the status-quo in order to evaluate the extent to which UCD is consistently, systematically and effectively implemented in development projects. The results can assist organisations in pinpointing their weaknesses and strengths relevant to UCD aspects and accordingly plan for improvement actions.

Thus this study has two aims: first, to investigate UMMs suitability for usage in agile projects to assess the organisation's UCD capability, second, to investigate the relationship between AUCDI success and usability maturity levels.

3 Research Approach

This section discusses the research approach chosen to achieve the research aims.

3.1 Comparative Study of Usability Maturity Models

A comparative study of UMMs was conducted to choose a UMM to assess the usability maturity level of AUCDI case studies. The following criteria were found relevant to compare the characteristics of the different UMMs:

Lightweight: The chosen UMM will be utilized to assess the usability maturity level of projects that uses agile methods, thus it should require low overhead so as not to disrupt any agile project time line; i.e, it should not consume considerable time to perform the assessment or require additional personnel.

Detailed English Documentation: The model should include detailed documentation of the maturity model definition and the assessment process. This documentation should provide explicit guidance to practitioners to conduct self assessment. Moreover, since the available UMMs were developed in various countries, the UMM should be documented in English.

Domain Independent: Some UMMs are for specific domains like telecommunication thus cannot be utilized in other domains. The model chosen should be suitable for utilisation irrespective of the organisation's business domain.

Empirically Evaluated: The model should have been empirically evaluated and iterated upon.

Table 1. Criteria for Choosing a Usability Maturity Model

UMM Model	Language	Detailed Documentation	Domain	Lightweight	Empirical Evaluation
Nielsen	English	Yes	Generic	Yes	No
UMM-HCS	English	Yes	Generic	Yes	Yes
Trillium	English	Yes	Telecommunication	No	Not published
ULMM	English	No	Generic	N/A	Not Published
HPI	English	No	Consumer Product Development	N/A	Not Published
UCDM	English	No	Information System Capability in UK Public Sector	N/A	Not Published
UMM-P	English	Yes	Generic	No	Yes
KESSU	English	No	Generic	N/A	Yes
DATech-UEPA	German	N/A	Manufacturing	N/A	N/A
HCD-PCM Design	Japanese	N/A	Generic	N/A	N/A
HCD-PCM Visioning	Japanese	N/A	Generic	N/A	N/A
OS-UMM	English	No	Open Source Projects	N/A	N/A

The UMMs were examined using the criteria identified above and Table 1 summarises the results of the comparison according to the comparison criteria.

The UMM pursued is documented in English, has a detailed documentation, can be used irrespective of the organisation's domain (generic), is lightweight, and was empirically evaluated. These criteria led to the exclusion of a number of UMMs and left us with only two UMMs: Nielsen Model and UMM-HCS. Although Nielsen model was not empirically evaluated, yet it was decided to utilise both models in five AUCDI case studies in order to provide richer comparative analysis. Results of utilising Nielsen model were reported in [26].

3.2 Choosing Five AUCDI Case Studies

Five case studies that integrated agile processes and UCD were chosen. A candidate list was formulated of five academic researchers and industrial practitioners who developed new AUCDI approaches and whose work on AUCDI was well received and highly referenced. The chosen case studies also reflected a "two tail" design [27] in which cases from both extremes (success and failure) are selected. Further details on the five case studies were reported in [26].

3.3 Utilising the Chosen UMMs in Five AUCDI Case Studies

UMM-HCS was used in assessing the usability maturity level of the AUCDI case studies. This occurred via formulating a set of open ended questions to evaluate the achievement of the different practices and conducting a set of one-to-one, Skype interviews. Answers to interview questions were used in evaluating the usability maturity level of each case study and comparing the results with the achieved practices in the different usability maturity levels in order to determine the closest usability maturity level. Those results are reported in section 5.

3.4 Synthesizing the Results of Utilisation of UMMs

The results of UMM-HCS utilisation were synthesised in order to investigate the following: the existence of a relationship between the success of AUCDI attempts and usability maturity level and the suitability of UMM-HCS for utilisation in assessing usability maturity in the context of agile projects.

4 Utilising UMM-HCS in AUCDI Case Studies

The European INUSE project developed UMM-HCS and derived it from a number of UMMs: Total Systems Maturity (TSM) [17], ULMM [8], User Centred Design Maturity (UCDM) [7] and Crosby [4]. It offers organisations an understanding of how organisation's usability maturity progress and allows organisations to measure their maturity and plan for improvement. UMM-HCS can be used as a stand alone model for assessing usability, or as a companion to ISO

15504-compliant process reference or any other process assessment model that does not have UCD as its focus [6].

UMM-HCS has 6 maturity levels, each maturity level is defined by a set of attributes, these attributes are embodied in a set of attitude, technology and / or management practices that are performed at that level. These practices are used in assessing the user centred approach of an organisation in regards to its working culture and systems development and support activities. This assessment occurs via a scoring scheme of 4 values: Not Achieved (N), Partially Achieved (P), Largely Achieved (L) and Fully Achieved (F)[6].

Table 2 shows UMM-HCS rating of realisation of each attribute in order to achieve a particular maturity level [6].

Table 2. UMM-HCS Maturity Level Ratings [6]

Scale	Process Attributes	Rating
Level A	Problem recognition	Fully or largely
	Performed processes	Fully or largely
Level B	Problem recognition	Fully
	Performed processes	Fully
	Quality in use awareness	Fully or largely
	User focus	Fully or largely
Level C	Problem recognition	Fully
	Performed processes	Fully
	Quality in use awareness	Fully
	User focus	Fully
	User involvement	Fully or largely
	HF technology	Fully or largely
	HF skills	Fully or largely
Level D	Problem recognition	Fully
	Performed processes	Fully
	Quality in use awareness	Fully
	User focus	Fully
	User involvement	Fully
	HF technology	Fully
	HF skills	Fully
	Integration	Fully or largely
	Improvement	Fully or largely
	Iteration	Fully or largely
Level E	Problem recognition	Fully
	Performed processes	Fully
	Quality in use awareness	Fully
	User focus	Fully
	User involvement	Fully
	HF technology	Fully
	HF skills	Fully
	Integration	Fully
	Improvement	Fully
	Iteration	Fully
	Human-centred leadership	Fully or largely
	Organisational Human-centredness	Fully or largely

UMM-HCS has an assessment recording form that is used by assessors to record the ratings of the different attributes. UMM-HCS documentation [6] contains details on the attributes and on the use of the recording form. UMM-HCS documentation [6] stated that the benefit of doubt should be used in assessing the achievement of practices and accordingly round up the rating to the higher level of achievement. UMM-HCS author was contacted for an updated version of the documentation and for clarifying some issues related to UMM-HCS model practices, terminology, assessment criteria and assessment method.

Answers to interview questions were used in evaluating the maturity level of each case study and results were reported in section 5.

5 Results

This section reports on applying UMM-HCS on five AUCDI case studies to assess their usability maturity level. The results of the evaluation per case study are shown in Tables 3, 4, 5, 6, and 7.

5.1 Maturity Level Evaluation of Case Studies via UMM-HCS

Table 8 shows the results of maturity level evaluation of UMM-HCS process attribute for CS1, CS2, CS3, CS4, and CS5.

Table 2 [6] showed the desired rating of each attribute in order to achieve the maturity level. On comparing Table 2 with the results of the AUCDI case studies reported in Table 8, it revealed that CS1 maturity level was "Level C", CS2 and CS4 maturity levels were "Level A" whereas CS3 maturity level was "Level B" and CS5 maturity level was "Unknown". The inability to identify CS5 maturity level is attributed to the inability to compute the collective rating of A.2 since the rating of its two constituent key practices A2.1 and A2.2 was "Fully" and "Partially" and the criteria assessment advice included in UMM-HCS documentation did not discuss how these values should be combined.

5.2 Revisiting UMM-HCS Study Aims

This section discusses the aims of the study in light of the results achieved.

Aim 1: Investigating the existence of a relationship between the success of AUCDI attempts and usability maturity level

It was not possible to achieve this aim via UMM-HCS due to problems exhibited with the model's rating system. Table 2 [6] shows the desired rating for each attribute in order to achieve the maturity level. It is clear from Table 2 [6] that UMM-HCS embraces a linear model of upgrading i.e., an organisation cannot be upgraded to maturity level i+1 unless it has largely or fully achieved all practices in maturity level i. The results of the five case studies shown in Tables 3, 4, 5, 6, and 7 reveal that the linear model of upgrading is contradictory to how organisation's perform since an organisation can score high in some of the practices related to a high maturity level even if the organisation is at a low maturity level. An example for that is CS2 whose maturity level was evaluated as "Level A" although it scored as "Fully" in all attributes except B.1-Quality in Use Awareness Attribute and B.2-User Focus Attribute.

Table 3. UMM-HCS Recording Form-Case Study 1

	**Level A Recognised**		
A.1	**Problem Recognition Attribute**	1	Rating
A1.1	Problem Recognition	Fully	
	Combined Rating for Attribute (A1.1):	Fully	
A.2	**Performed Processes Attribute**		
A2.1	Information collection	Fully	
A2.2	Performance of relevant practices	Fully	
	Combined Rating for Attribute (A2.1 to 2.2):	Fully	
	Combination of Ratings for this Level:		Fully
	**Level B Considered**		
B.1	**Quality in Use Awareness Attribute**	1	Rating
B1.1	Quality in use training	Fully	
B1.2	Human-centred methods training	Fully	
B1.3	Human-system interaction training	Fully	
	Combined Rating for Attribute (B1.1 and 1.3):	Fully	
B.2	**User Focus Attribute**		
B2.1	User consideration training	Fully	
B2.2	Context of use training	Fully	
	Combined Rating for Attribute (B2.1 and 2.2):	Fully	
	Combination of Ratings for Level:		Fully
	**Level C Implemented**		
C.1	**User Involvement Attribute**	1	Rating
C1.1	Active involvement of users	Fully	
C1.2	Elicitation of user experience	Fully	
C1.3	End users define quality-in-use	Largely	
C1.4	Continuous evaluation	Fully	
	Combined Rating for Attribute (C1.1 to 1.4):	Fully	
C.2	**HF Technology Attribute**		
C2.1	Provide appropriate human-centred methods	Fully	
C2.2	Provide suitable facilities and tools	Fully	
C2.3	Maintain quality in use techniques	Largely	
	Combined Rating for Attribute (C2.1 to 2.3):	Fully	
C.3	**HF Skills Attribute**		
C3.1	Decide on required skills	Partially	
C3.2	Develop appropriate skills	Largely	
C3.3	Deploy appropriate staff	Largely	
	Combined Rating for Attribute (C3.1 to 3.3):	Largely	
	Combination of Ratings for this Level:		Fully
	**Level D Integrated**		
D.1	**Integration Attribute**	1	Rating
D1.1	Integrate HF processes	Partially	
D1.2	Facilitate interface between HF and the organisation	Largely	
D1.3	Use appropriate representations	Largely	
	Combined Rating for Attribute (D1.1 to 1.3):	Largely	
D.2	**Improvement Attribute**		
D2.1	Ensure design feedback	Fully	
D2.2	Change based on feedback	Largely	
D2.3	Timing of feedback	Fully	
	Combined Rating for Attribute(D2.1 to 2.3):	Fully	
D.3	**Iteration Attribute**		
D3.1	Minimize risks by iteration of design	Largely	
D3.2	Manage iteration of design solutions	Partially	
D3.3	Use design objectives to control iteration	Largely	
	Combined Rating for Attribute (D3.1 to 3.3):	Largely	
	Combination of Ratings for this Level:		Largely
	**Level E Institutionalized**		
E.1	**Human-Centred Leadership Attribute**	1	Rating
E1.1	Manage usability programme	Not achieved	
E1.2	Systematic improvement in quality in use	Not achieved	
E1.3	Human-centred improvement of organisation	Not achieved	
	Combined Rating for Attribute (E1.1 to 1.3):	Not achieved	
E.2	**Organisational Human-Centredness Attribute**		
E2.1	Organisational implementation of user-centred practices	Not achieved	
E2.2	Acceptance of human-centred skills	Partially	
	Combined Rating for Attribute (E2.1 to 2.2):	Partially	
	Combination of Ratings for this Level:		Partially

Table 4. UMM-HCS Recording Form-Case Study 2

	Level A Recognised		
A.1	**Problem Recognition Attribute**	1	Rating
A1.1	Problem Recognition	Fully	
	Combined Rating for Attribute (A1.1):	**Fully**	
A.2	**Performed Processes Attribute**		
A2.1	Information collection	Fully	
A2.2	Performance of relevant practices	Fully	
	Combined Rating for Attribute (A2.1 to 2.2):	**Fully**	
	Combination of Ratings for this Level:		Fully
	Level B Considered		
B.1	**Quality in Use Awareness Attribute**	1	Rating
B1.1	Quality in use training	Partially	
B1.2	Human-centred methods training	Not achieved	
B1.3	Human-system interaction training	Not achieved	
	Combined Rating for Attribute (B1.1 and 1.3):	**Not achieved**	
B.2	**User Focus Attribute**		
B2.1	User consideration training	Not achieved	
B2.2	Context of use training	Not achieved	
	Combined Rating for Attribute (B2.1 and 2.2):	**Not achieved**	
	Combination of Ratings for Level:		Not achieved
	Level C Implemented		
C.1	**User Involvement Attribute**	1	Rating
C1.1	Active involvement of users	Fully	
C1.2	Elicitation of user experience	Fully	
C1.3	End users define quality-in-use	Fully	
C1.4	Continuous evaluation	Fully	
	Combined Rating for Attribute (C1.1 to 1.4):	**Fully**	
C.2	**HF Technology Attribute**		
C2.1	Provide appropriate human-centred methods	Fully	
C2.2	Provide suitable facilities and tools	Fully	
C2.3	Maintain quality in use techniques	Fully	
	Combined Rating for Attribute (C2.1 to 2.3):	**Fully**	
C.3	**HF Skills Attribute**		
C3.1	Decide on required skills	Fully	
C3.2	Develop appropriate skills	Fully	
C3.3	Deploy appropriate staff	Largely	
	Combined Rating for Attribute (C3.1 to 3.3):	**Fully**	
	Combination of Ratings for this Level:		Fully
	Level D Integrated		
D.1	**Integration Attribute**	1	Rating
D1.1	Integrate HF processes	Largely	
D1.2	Facilitate interface between HF and the organisation	Fully	
	Combined Rating for Attribute (D1.1 to 1.3):	**Fully**	
D.2	**Improvement Attribute**		
D2.1	Ensure design feedback	Fully	
D2.2	Change based on feedback	Fully	
D2.3	Timing of feedback	Fully	
	Combined Rating for Attribute(D2.1 to 2.3):	**Fully**	
D.3	**Iteration Attribute**		
D3.1	Minimize risks by iteration of design	Fully	
D3.2	Manage iteration of design solutions	Fully	
D3.3	Use design objectives to control iteration	Fully	
	Combined Rating for Attribute (D3.1 to 3.3):	**Fully**	
	Combination of Ratings for this Level:		Fully
	Level E Institutionalized		
E.1	**Human-Centred Leadership Attribute**	1	Rating
E1.1	Manage usability programme	Fully	
E1.2	Systematic improvement in quality in use	Fully	
E1.3	Human-centred improvement of organisation	Fully	
	Combined Rating for Attribute (E1.1 to 1.3):	**Fully**	
E.2	**Organisational Human-Centredness Attribute**		
E2.1	Organisational implementation of user-centred practices	Fully	
E2.2	Acceptance of human-centred skills	Fully	
	Combined Rating for Attribute (E2.1 to 2.2):	**Fully**	
	Combination of Ratings for this Level:		Fully

Table 5. UMM-HCS Recording Form-Case Study 3

	Level A Recognised		
A.1	**Problem Recognition Attribute**	1	Rating
A1.1	Problem Recognition	Fully	
	Combined Rating for Attribute (A1.1):	Fully	
A.2	**Performed Processes Attribute**		
A2.1	Information collection	Fully	
A2.2	Performance of relevant practices	Fully	
	Combined Rating for Attribute (A2.1 to 2.2):	Fully	
	Combination of Ratings for this Level:		Fully
	Level B Considered		
B.1	**Quality in Use Awareness Attribute**	1	Rating
B1.1	Quality in use training	Fully	
B1.2	Human-centred methods training	Fully	
B1.3	Human-system interaction training	Not achieved	
	Combined Rating for Attribute (B1.1 and 1.3):	Fully	
B.2	**User Focus Attribute**		
B2.1	User consideration training	Largely	
B2.2	Context of use training	Largely	
	Combined Rating for Attribute (B2.1 and 2.2):	Largely	
	Combination of Ratings for Level:		Fully
	Level C Implemented		
C.1	**User Involvement Attribute**	1	Rating
C1.1	Active involvement of users	Fully	
C1.2	Elicitation of user experience	Fully	
C1.3	End users define quality-in-use	Largely	
C1.4	Continuous evaluation	Fully	
	Combined Rating for Attribute (C1.1 to 1.4):	Fully	
C.2	**HF Technology Attribute**		
C2.1	Provide appropriate human-centred methods	Fully	
C2.2	Provide suitable facilities and tools	Fully	
C2.3	Maintain quality in use techniques	Largely	
	Combined Rating for Attribute (C2.1 to 2.3):	Fully	
C.3	**HF Skills Attribute**		
C3.1	Decide on required skills	Largely	
C3.2	Develop appropriate skills	Partially	
C3.3	Deploy appropriate staff	Largely	
	Combined Rating for Attribute (C3.1 to 3.3):	Largely	
	Combination of Ratings for this Level:		Fully
	Level D Integrated		
D.1	**Integration Attribute**	1	Rating
D1.1	Integrate HF processes	Partially	
D1.2	Facilitate interface between HF and the organisation	Largely	
D1.3	Use appropriate representations	Largely	
	Combined Rating for Attribute (D1.1 to 1.3):	Largely	
D.2	**Improvement Attribute**		
D2.1	Ensure design feedback	Fully	
D2.2	Change based on feedback	Largely	
D2.3	Timing of feedback	Fully	
	Combined Rating for Attribute (D2.1 to 2.3):	Fully	
D.3	**Iteration Attribute**		
D3.1	Minimize risks by iteration of design	Largely	
D3.2	Manage iteration of design solutions	Partially	
D3.3	Use design objectives to control iteration	Largely	
	Combined Rating for Attribute (D3.1 to 3.3):	Largely	
	Combination of Ratings for this Level:		Largely
	Level E Institutionalized		
E.1	**Human-Centred Leadership Attribute**	1	Rating
E1.1	Manage usability programme	Partially	
E1.2	Systematic improvement in quality in use	Partially	
E1.3	Human-centred improvement of organisation	Partially	
	Combined Rating for Attribute (E1.1 to 1.3):	Partially	
E.2	**Organisational Human-Centredness Attribute**		
E2.1	Organisational implementation of user-centred practices	Largely	
E2.2	Acceptance of human-centred skills	Largely	
	Combined Rating for Attribute (E2.1 to 2.2):	Largely	
	Combination of Ratings for this Level:		Largely

Table 6. UMM-HCS Recording Form-Case Study 4

	Level A Recognised		
A.1	Problem Recognition Attribute	1	Rating
A1.1	Problem Recognition	Fully	
	Combined Rating for Attribute (A1.1):	Fully	
A.2	Performed Processes Attribute		
A2.1	Information collection	Fully	
A2.2	Performance of relevant practices	Fully	
	Combined Rating for Attribute (A2.1 to 2.2):	Fully	
	Combination of Ratings for this Level:		Fully
	Level B Considered		
B.1	Quality in Use Awareness Attribute	1	Rating
B1.1	Quality in use training	Partially	
B1.2	Human-centred methods training	Partially	
B1.3	Human-system interaction training	Not achieved	
	Combined Rating for Attribute (B1.1 and 1.3):	Partially	
B.2	User Focus Attribute		
B2.1	User consideration training	Partially	
B2.2	Context of use training	Partially	
	Combined Rating for Attribute (B2.1 and 2.2):	Partially	
	Combination of Ratings for Level:		Partially
	Level C Implemented		
C.1	User Involvement Attribute	1	Rating
C1.1	Active involvement of users	Largely	
C1.2	Elicitation of user experience	Fully	
C1.3	End users define quality-in-use	Fully	
C1.4	Continuous evaluation	Fully	
	Combined Rating for Attribute (C1.1 to 1.4):	Fully	
C.2	HF Technology Attribute		
C2.1	Provide appropriate human-centred methods	Largely	
C2.2	Provide suitable facilities and tools	Largely	
C2.3	Maintain quality in use techniques	Largely	
	Combined Rating for Attribute (C2.1 to 2.3):	Largely	
C.3	HF Skills Attribute		
C3.1	Decide on required skills	Largely	
C3.2	Develop appropriate skills	Partially	
C3.3	Deploy appropriate staff	Largely	
	Combined Rating for Attribute (C3.1 to 3.3):	Largely	
	Combination of Ratings for this Level:		Largely
	Level D Integrated		
D.1	Integration Attribute	1	Rating
D1.1	Integrate HF processes	Not achieved	
D1.2	Facilitate interface between HF and the organisation	Partially	
D1.3	Use appropriate representations	Partially	
	Combined Rating for Attribute (D1.1 to 1.3):	Partially	
D.2	Improvement Attribute		
D2.1	Ensure design feedback	Fully	
D2.2	Change based on feedback	Fully	
D2.3	Timing of feedback	Fully	
	Combined Rating for Attribute(D2.1 to 2.3):	Fully	
D.3	Iteration Attribute		
D3.1	Minimize risks by iteration of design	Fully	
D3.2	Manage iteration of design solutions	Fully	
D3.3	Use design objectives to control iteration	Largely	
	Combined Rating for Attribute (D3.1 to 3.3):	Fully	
	Combination of Ratings for this Level:		Fully
	Level E Institutionalized		
E.1	Human-Centred Leadership Attribute	1	Rating
E1.1	Manage usability programme	Partially	
E1.2	Systematic improvement in quality in use	Not achieved	
E1.3	Human-centred improvement of organisation	Not achieved	
	Combined Rating for Attribute (E1.1 to 1.3):	Not achieved	
E.2	Organisational Human-Centredness Attribute		
E2.1	Organisational implementation of user-centred practices	Partially	
E2.2	Acceptance of human-centred skills	Partially	
	Combined Rating for Attribute (E2.1 to 2.2):	Partially	
	Combination of Ratings for this Level:		Partially

Table 7. UMM-HCS Recording Form-Case Study 5

	Level A Recognised		
A.1	**Problem Recognition Attribute**	1	Rating
A1.1	Problem Recognition	Partially	
	Combined Rating for Attribute (A1.1):	Partially	
A.2	**Performed Processes Attribute**		
A2.1	Information collection	Fully	
A2.2	Performance of relevant practices	Partially	
	Combined Rating for Attribute (A2.1 to 2.2):	Unknown	
	Combination of Ratings for this Level:		Unknown
	Level B Considered		
B.1	**Quality in Use Awareness Attribute**	1	Rating
B1.1	Quality in use training	Partially	
B1.2	Human-centred methods training	Partially	
B1.3	Human-system interaction training	Not achieved	
	Combined Rating for Attribute (B1.1 and 1.3):	Partially	
B.2	**User Focus Attribute**		
B2.1	User consideration training	Partially	
B2.2	Context of use training	Partially	
	Combined Rating for Attribute (B2.1 and 2.2):	Partially	
	Combination of Ratings for Level:		Partially
	Level C Implemented		
C.1	**User Involvement Attribute**	1	Rating
C1.1	Active involvement of users	Partially	
C1.2	Elicitation of user experience	Partially	
C1.3	End users define quality-in-use	No	
C1.4	Continuous evaluation	Partially	
	Combined Rating for Attribute (C 1.1 to 1.4):	Partially	
C.2	**HF Technology Attribute**		
C2.1	Provide appropriate human-centred methods	Partially	
C2.2	Provide suitable facilities and tools	Fully	
C2.3	Maintain quality in use techniques	Partially	
	Combined Rating for Attribute (C2.1 to 2.3):	Partially	
C.3	**HF Skills Attribute**		
C3.1	Decide on required skills	Not achieved	
C3.2	Develop appropriate skills	Partially	
C3.3	Deploy appropriate staff	Partially	
	Combined Rating for Attribute (C3.1 to 3.3):	Partially	
	Combination of Ratings for this Level:		Partially
	Level D Integrated		
D.1	**Integration Attribute**	1	Rating
D1.1	Integrate HF processes	Not achieved	
D1.2	Facilitate interface between HF and the organisation	Not achieved	
D1.3	Use appropriate representations	Partially	
	Combined Rating for Attribute (D1.1 to 1.3):	Not achieved	
D.2	**Improvement Attribute**		
D2.1	Ensure design feedback	Partially	
D2.2	Change based on feedback	Not achieved	
D2.3	Timing of feedback	Not achieved	
	Combined Rating for Attribute (D2.1 to 2.3):	Not achieved	
D.3	**Iteration Attribute**		
D3.1	Minimize risks by iteration of design	Partially	
D3.2	Manage iteration of design solutions	Not achieved	
D3.3	Use design objectives to control iteration	Not achieved	
	Combined Rating for Attribute (D3.1 to 3.3):	Not achieved	
	Combination of Ratings for this Level:		Not achieved
	Level E Institutionalized		
E.1	**Human-Centred Leadership Attribute**	1	Rating
E1.1	Manage usability programme	Not achieved	
E1.2	Systematic improvement in quality in use	Not achieved	
E1.3	Human-centred improvement of organisation	Not achieved	
	Combined Rating for Attribute (E1.1 to 1.3):	Not achieved	
E.2	**Organisational Human-Centredness Attribute**		
E2.1	Organisational implementation of user-centred practices	Not achieved	
E2.2	Acceptance of human-centred skills	Partially	
	Combined Rating for Attribute (E2.1 to 2.2):	Partially	
	Combination of Ratings for this Level:		Partially

Table 8. All Case Studies-UMM-HCS Process Attribute Maturity Level Evaluation

Process Attribute	Rating-CS1	Rating-CS2	Rating-CS3	Rating-CS4	Rating-CS5
Problem Recognition	Fully	Fully	Fully	Fully	Partially
Performed Process	Fully	Fully	Fully	Fully	Unknown
Quality in Use Awareness	Fully	Not achieved	Fully	Partially	Partially
User Focus	Fully	Not achieved	Largely	Partially	Partially
User Involvement	Fully	Fully	Fully	Fully	Partially
HF Technology	Fully	Fully	Fully	Largely	Partially
HF Skills	Largely	Fully	Largely	Largely	Partially
Integration	Largely	Fully	Largely	Partially	Not achieved
Improvement	Fully	Fully	Fully	Fully	Not achieved
Iteration	Largely	Fully	Largely	Fully	Not achieved
Human Centred Leadership	No	Fully	Partially	Not achieved	Not achieved
Organisational Human Centredness	Partially	Fully	Largely	Partially	Partially
Maturity Level	Level C	Level A	Level B	Level A	Level Unknown

Aim 2: Investigating whether UMM-HCS is suitable for utilisation in assessing usability maturity in the context of Agile projects

The following criteria were set in order to investigate the suitability of UMM-HCS for utilisation in assessing usability maturity in the context of agile projects:

CR1: The model does not conflict with Agile values and principles

This criteria was set in order to maintain the agility of the development process in case of utilising UMM-HCS. Practice E1.1, "Manage usability programme. Management of the whole programme of human centred processes on all projects in a department or organisation" could pose a conflict with the agile value of "Individuals and interactions over processes and tools", however, this practice also works in support of another agile principle "Continuous attention to technical excellence and good design enhances agility" since the aim of practice E1.1 is to improve the quality of usability across all products.

Moreover, most of UMM-HCS practices are in support of agile principles. For example, the agile principle "Our highest priority is to satisfy the customer through early and continuous delivery of valuable software." is supported by practices A2.1, A2.2, C1.1, C1.2, C1.4, D2.1, D2.2, and D3.1. The agile principle "Welcome changing requirements, even late in development. Agile processes harness change for the customer's competitive advantage." is supported by practices D2.1, D2.2, and D2.3. The agile principle "Deliver working software frequently, from a couple of weeks to a couple of months, with a preference to the shorter timescale." is supported by practice C1.4. The agile principle "At regular intervals, the team reflects on how to become more effective, then tunes and adjusts its behaviour accordingly." is supported by practices C2.3 and E1.2.

Thus CR1 is satisfied by UMM-HCS since the model does not conflict with agile values and principles.

CR2: The model integrates UCD activities into the overall project plan and throughout the software development life cycle

Criteria CR2 was considered as critical for judging the suitability of UMM-HCS for utilisation in assessing usability maturity in the context of agile projects since one of the AUCDI main challenges is the timing of performing the different UCD activities and how to make UCD activities more lightweight in order to accommodate the agile processes iterative and incremental nature [25].

UMM-HCS was not developed for a particular software development life cycle; thus the model focus is on declaring the important attributes and practices for usability maturity rather than clarifying the timing or frequency for conducting these practices along the project or the phases of the development life cycle. This is of specific importance in case of agile methods since a significant part of the integration challenges are related to the iterative, incremental, tight time line nature of agile development processes as illustrated in [25].

Thus CR2 is not satisfied since UMM-HCS does not state clear timings and milestones along the agile development cycle for UCD activities inclusion.

6 Conclusion

A variety of UMMs exist, however, published UMM research is limited [15]. Up to our knowledge none of the available UMMs was initially created for use in an agile development process thus they lack details on the timing and the lightweight method for applying the different UCD practices along the agile development life cycle. This is of specific importance in case of agile since a significant part of the AUCDI challenges are related to the timing and lightweight method of performing the different UCD activities in order to accommodate the agile processes iterative and incremental nature [25].

The application of UMM-HCS on five AUCDI case studies in order to investigate the relationship between the success of AUCDI attempts and usability maturity level gave an indication that it was not possible to achieve this aim due to problems exhibited with UMM-HCS rating system. UMM-HCS embraces a linear upgrading model that led to discarding considerable achieved attributes by the case studies. Moreover, the results of the AUCDI case studies gave an indication that the linear upgrading model is contradictory to how organisation's perform since an organisation can score high in some of the practices related to a high maturity level even if the organisation is at a low maturity level.

Although UMM-HCS does not conflict with agile values and principles yet it does not address the requirements, activities, and challenges identified within the AUCDI domain. These issues need to be taken into consideration by any researcher who considers developing a usability maturity model for the agile process. Examples of AUCDI challenges that are not approached by UMM-HCS models are: practices regarding the communication, coordination, and collaboration between UCD practitioners and agile developers in order to synchronize and complete their work, and practices related to design modularization. Another issue that needs addressing is the activities of some team roles, for example, XP coach and Scrum master, etc whose role can impact the integration process.

References

1. Beyer, H., Holtzblatt, K., Baker, L.: An Agile customer-centered method: rapid contextual design. In: Zannier, C., Erdogmus, H., Lindstrom, L. (eds.) XP/Agile Universe 2004. LNCS, vol. 3134, pp. 50–59. Springer, Heidelberg (2004)
2. Coallier, F.: TRILLIUM: A Model for the Assessment of Telecom Product Development & Support Capability. Software Process Newsletter **2**, 13–18 (1995)
3. Constantine, L.: Process Agility and Software Usability: Towards Lightweight Usage Centred Design (2001b)
4. Crosby, P.: Quality is Free: The Art of Making Quality Certain. McGraw Hill, New York (1987)
5. Detweiler, M.: Managing UCD within Agile Projects. Interactions **14**(3), 40–42 (2007)
6. Earthy, J.: Usability Maturity Model: Human Centredness Scale:INUSE Project Deliverable D5.1.4 Version 1.2. Technical report, Llyod's Register, London (1998)
7. Eason, Haker: User Centred Design Maturity. Internal Working Document. Technical report, Department of Human Sciences. Loughborough University (1997)
8. Flanagan, G., Rauch, T.: Usability management maturity, part 1: self assessment: how do you stack up? In: CHI 95 Conference Companion (4), October 1995
9. Gupta, A.: Humanware Process Improvement Framework: Interfacing User Centred Design and the Product Creation Process at Philips. Position paper at Human Centred Process Improvement Group (HCPIG) meeting, UK (1997)
10. Rauch, T., Flanagan, G.: Usability management maturity, part 2: usability techniques - what can you do? In: CHI 95 Conference Companion (1995)
11. Fowler, M.: The New Methodology, December 2005
12. Gottschalk, P.: Maturity Levels for Interoperability in Digital Government. Government Information Quarterly **26**, 75–81 (2009)
13. Gould, J., Lewis, C.: Designing for Usability: Key Principles and What Designers Think. Communications of ACM **28**(3), 300–311 (1985)
14. Iversen, J., Nielsen, P.A., Norbjerg, J.: Situated Assessment of Problems in Software Development. ACM SIGMIS Database - Special Issue on Infomration Systems **30**(2), 66–81 (1999)
15. Jokela, T., Siponen, M., Hirasawa, N., Earthy, J.: A Survey of Usability Capability Maturity Models: Implications for Practice and Research. Behaviour and Information Technology **25**(3), 263–282 (2006)
16. Jokela, T., Abrahamsson, P.: Modelling usability capability - introducing the dimensions. In: Bomarius, F., Oivo, M. (eds.) PROFES 2000. LNCS, vol. 1840, pp. 73–87. Springer, Heidelberg (2000)
17. Jones, B.S.: Total Systems Maturity. Internal Report. Version 2. BAeSEMA; Glasgow (1995)
18. Lee, J.C., McCrickard, S., Stevens, T.: Examining the foundations of agile usability with extreme scenario-based design. In: Agile Conference, pp. 3–10 (2009)
19. McClelland, I., Gelderen, T., Taylor, B., Hefley, B., Gupta, A.: Humanware Process Improvement - Institutionalising the Principles of User Centred Design
20. Mettler, T.: Maturity Assessment Models: A Design Science Research Approach. International Journal of Society Systems Science **3**, 81–98 (2011)
21. Nielsen, J.: Neilsen's Alertbox: Corporate Usability Maturity: Stages, pp. 1–4 (2006)
22. Raza, A., Capretz, L.-F., Ahmed, F.: An Open Source Usability Maturity Model (OS-UMM). Computers in Human Behavior **28**(4), 1109–1121 (2012)

23. Rosemann, M., deBruin, T.: Towards a business process management maturity model. In: European Conference on Information Systems, Germany (2005)
24. Salah, D., Paige, P., Cairns, P. : A practitioner perspective on integrating agile and user centered design. In: The British HCI Conference (HCI 2014), UK (2014)
25. Salah, D., Paige, P., Cairns, P.: A systematic literature review for agile development processes and user centred design integration. In: The International Conference on Evaluation and Assessment in Software Engineering, London, UK (2014)
26. Salah, D., Paige, R., Cairns, P.: Integrating agile development processes and user centred design- a place for usability maturity models? In: Sauer, S., Bogdan, C., Forbrig, P., Bernhaupt, R., Winckler, M. (eds.) HCSE 2014. LNCS, vol. 8742, pp. 108–125. Springer, Heidelberg (2014)
27. Yin, R.: Case Study Research: Design and Methods. Beverly Hills, London (2009)

Assessment and Maturity Models

Causes of Continuity and Participation Problems in Process Improvement with Staged Maturity Models

Algan Uskarci[✉] and Onur Demirörs

Informatics Institute, Middle East Technical University, Ankara, Turkey
`algan.uskarci@gmail.com, demirors@metu.edu.tr`

Abstract. Staged maturity model based process improvement have been widely employed and analyzed over the past few decades. However the participation of the employees and the continuity of process improvement activities while employing these models is an unexplored aspect of software process improvement research. In this paper we try to identify the causal factors resulting in the shortcomings of staged maturity models with respect to the continuity, extent, and employee participation of process improvement activities. We propose a preliminary set of activities and improvements that can be employed to alleviate the documented problems.

Keywords: Software process improvement · Staged maturity models · Employee participation · Continuous improvement

1 Introduction

Maturity models have been used extensively for software process improvement for the last 35 years since Crosby first proposed them [1]. The initial crude definitions of the staged models have evolved over time to more advanced frameworks such as CMMI (Capability Maturity Model Integration) [2] that is developed based on the early works of Humphrey [3] and ISO-33000 family of standards [4] that have supplanted ISO-15504 [5]. These frameworks have been extensively used for the last two decades for process improvement activities. In parallel with the large scale adoption of maturity models their relationship with process improvement is extensively studied by both academia and the business world to emphasize their advantages and shortcomings. However, research activities specifically targeting the continuity and the employee participation characteristics of process improvement while employing maturity model based approaches are scarce. Wendler conducted an extensive survey of 237 maturity model related publications [6]. A wide range of research questions from applied field to publication forum is considered by the survey. One of the categorizations of the publications used by Wendler is based on the research content. However, even this categorization does not include the continuity or the extent of process improvement as a separate category. Overall, the publications surveyed do not convey the research of the continuity of improvement efforts or the extent of process improvement.

Despite our rigorous efforts to reach contradicting evidence from previous research endeavors, we had came to the conclusion that, although the models suggest in the contrary, as the nature of the models are discrete (in the form of capability levels) improvements can happen in discrete steps. Furthermore we had showed the problems faced with respect to the participation and extent of process improvement activities. Unfortunately these are frequently less discussed difficulties related with model-based improvement. [7]

Our goal in this study is to elaborate on the problems that we had presented in our previous studies and identify the underlying factors that cause these problems. By identifying these causal factors we propose a set of possible improvements in order to establish a remedy for these problems. The actual implementation and validation of these solution proposals are a work in progress and therefore are not in the scope of this study.

2 Previous Research and Problem Definition

Our previous research conducted in order to identify the problems regarding the continuity, extent, and employee participation of process improvement activities while employing staged maturity models is given in [7] and [8]. A summary of our research is presented here in order to define the problems with staged maturity models.

We had performed a case study in two phases. In the first phase we had explored the answers of the following questions:

- How do the staged models enforce continuous process improvement?
- How do the staged models enforce organization wide commitment?
- How do the staged models enforce process wide improvement?

For this purpose we analyzed the process improvement activities of a CMMI level-3 software and electronics company operating in the defense industry sector in Turkey. We have specifically studied the commitment of the company employees to process improvement activities in various aspects. The process improvement database maintained by the company was analyzed for this purpose.

We had seen that the software developers and engineers, which form the majority of the company, have a much lower contribution to process improvement than the other role groups such as quality assurance engineers, although the processes are enforced in the first place to mold the way that they produce their software products. Therefore it was observed that the staged model based initiative has not been successful in enforcing organization wide process improvement commitment. The current situation is a *process-wise oligarchy* where a minority manages the processes for a majority who use them. It might not be the goal of the company to establish a *process-wise democracy* where every employee has equal commitment and voice in the process improvement; however, it had been concluded that the organization wide process improvement commitment is not enabled for the organization.

It was also observed that process improvement suggestions are concentrated before the maturity level assessment periods. This results in most of the database entries being submitted in only a short period of time over a course of many years. Therefore it was not possible to state that the maturity model based approaches enforced continuous process improvement for the organization.

The second phase of the case study builds on the findings of the previous phase by analyzing the opinions of the employees of the target company in order to answer the following question:

- How is software process improvement contribution related to an employee's education, experience and role within the organization?

A questionnaire had been created and distributed to the employees of the company. The questionnaire consisted of two parts. The first part contained 15 questions with 5-level Likert scale answers (Coded as 1 for Strongly Disagree to 5 for Strongly Agree). These questions aimed to document the opinion of the employees regarding the

Table 1. Questionnaire Part I

Code	Question
SPIRequired	Process improvement activities are required and important for the success of organizations.
SPIContinous	Process improvement activities shall be performed continuously independent of maturity level assessments.
ProcessesMature	Processes of my organization do not need to be improved.
AllParticipate	All members of the organization shall participate in process improvement activities.
SmallTeam	A small dedicated team shall perform process improvement activities while minimally disturbing the rest of the organization.
RoleBased	Participation ratio in process improvement activities shall be based on the employee's role.
SeniorityBased	Participation ratio in process improvement activities shall be based on the employee's seniority and experience.
HeavyWorkload	I cannot spare time for process improvement activities because of my heavy workload.
NotJustified	The gains obtained from process improvement activities is not high enough to justify the effort dedicated to them.
SPIKnowledge	I have adequate knowledge about what I can do for the improvement of my organization's processes.
PTIKnowledge	I have adequate knowledge about the Process and Technology Improvement Database (PTI DB).
PTIBeneficial	PTIDB is beneficial in continuous process improvement activities.
PTISufficient	PTIDB is sufficient in continuous process improvement activities.
PTIContent	I know the possible content of suggestions that I can submit to PTIDB.
PTIEvaluation	I think that the suggestions I have submitted/plan to submit to the PTIDB are evaluated in an adequate way.

process improvement activities and the improvement database used within the organization. The questions of the first part of the questionnaire are given in Table 1 together with the associated codes, which will be used for the rest of this study.

The second part of the questionnaire consisted of 8 questions, which obtained personal information about the employee as presented in Table 2.

Table 2. Questionnaire Part II

Code	Question
Sex	Sex
University	University
Department	Department
TargetExp	Employment duration in target company
MaturityExp	Employment duration in an organization with a maturity level certificate (CMMI, ISO 15504 etc.) other than the target company
NonMaturityExp	Employment duration in an organization without a maturity level certificate (CMMI, ISO 15504 etc.) other than the target company
Role	Role
PTISubmission	PTIDB Submission Count

We performed a factor analysis [9] on the questionnaire results in order to identify the underlying approaches of target company employees regarding the staged models and process improvement activities. We obtained findings that support or at least align with the findings of the first phase of our research.

After the research for the first company was published we extended our research to a second target company. The company was chosen so that it has a similar profile with the first target company. The same research method was applied and the results obtained from both phases were in line with the results obtained from the first target company.

All our findings coupled with our experience in the field of software process improvement, established that the staged maturity model based approaches in software process improvement fails to enable a continuous process improvement with a high participation ratio of the employees.

3 Causal Factors and Solution Proposals

In order to form a more sound solution to the presented problems, we explore the causes to the problems of continuity and participation in process improvement activities. We postulate that the underlying cause of the problems we have encountered so far is the lack of three separate but interrelated dimensions as given in Fig. 1. These are the lack of *awareness* of the employees regarding the processes of the organization and process improvement in general, lack of *motivation* of the employees to participate in process improvement and the lack of established *model support* for continuous process improvement in the organization.

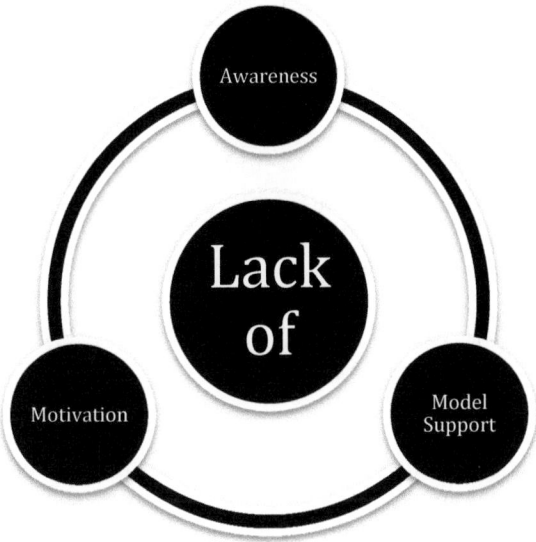

Fig. 1. Root Causes of Documented Problems

3.1 Awareness

Revisiting the questionnaire findings from our previous target companies, it is seen that the general view of the employees seems to support the process improvement activities and the continuity of these activities. The mean values of the answers to all questions are presented in Table 3. The questions coded as SPIRequired and SPIContinous have mean values of higher than 4. However it shall be noted that the SPIKnowledge mean value is approximately one point lower than these values. This shows that the employees support continuous process improvement even if they think that their SPI knowledge is not high. Furthermore, there seems to be some confusion among employees regarding participation in process improvement activities. The average view supports both large scale (AllParticipate), role based (RoleBased) and seniority based (SeniorityBased) participation but these views are expected to be contradictory. Also the mean value for the answer to the smaller team size for process improvement (SmallTeam) is quite high.

Table 3. Questionnaire Answers' Mean Values

Code	Mean Value
SPIRequired	4.31
SPIContinous	4.14
AllParticipate	3.81
RoleBased	3.70
PTIBeneficial	3.65
SeniorityBased	3.24
PTIKnowledge	3.23
PTIContent	3.23
PTIEvaluation	3.22
HeavyWorkload	3.17
SPIKnowledge	3.17
SmallTeam	3.08
PTISufficient	2.77
ProcessesMature	2.16
NotJustified	1.95

Combining these mean values with our findings from our previous research, we see that contradicting views are observed among the employees and different approaches are predominant between different role groups. We believe that training is an important tool for resolving these problems. Another point worth mentioning is the role-based variation. As proposed in our previous studies a strong candidate for explaining this variation is the exposure of the different roles to process improvement activities either through their daily activities or the periodic appraisals performed in the organizations. The training and exposure factors given here are collectively named as *awareness* dimension given above. It is postulated that by increasing effective training and exposure to processes and process improvement activities, the overall awareness of the employees will be increased. The specific suggestions for overcoming the problems in the *awareness* dimension are presented in Table 4.

Table 4. Solutions for the Problems in Awareness Dimension

Appraisal Team Rotation	
Rationale	*Explanation*
The periodic appraisals performed for obtaining and maintaining maturity levels are usually performed by a group of people mostly consisting of the role groups such as quality engineers or configuration managers. This might be a contributing factor for the participation ratio discrepancies between the different role groups.	The appraisal team membership shall be rotated between the role groups and members of the organization. Different persons shall be utilized at each periodic appraisal.

Table 4. (*Continued*)

Extensive Training	
Rationale	*Explanation*
Current organizational training programs usually focus on teaching the employees how to do their jobs. An extensive training approach with a focus on the institutionalized processes might be beneficial in raising awareness.	Training courses that focus on the written-down versions of institutionalized processes will increase the employee's awareness regarding the organizational process assets. These trainings must also focus on the process improvement channels used in the organization so that the employee will be able to participate in the improvement activities.

Process Action Teams	
Rationale	*Explanation*
Process Action Teams (PATs) are formed cross-functionally to improve a process or to address a process related issue. Experience shows that these teams contribute to raising process related-awareness in team members who are not usually exposed to organizational processes.	PATs may be formed with goals set by the management. In addition to the quality engineers and configuration managers, employees from engineering groups must be assigned to these teams to increase their awareness.

Periodic Reminders	
Rationale	*Explanation*
Formal organizational trainings for specific subjects might not be performed with a high frequency. The employees will be accustomed to the daily routine with time and stop referring to the organizational process assets.	Periodic publications such as weekly e-mails or bulletins may be used to remind the employees of the organizational process asset library items. These periodic reminders might also include pop-quizzes related to organizational processes, which might also support the gamification approach presented below.

Management Support	
Rationale	*Explanation*
Usually process improvement incentives within organizations are assigned to a small group of employees by the management. Organization wide participation requires support on the management side.	Yearly process improvement plans and objectives might be shared with the whole organization and the management might encourage all the employees (not only a small group) to actively pursue these objectives according to the plan.

3.2 Motivation

Although the employees support continuous process improvement as presented by the questionnaire answers this support does not result in actual contribution as we have explored in previous phases. This shows that the employees are not motivated to personally engage in process improvement activities despite believing its benefits for the company they work for. This brings us to the motivation dimension we have stated above. Our solution proposal for motivation is to employ a gamification approach [10]. We propose a reputation system where active participation in process improvement activities results in points in the name of the employee. In addition to the points, a badge system will enable the employees to earn badges based on the points accumulated or different tasks completed. The point and badge listings will be publicly available for all employees to see and compare which will hopefully result in competition between employees. Furthermore, the organizational management might use the points and badges as a means of measuring performance or allocating bonus payments or benefits. A recommended list of points and badges that can be used as a staring point is given in Table 5.

Table 5. Recommended Reputation Gains

Action	Reputation Gain
Submitting a PTI	10 points
Adding comment to a PTI submitted by someone else	1 point
Submitted PTI chosen for implementation	20 points
Completing a specific organizational training course	30 points
Participating in a PAT	50 points
Completing the Pop-Quiz of a periodic reminder	Varies (based on success)
Participating in a Process Appraisal Team	100 points or Badge
Gaining Most Points in a Period of Time	Badge
Making Most PTI Submissions in a Period of Time	Badge
Adding Most Comments to PTIs in a Period of Time	Badge
Most PTIs chosen for implementation in a Period of Time	Badge
Most PAT Participations	Badge
Reaching pre-determined PTI submission counts (e.g. 5/20/50/100)	Badge
Most Novel Idea for a PTI	Badge

3.3 Model Support

The last dimension we have postulated is the support of the employed process models. Since our target companies have both been using CMMI, it will be used for explaining this dimension. CMMI-DEV version 1.3 [2] gives two process areas as related to process improvement activities. Organizational Process Focus (Maturity Level 3) process area states "The organization encourages participation in process improvement activities by those who perform the process" in the introductory notes section. However, the rest of the process area does not clearly enforce participation by those who perform the processes. One of the focuses of this process area is periodic appraisals. It might be possible to support an increase in exposure by modifying the appraisal methods used. The model does not enforce periodicity or the team composure for these appraisals. We suggest that the model might be updated to support our "Appraisal Team Rotation" suggestion detailed above. Overall, this process area fails to enforce continuous and highly participated process improvement. It is our understating that the authors of the model assume that all stakeholders will participate "somehow" by supplying improvement suggestions. Unfortunately our previous studies have shown that this is not the situation in the target organizations.

The second process area is Organizational Performance Management (Maturity Level 5). This process area extends the Organizational Process Focus practices by focusing on process improvement based on a quantitative understanding. Also the definitions of improvements are elaborated and much more in focus then Organizational Process Focus. However it is still assumed that the members of the organization will supply the improvement suggestions. There is no mechanism in place to enforce continuity or large-scale participation. The method suggested for collecting improvement suggestions is based on comparing organizational performance data with business objectives and submit suggestions for negating any shortcomings. One sub-practice in Specific Practice (SP) 2.1 Elicit Suggested Improvements states the following for clarifying sources of suggestions;

> *"These suggestions document potential improvements to processes and technologies. Managers and staff in the organization as well as customers, end users, and suppliers can submit suggestions. The organization can also search the academic and technology communities for suggested improvements. Some suggested improvements may have been implemented at the project level before being proposed for the organization."*

This paragraph is one of the rare explanations in the CMMI model that specifically targets our research questions. However it does not specifically enforce the continuity or range of improvement suggestions.

The general problem with CMMI seems to derive from the fact that the process improvement approach presented relies on the organization performing a gap analysis with the model and then perform the activities to close this gap. However we believe that the intrinsic improvements originating from within the organization is also highly beneficial but CMMI fails to provide a consolidated mechanism to enable effective participation within the organization. It is interesting that a widely trendsetting model such as CMMI fails to address the problems that we have observed.

We suggest that the Organizational Performance Management process area of CMMI be split in two. Activities that depend on the statistical performance data of the organization be kept at maturity level 5. However the definition and management of improvements shall be moved to the Organizational Process Focus process area of maturity level 3. Since maturity level 3 establishes institutionalized processes, their improvement shall also start at that maturity level to lay the foundation of a continuous process improvement environment with large-scale participation. We also suggest that the model should focus on the process improvement more thoroughly by defining and encouraging the continuity and participation aspects in sub-practices.

A further improvement opportunity for the maturity models might also be to change the way appraisals are handled by the model. Widely used models usually come together with an appraisal model. In the case of CMMI the appraisal methodology is called SCAMPI (Standard CMMI Appraisal Method for Process Improvement) [11]. We have seen that the periodic appraisals performed based on SCAMPI results in discontinuities in the process improvement activities in the organizations. Instead of a full scale appraisal performed for all process areas of the organization a new approach for a continuous appraisal of the process areas might be beneficial in overcoming the continuity problems in process improvement.

4 Conclusion

Our aim was to elaborate on the problems that we had presented in our previous studies regarding the continuity, extent, and employee participation of process improvement activities while employing staged maturity models. Previously we had presented that the process improvement activities are not continuous for organizations depending on staged maturity models such as CMMI. Furthermore, the employee participation in these activities is highly dependent on the role of the employee and software engineers who actually use the processes do not participate in their improvement.

As identification of the underlying factors that cause these problems, we put forward the lack of three separate but interrelated properties. These are the lack of *awareness* of the employees regarding the processes of the organization and process improvement in general, lack of *motivation* of the employees to participate in process improvement and the lack of established *model support* for continuous process improvement in the organization. We propose a set of possible improvements in order to establish a remedy for each these problems.

In order to overcome the lack of awareness of employees, we suggest using techniques and improvements such as appraisal team member rotation for each consecutive appraisal activity, extensive training focusing on improvement aspect of organization's established processes, forming of process action teams with large scale participation of different role groups, broadcasting of process and improvement related periodic reminders, and management support of process improvement activities with a focus on the problems that we have documented.

For increasing the motivation of employees we propose a gamification approach with a reputation system where active participation in process improvement activities results in points and badges in the name of the employee. A publicly available list of points and badges gained by employees will hopefully result in competitive environment for process improvement.

Finally, in order to overcome lack of the model support of CMMI regarding the continuity and participation issues of process improvement, we suggest a set of improvements for the Organizational Process Focus and Organizational Performance Management process areas.

The actual implementation and validation of these solution proposals are a work in progress and therefore are not in the scope of this study. We plan to implement these activities in a serial manner so that we can actually evaluate their benefits separately. Our first target is to focus on the lack of motivation by employing the gamification approach. We hope that the suggestions put forward by us will enable improvement suggestions for the maturity models themselves. Furthermore, the practices and techniques that we are evaluating might also be beneficial in other areas of organizational management where continuous participation of employees is a critical issue.

References

1. Crosby, P.B.: Quality is Free: The Art of Making Quality Certain. McGraw-Hill, New York (1979)
2. Software Engineering Institute. CMMI Version 1.3 Information Center, February 25, 2015. http://cmmiinstitute.com/resources/cmmi-development-version-13
3. Humphrey, W.S.: Managing the Software Process. Addison-Wesley Reading Mass (1989)
4. International Organization for Standardization. ISO/IEC 33001:2015, April 7, 2015. http://www.iso.org/iso/home/store/catalogue_tc/catalogue_detail.htm?csnumber=54175
5. International Organization for Standardization. ISO/IEC 15504-1:2004, February 25, 2015. http://www.iso.org/iso/iso_catalogue/catalogue_tc/catalogue_detail.htm?csnumber=38932
6. Wendler, R.: The Maturity of Maturity Model Research: A Systematic Mapping Study. Information and Software Technology **54**(12), 1317–1339 (2012)
7. Uskarcı, A., Demirörs, O.: A case study on employee perceptions of organization wide continuous process improvement activities. In: Mas, A., Mesquida, A., Rout, T., O'Connor, R.V., Dorling, Alec (eds.) SPICE 2012. CCIS, vol. 290, pp. 26–37. Springer, Heidelberg (2012)
8. Uskarci, A., Demirors, O.: Do staged models enable organization wide continuous process improvement? In: 2011 IEEE International Conference on Quality and Reliability (ICQR), pp. 20–24 (2011)
9. Field, A.: Discovering Statistics Using SPSS, 3rd edn. Sage Publications, London (2009)
10. Groh, F.: Gamification: State of the art definition and utilization. Institute of Media Informatics Ulm University, pp. 39 (2012)
11. Software Engineering Institute. Standard CMMI Appraisal Method for Process Improvement (SCAMPI) Version 1.3b: Method Definition Document for SCAMPI A,B, and C., February 25, 2015. http://cmmiinstitute.com/resources/standard-cmmi-appraisal-method-process-improvement-scampi-version-13b-method-definition

Towards a Maturity Model for ISO/IEC 20000-1 Based on the TIPA for ITIL Process Capability Assessment Model

Alain Renault(✉), Stéphane Cortina, and Béatrix Barafort(✉)

Luxembourg Institute of Science and Technology, Esch-sur-Alzette, Luxembourg
{alain.renault,stephane.cortina,beatrix.barafort}@list.lu

Abstract. Since the publication of ISO/IEC 15504-7 (*"Assessment of organizational maturity"*) in 2008, there have been few known instances of development of ISO compliant Organizational Maturity Models. As more and more Management Systems standards documenting requirements on processes from various fields of activity are being developed, maturity models can be used as a means to support organizations' route to compliance, and to understand their readiness to certification. This article outlines the design and engineering of a maturity model for ITSM (IT Service Management), targeting compliance to the ISO/IEC 20000-1. The design and engineering of the maturity model artefact has followed and fulfils ISO/IEC 15504-7 and ISO/IEC 33004 requirements for Organizational Maturity Models. These works extend the Transformation Process for Process Assessment Models Design and Engineering with Maturity Model activities.

Keywords: Maturity model · ITSM · TIPA · Process assessment · Transformation process · ISO/IEC 20000

1 Introduction

Though the original edition of the ISO/IEC 15504 [1][2] was clearly based on the basic concepts from ISO 9000 [3] and ISO 9001 [4] (as formulated in the ISO Requirements Specification for a Software Process Assessment Standard in June 1993 [5]), advocates of management system standards are often considering the process assessment approach described in ISO/IEC 15504 as incompatible and worthless.

However, the publication of Cobit5 [6] and the rapid growth of the Tudor's IT Process Assessment (TIPA) framework [7] for ITIL on the market seem to have contributed to a better understanding of what process models are. In the IT Service Management field, TIPA for ITIL [8] is a good example of the value that ISO/IEC 15504-based assessments can bring either when monitoring the adoption of IT Infrastructure Library (ITIL) practices, or when working towards compliance to the requirements of a management system standard (such as ISO/IEC 20000-1). Process assessment has proved its value through a massive adoption in some sectors of the industry with CMMI [9][10][11], Automotive Spice [12], and more recently with the release of TIPA for ITIL. As stated in the ISO/IEC 15504-2 standard [13], process assessment is applicable in the following circumstances: *"a) by or on behalf of an organization with the objective of understanding the state of its own processes for process improvement; b) by or on behalf of an organization with the objective of determining the suitability of its own processes for a particular requirement or class of requirements; c) by or on behalf of one organization with the objective of determining the suitability of another organization's processes for a particular contract or class of contracts."*

In all three cases, the main components of the assessment output are the process profiles, which provide a structured representation of an individual process capability. These process profiles are then compared with the target profile defined prior to the assessment based on the organization's expectations and constraints. This enables measuring the benefits of efforts previously undertaken, and understanding the gaps still to be covered to reach the target situation.

Many organizations do also recognize the value of an ISO/IEC 20000-1 [14] certification as a means to publically demonstrate their excellence, or at least the compliance of their IT service management system to the standard's requirements.

In that context, more and more organizations from the TIPA community already engaged in a process improvement process, came and asked the same following question: "what capability level should my ITIL processes reach to meet ISO/IEC 20000-1 requirements?"

Thus this paper explains the **underlying process to design an organizational maturity model in the specific domain of IT Service Management**. It outlines the extension of the Transformation Process [15], initially used for the design of Process Assessment Models (PAMs) [16][17] in this domain, to the design and engineering of Maturity Models. It also depicts how this extended transformation process has been applied to create a maturity model covering all the requirements of ISO/IEC 20000-1.

The Transformation Process extension for Maturity Model contributes to solving the initial problem identified within the TIPA R&D initiative: *"how to improve ITSM processes?"*. As explained in detail in [18], we had already translated ITIL best practices into a set of processes that companies can deploy for measuring the performance and capability of these processes. This paper describes how to design and engineer a maturity model for IT Service Management, targeting compliance to the ISO/IEC 20000-1 and based on the processes defined in the "TIPA® for ITIL" process assessment model, with a management system mindset.

This paper is organized as follows: section 2 presents related works; section 3 introduces the ISO requirements for maturity model design and associated constraints; then section 4 describes the extended Transformation Process for Maturity Model Design and Engineering in the ITSM domain before discussing design choices and concluding.

2 Related Work

To date, dozens of Capability Maturity Models have been developed in several domains, including those related to IT. The Capability Maturity Model Integrated (CMMI) [9] and the ISO/IEC 15504 standard series for Process Assessment contributed to their spreading, particularly for Software Engineering in the 1990's and more widely for IT purposes in the 2000's. We can particularly mention Capability Maturity Models for IT Service Management purposes such as: IT Service Capability Maturity Model (ITSCMM) [19], Capability Maturity Model Integration for Services (CMMI-SVC)[11], Maturity Model for Implementing ITIL v3 [20][21], a Process Reference Model (ISO/IEC 20000-4)[22] and a Process Assessment Model (ISO/IEC 15504-8)[23] for IT Service Management, and Cobit5 Process Assessment Model [6].

Despite this wide range of models, there are few publications on the engineering of such models. Moreover, process models design and engineering remain an emerging discipline [24][25] and a sound systematic method for developing such models [26][27][28] is still missing. There was thus a need for demonstrating quality, efficiency and effectiveness of the produced artefacts and of their intended usage on the field for resolving the identified problem in a Design Science perspective. In addition various capability models and exemplar process models have been (are currently being) developed by the International Standardization Organization but little guidance exists for maturity model engineering and usage.

In this context and with the market need for an ITIL-based maturity model for IT Service Management targeting compliance to the ISO/IEC 20000-1, the Transformation process initially designed for capability process models, has been extended to the organizational maturity aspects for ITSM.

3   ISO Requirements for Maturity Model Design and Associated Constraints

The Initial ISO/IEC 15504-7
The ISO/IEC 15504-7 standard [29] defines the conditions for an assessment of Organizational Maturity. The standard establishes a framework for determining overall Organizational Maturity, based upon assessed profiles of process capability, and defines the conditions under which such assessments are valid.

The standard also sets requirements and contains guidance on implementing the requirements for constructing an Organizational Maturity Model. The standard outlines that processes can be categorized into 5 process sets based on their contributions to the business goals of the organization. The set of fundamental processes that support the business is called the basic process set. The standard also defines a scale for organizational maturity, representing *"the extent to which the organization has explicitly and consistently performed, managed and established its processes with predicable performance and demonstrated the ability to change and adapt the performance of the processes fundamental to achieving the organization's business goals"*. Maturity levels range from *"immature (level 0)"* to *"innovating (level 5)"*.

Each organizational maturity level beyond level 1 is characterized by the implementation, at an appropriate level of process capability, of a further set of processes (called extended process set) that drive the achievement of the capabilities relevant to that maturity level.

The standard requires that Organizational Maturity Models shall be based upon one or more specified Process Assessment Model(s). The Organizational Maturity Model shall specify the elements, drawn from the specified Process Assessment Model(s) that constitute the elements of the Organizational Maturity Model, and the relationships between these elements and the organizational Maturity Levels.

Transition to ISO/IEC 33004

The revision of the ISO/IEC 15504 series lead to a sound revamping of the clauses related to process and maturity models in the new ISO/IEC 33004 [30] published in March 2015. Compared to the original ISO/IEC 15504-7, the new ISO/IEC 33004 is more open and can be seen as a meta-model for building process and maturity models.

Whereas ISO/IEC 15504-7 was defining a scale for organizational maturity, ISO/IEC 33004 sets requirements on how to design such a maturity scale, emphasizing that the maturity model *"shall define an ordinal scale for organizational process maturity, [..] shall specify a maturity level for each point on the ordinal scale, and [..] shall specify a continuous set of maturity levels, representing increasing levels of organizational process maturity, starting at the basic maturity level"*. This gives anyone the liberty to define its own maturity scale.

The standard goes further and states that a maturity model *"shall define the rules for deriving an organizational process maturity level rating from the set of process profiles that result from an assessment"*. These rules are thus no longer set in stone as requirements of the standard itself, and can thus also be implemented differently based on the context.

The standard does however keep the same approach for the design of maturity models: they remain derived from one or more specified process assessment model(s) and identify the process sets associated with each of the levels in a scale of organizational process maturity, and relate to the growing ability of an organization to achieve higher levels of a specific process quality characteristic.

4 The Maturity Model Artefact Design and Engineering in the ITSM Domain

The context of the original request was: deriving the maturity level of an organization wishing to demonstrate its maturity and its readiness towards an ISO/IEC 20000-1 certification while using ITIL processes to structure its improvement program.

This characterizes the community of interest for the maturity model and its intended usage but also gives birth to a number of issues or challenges:

1. ISO/IEC 20000-1 sets requirements on management system that are not defined as such in ITIL.
2. ITSM processes are defined differently in ISO/IEC 20000-1 and ITIL.
3. ISO/IEC 20000-1 requirements may or may not be present in ITIL processes.
4. There is no consensus on an implementation order for these processes (no silver bullet).

Based on the context, issues and challenges previously stated, an ISO/IEC 33004-compliant Maturity Model for ITSM was designed. So this Maturity Model has to be based on one or several specified PAMs: it relies on two existing Process Assessment Models. On the one side, the TIPA PAM for ITIL which contains 26 ITSM processes and addresses the practices described in ITIL 2011 [31] (such as Service level management, Catalogue management, Incident management…). On the other side, the draft ISO/IEC 33070-4 PAM for Information security management [32], which among others, embeds 12 processes describing all the practices common to all management systems (such as internal audit, communication management, management review…) [Figure 1]. These two models contain processes that are described according to the guidance coming from [33]. Still under development, the PAM for Information security management will be the first PAM targeting a Management System Standard (MSS) following the new structure required by ISO in its directives [34].

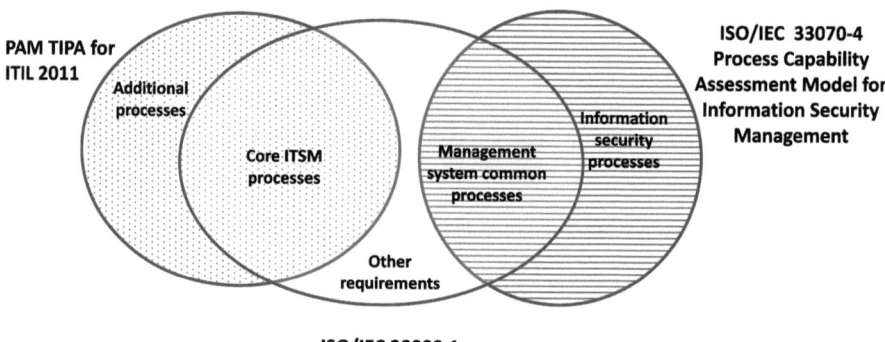

Fig. 1. Coverage of ISO/IEC 20000-1

For that, a specific design process was set up, extending the Transformation Process used for designing Process Reference and Process Assessment Models. This extended Transformation Process (see Figure 2) consists in the following steps:

1. Identifying elementary requirements
2. Identifying the processes which cover the elementary requirements
3. Identifying the (base or generic) practices addressing these elementary requirements
4. Defining the maturity scale
5. Agreeing on the consolidation rules
6. Assigning each process to a maturity level
7. Identifying optional and conditional processes

Each step of this extended Transformation Process is further described below.

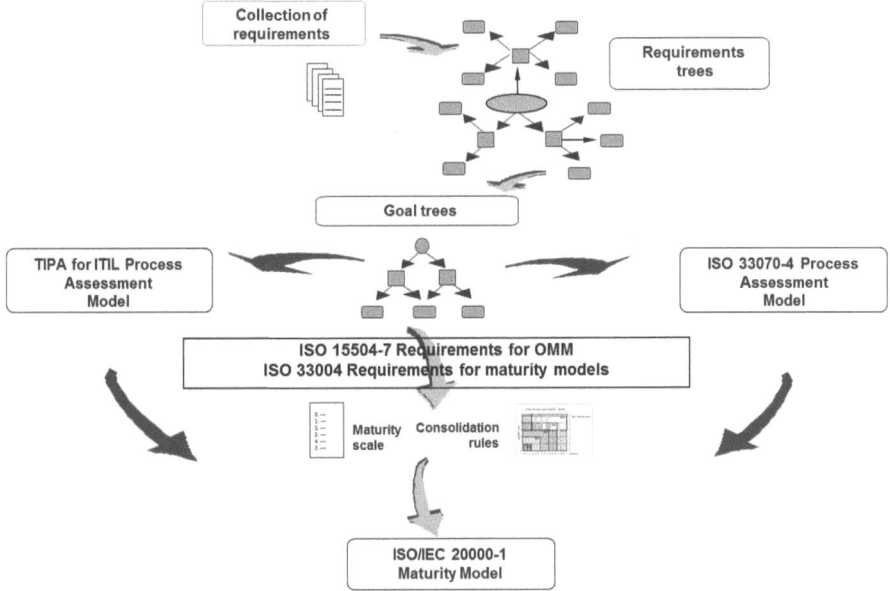

Fig. 2. Extended Transformation Process

Step1: Identifying elementary requirements
The ISO/IEC 20000-1 standard was first analyzed in order to structure its content as a flat list of elementary requirements. For that, each "shall" statement was examined and broken down into one or several elementary requirements.

For example, the sentence *"The service provider shall create, implement and maintain a service continuity plan(s) and an availability plan(s)"*, was decomposed into six elementary requirements: *The service provider shall create a service continuity plan(s) / The service provider shall implement a service continuity plan(s) / The service provider shall maintain a service continuity plan(s) / The service provider shall create an availability plan(s) / The service provider shall implement an availability plan(s) / The service provider shall maintain an availability plan(s).*

An elementary requirement is made up of one subject, one "shall", one verb and one (or more) complement(s). More than 400 elementary requirements were derived from the original document.

Step2: Identifying the processes which cover the elementary requirement
Each elementary requirement identified in step1 was then associated to one specific process coming from one of the two process assessment models used as inputs. For that the authors analyzed the meaning of each elementary requirement. When the requirement covered an ITSM practice, it was associated to one (or more) of the 26 ITIL processes (described in the TIPA PAM for ITIL). When the elementary requirement depicted an activity related to the implementation of the service management system, it was associated to one of the 12 management system common processes (described in [32]). When the elementary requirement described an interaction or an exchange between processes, it was associated to several processes (eventually coming from the two PAMs). For example, the elementary requirement *"The service provider shall assess the*

impact of request for change on the service continuity plan(s)" was associated to both Change Management and IT Service Continuity Management processes.

Step3: Identifying the (base or generic) practice which address the elementary requirement

Once each elementary requirement has been associated to a process, the authors drilled down into that process to select the most appropriate base practice addressing the elementary requirement. When no base practice could be considered as indicator of the achievement of the elementary requirement, the authors tried to associate it to a generic practice (i.e. an indicator of a capability level upper than one).

This step permitted to highlight the following findings:

- There were 22 elementary requirements that were not covered by any process of the two PAMs.
- No elementary requirement from ISO/IEC 20000-1 is mapped to a capability level upper than 3.
- No elementary requirement from ISO/IEC 20000-1 is mapped to the following ITIL processes: IT Service Strategy Management, Demand Management, Knowledge Management, Event Management, and Access Management.

Step4: Defining the maturity scale

ISO/IEC 33004 requires defining an ordinal scale for organizational process maturity and then specifying a maturity level for each point on the ordinal scale. Each maturity level needs then to be defined with a unique identification and description.

The authors decided to start with the 6-levels ordinal scale originally defined in ISO/IEC 15504-7. Based on their experience, they reviewed the definition of levels 1 to 5, keeping in mind the objective of the maturity model (i.e. preparing for ISO/IEC 20000 certification).

The name of each maturity level is an adjective that can be used to qualify an organization reaching that particular maturity level. For example, an IT service provider reaching the maturity level 2 can be seen as a "managed organization".

The maturity scale is presented in the Table 1 below.

Table 1. ISO/IEC 20000-1 Maturity levels

#	Maturity level	Description
0	Immature	The organization does not demonstrate effective implementation of the processes that are fundamental for providing IT services, according to business expectations.
1	Reactive	The reactive organization is capable of operating and supporting identified and agreed IT services. The organization demonstrates achievement of the purpose of the processes that are fundamental for providing IT services, according to business expectations.
2	Managed	The managed organization is capable of proactively operating and supporting existing, new, or changed IT services. The organization demonstrates management of the resources and processes for providing and supporting existing, new, or changed IT services, according to business expectations.

Table 1. (*Continued*)

3	Integrated	The organization is capable of providing consistent design, transition and operation of existing, new, or changed services with integrated processes. The organization demonstrates effective definition and deployment of the IT service management processes that are integrated in a controlled management system.
4	Governed	The organization understands current and future market expectations and can guarantee its ability to meet them. The organization demonstrates objective control of its fundamental processes. The organization's strategy is translated in a portfolio of services that governs the performance and management of the processes and management system. It operates an effective influence on market demand accordingly.
5	Optimizing	The organization is continually improving its services according to its strategy. The organization demonstrates the ability to optimize its processes and its IT services.

Step5: Agreeing on the consolidation rules
An organization's maturity level is derived from a set of process profiles that result from an assessment. ISO/IEC 33004 requires each maturity model to define the rules for doing so. These *consolidation rules* were initially described in ISO/IEC 15504-7.

Here it was agreed to keep the ISO/IEC 15504-7 consolidation rules as they fit with our context and comply with the requirements contained in ISO/IEC 33004. These rules can be summarized in Table 2 below.

Table 2. Maturity level achievement consolidation rules

To achieve Maturity Level 1	All processes assigned to level 1 shall achieve process capability level (PCL) 1 or higher.
To achieve Maturity Level 2	All processes assigned to levels 1 and 2 shall achieve PCL 2 or higher.
To achieve Maturity Level 3	All processes assigned to levels 1, 2 and 3 shall achieve PCL 3 or higher.
To achieve Maturity Level 4	All processes assigned to levels 1, 2, 3, and 4 shall achieve PCL 3 or higher. One or more processes in the basic process set shall achieve PCL 4 or higher.
To achieve Maturity Level 5	All processes shall achieve PCL 3 or higher. One or more of the processes in the basic process set shall achieve PCL 5.

Step6: Assigning each process to a maturity level
As defined in ISO/IEC 33001 [35], a maturity model is *"a model, derived from one or more specified process assessment model(s) that identifies the process sets associated with the levels in a specified scale of organizational process maturity."*

During this step, the authors assigned each process from both PAMs to one of the maturity levels previously defined. These design choices were based on the mapping done during step2 and step3, with the intent to have a consistent set of processes contributing to the achievement of each level (defined during step4). These design choices will be discussed during the following section of this paper.

Step7: Identifying optional and conditional processes
In order to make a maturity model more flexible and usable in different contexts, some of its processes can be identified as 'optional' or 'conditional'. In our case, optional processes are those that are not required to comply with the requirements of ISO/IEC 20000-1 (i.e. the processes without any associated elementary requirement identified during step3, such as *event management* or *access management* processes that are present in ITIL 2011). Conditional processes (processes that can be omitted under certain circumstances) have not been used in our specific context.

5 Discussions

Why were these previously described consolidation rules set?
During the construction of the maturity model for ITSM, it was agreed by the authors to keep the consolidation rules previously defined in ISO/IEC 15504-7. This choice was made in order to avoid confusion, particularly for people who were already familiar with the concept of Organizational Maturity Model described in ISO/IEC 15504-7.

As the maturity model requirements set by the ISO/IEC 33004 are not yet broadly deployed for new Maturity Model releases, there was a lack of hindsight. But the practice and feedback we are expecting from the ITSM community will definitively enable to refine this expert judgment.

Why were these maturity levels determined?
Most popular maturity models on the market have defined a maturity scale ranging from 1 to 5, ISO/IEC 15504-7 having added a level 0. Even if these levels are defined differently and may have different meanings, people do unconsciously know or feel what these levels represent in term of maturity of their organization. Our maturity model needed to keep that structure to ease its adoption on the market. However keeping the additional "immature" value as level 0 on the ordinal scale of maturity seems as important to remain aligned with the standards philosophy. So we ended up with a 6 points ordinal scale ranging from level 0 (immature) to level 5 (optimizing) to which processes needed to be assigned.

The structure of the maturity scale reflects the path of organizations progressing towards an ISO/IEC 20000-1 certification. The journey starts with an immature organization aiming to have more confidence in their ability to reactively perform their activities. More efforts will contribute to setting up a managed organization with repeatable fulfilled process outcomes.

Mature IT service management processes (defined and deployed) supported by a mature management system define a "Level 3 – Integrated" organization, in which all requirements of ISO/IEC 20000-1 are met. The maturity scale was then challenged to evaluate the value of keeping levels 4 and 5.

Some organization may however wish or need to go further and implement activities and processes that are documented in ITIL but not required in the ISO/IEC 20000-1, deserving to be qualified as "Governed" (Level 4) or "Optimizing" (Level 5). These two upper levels were then kept to host optional processes.

Why did the processes be assigned to such and such maturity levels?
During step6 the authors associated each process described in the two selected PAMs to one of the five maturity levels defined during step4. This was driven by the purpose of these processes as well as by the meaning of each maturity level. For example, to determine the processes to be associated with maturity level 1, we tried to answer the following question: what are the processes required by a reactive organization? Incident management? Request fulfilment? For maturity level 2, the authors determined which processes are necessary for an organization to be considered as managed. A key indicator of maturity level 3 is the existence of a management system. By nature, the processes supporting a management system (for example management review, internal audit, or documentation management), bring value once they are uniformly defined and deployed within the assessed organization. In other words, to be efficient, these processes should individually reach a process capability level of 3. For that reason, and according to the previously defined consolidation rules, the authors decided to assign most of the management system common processes to the maturity level 3. Thus, all the processes mapped to requirements from the ISO/IEC 20000-1 standard were allocated to levels 1 to 3, and the remaining processes from the TIPA for ITIL PAM were defined as optional processes and assigned to maturity levels 4 and 5.

This work was mainly based on the authors' judgment and on their experience. This activity was however more influenced by the consolidation rules (step5) than by the results of the mapping performed during step3. The feedback and validation on the field will enable to rationale and document this further.

Was the maturity model a good option to prepare for ISO/IEC 20000-1 certification?
The maturity model offers a structured approach that can help organizations implement a staged approach towards the targeted certification. The suggested journey can help organizations implement consistent set of processes depending on their business objectives, and hopefully get certified once level 3 covered.

Steps 2 and 3 of the extended transformation process connect the elementary requirements from the standards to (generic or base) practices from the process assessment models used. The requirements are so contributing to the process capability. But for reaching maturity level 1 (or any higher level) all processes of the basic (or any further extended) process set is expected to have reached the appropriate capability level (according to the consolidation rules), which means that the highest process attributes targeted can be either largely or fully implemented.

In the ISO/IEC 20000-1 certification mindset, traceability to requirements has to be demonstrated. The mapping that was performed for the ITSM maturity model development ensured this but appropriate additional tools and views may have to be considered for enhancing the improvement power and complementary qualities of a process maturity approach compared to a certification (audit) preparation.

6 Conclusion

Maturity Models are powerful tools for organizations that want to demonstrate their excellence through a staged approach of (third-party) assessments. They can also be used to target the scope of these assessments and so set a structure for improvement initiatives as they are supposed to provide consistent set of processes for each level of maturity. However, as each context is unique, there are no "silver bullets" and one can always argue that the set of processes defined for each level does not suit them. We are proposing a maturity model for ISO/IEC 20000-1 based on the IT service management processes as defined in ITIL 2011 [31] (and structured in the TIPA for ITIL PAM) and on the management system activities as recommended in the Annex SL from ISO [34] (and presented as processes in [32]). This maturity model shows how an organization can evolve from *reactive* (level 1) to *managed* (level 2), and *integrated* (level 3) where it covers the ISO/IEC 20000-1 requirements, including the ones covering the management system. The organization can even go further to level 4 (*governed*), and ultimately to level 5 (*optimizing*). The maturity model helps organizations to understand their readiness towards ISO/IEC 20000-1 compliance, and presents the gap they need to cover before they can claim official recognition through an ISO/IEC 20000-1 certification. The maturity model enables to understand the capability level that processes need to reach to meet ISO/IEC 20000-1 requirements. Experimentations and validation are in progress on the field with early-adopters of the maturity model with a sample of organizations from the relevant community of interest. So the model is still subject to modification and is not presented in details in this paper. Future works will consist in analyzing the feedback from the experimentation and validation phases and share the conclusion with the scientific community through publication.

References

1. ISO/IEC 15504-1:1998 Information Technology — Software process assessment — Part 1: Concepts and introductory guide (1998)
2. ISO/IEC 15504-2:1998 Information Technology — Software process assessment — Part 2: A reference model for processes and process capability (1998)
3. ISO 9000:1987 Quality management and quality assurance standards — Guidelines for selection and use (1987)
4. ISO 9001:1987 Quality systems — Model for quality assurance in design/development, production, installation and servicing (1987)
5. ISO/IEC JTC1/SC7/WG10/N017R Requirements specification for a software process assessment standard (1993)
6. ISACA. CObit5 (2013). http://www.isaca.org/COBIT/Pages/Product-Family.aspx
7. Public Research Center Henri Tudor. ITSM Process Assessment Supporting ITIL. Van Haren Publishing (2009). ISBN: 9789087535643
8. TIPAonline. http://www.tipaonline.org

9. "CMMI for Development, Version 1.3" (PDF). CMMI-DEV (Version 1.3, November 2010). Carnegie Mellon University Software Engineering Institute (2010)
10. "CMMI for Acquisition, Version 1.3" (PDF). CMMI-ACQ (Version 1.3, November 2010). Carnegie Mellon University Software Engineering Institute (2010)
11. "CMMI for Services, Version 1.3" (PDF). CMMI-SVC (Version 1.3, November 2010). Carnegie Mellon University Software Engineering Institute (2010)
12. Automotive Spice. http://www.automotivespice.com/
13. ISO/IEC 15504-2:2003 Information Technology — Process assessment — Performing an assessment (2003)
14. ISO/IEC TR 20000-1:2011. Information Technology — Service management — Service management system requirements (2011)
15. Barafort, B., Renault, A., Picard, M., Cortina, S.: A transformation process for building PRMs and PAMs based on a collection of requirements – example with ISO/IEC 20000. In: Proceedings of the International Conference SPICE 2008, Nuremberg, Germany (2008)
16. Cortina, S., Picard, M., Valdés, O., Renault, A.: A challenging process models development: the ITIL v3 lifecycle processes. In: Proceedings of the International Conference SPICE 2010, Pisa, Italy (2010)
17. Cortina, S., Mayer, N., Renault, A., Barafort, B.: Towards a process assessment model for management system standards. In: Mitasiunas, A., Rout, T., O'Connor, R.V., Dorling, A. (eds.) SPICE 2014. CCIS, vol. 477, pp. 36–47. Springer, Heidelberg (2014)
18. Renault, A., Barafort, B.: TIPA for ITIL – from genesis to maturity of SPICE applied to ITIL 2011. In: Proceedings of the International Conference EuroSPI 2014, Luxembourg (2014)
19. Niessinka, F., Clerca, V., Tijdinka, T., van Vliet, H.: IT Service Capability Maturity Model. Vrije Universiteit (2005)
20. Pereira, R., da Silva, M.M.: ITIL maturity model. In: Proceedings of the 5th Iberian Conference on Information Systems and Technologies (CISTI) (2010)
21. Pereira, R., Mira da Silva M.: A Maturity Model for Implementing ITIL v3. In: 6th World Congress on Services (SERVICES-1), USA (2010)
22. ISO/IEC TR 20000-4:2010. Information Technology — Service management — Process reference model (2010)
23. ISO/IEC 15504-8:2012 Information Technology — Process assessment — An exemplar process assessment model for IT service management (2012)
24. Mettler T.: A Design Science Research Perspective on Maturity Models in Information Systems. https://www.alexandria.unisg.ch/Publikationen/214531
25. Becker, J., Knackstedt, R., Pöppelbuß, J.: Developing maturity models for IT management – a procedure model and its application. Journal Business & Information Systems Engineering (BISE) **1**(3). B&ISE (2009)
26. Stallinger, F., Plösch, R.: Towards methodological support for the engineering of process reference models for product software. In: Mitasiunas, A., Rout, T., O'Connor, R.V., Dorling, A. (eds.) SPICE 2014. CCIS, vol. 477, pp. 24–35. Springer, Heidelberg (2014)
27. Salviano, C.F., Zoucas, A.C., Silva, J.V.L., Alves, A.M., Wangenheim, C.G., Thiry, M: A method framework for engineering process capability models. In: Proceedings of the International Conference EuroSPI 2009, Madrid (2009)
28. Figueiredo, A.M., Salviano, C.F.: Evolving a method framework for engineering process assessment models. In: Mitasiunas, A., Rout, T., O'Connor, R.V., Dorling, A. (eds.) SPICE 2014. CCIS, vol. 477, pp. 12–23. Springer, Heidelberg (2014)

29. ISO/IEC TR 15504-7:2008. Information Technology — Process assessment — Assessment of organizational maturity (2008)
30. ISO/IEC 33004. Information Technology — Process assessment — Requirements for process reference, process assessment and maturity models (2015)
31. The Cabinet Office. ITIL Lifecycle Publication Suite. The Stationery Office Edition (2011)
32. ISO/IEC PDTS2 33070-4. Information Technology — Process assessment — Process capability assessment model for Information Security Management
33. ISO/IEC TR 24774. Systems and software engineering – Life cycle management – Guidelines for process description (2010)
34. ISO/IEC Directives, Part1. Annex SL (2014)
35. ISO/IEC 33001. Information Technology — Process assessment — Concepts and terminology (2015)

Process and Education

Towards the Development of a Framework for Encouraging the Learning of SPICE Model by Using Knowledge Graphs

Alvaro Fernández Del Carpio[1(✉)] and Leonardo Bermón Angarita[2]

[1] Universidad La Salle, Arequipa, Perú
alfernandez@ulasalle.edu.pe
[2] Universidad Nacional de Colombia, Manizales, Colombia
lbermona@unal.edu.co

Abstract. Software process learning is a relevant aspect on software process improvement. In this paper, we present a framework based on knowledge graphs, in order to evaluate the expertise on ISO 15504 software model (SPICE). Having identified some papers related to the target of the research, we have proposed a framework with modules related to mechanisms, to extract both: information from IT workers and SPI models, for generating the corresponding knowledge graphs and matching them, to determine strengths and weaknesses in the learning process of the SPICE model.

Keywords: Software process · SPI · ISO/IEC 15504 · SPICE · Knowledge graphs · Learning · Education

1 Introduction

Software process is an important discipline in the body of knowledge of software engineering. Though, many process models are found in the literature and are widely known and used by industry members, these models require special techniques and mechanisms, so the beginners can learn and effectively use them, during software development projects. Furthermore, it is necessary to research on new techniques, in order to assess if the knowledge acquired by learners matches, the knowledge of standard models used. This paper aims to research the development of a framework, which uses knowledge graphs, to assess the degree of learning about a specific software process. The selected software process model was the ISO 15504 (SPICE) model. This model is one of the most well known software process models, that is referenced by software development organizations.

This paper is organized as follows: First, it is presented a background about the main concepts underlying the proposed framework. Next, the working method is described with a set of papers related to the research subject. Then, the results of the working method are shown. In the next section, the proposed framework is explained, with its main elements and functions. After that, the validation of the study is presented. Finally, the conclusions and future researches are presented.

2 Background

This section contains a brief description of the main concepts of our research. First, it addresses the some issues related to software process and learning, and then, the SPICE model is described. Finally, the concept of knowledge graph is presented.

2.1 Software Process and Learning

A software process can be defined as: "a coherent set of policies, organizational structures, technologies, processes and artifacts required to design, develop, install and maintain a software product" [1]. Software process management involves the following activities: process definition, process control, process measurement, process improvement and process execution [2].

Initially, we started learning about software process, mainly focused on adding it to the discipline of software engineering. Therefore, it was included in the final versions of SWEBOK [3]. While knowledge areas are defined by what to teach, there is no way to teach, leaving wide open pedagogical choices in between, say, reading vs. practice, teacher-centered vs. student-centered, individual learning vs. team learning, context-free project case vs. project located case, etc. [4].

In order for learning to be effective, the process should be easy to understand, the contents of processes must be flexible and easily modifiable to be applied in different projects, and also, they should have well defined interfaces to other related processes [5].

Lyytinen and Robey [6] refer to the failure of organizations, to learn from their own previous experience, as a reason for the recurrence in problems of IS development. They argue that learning from experience is against the common practice, because the necessary motivation is not there to do it.

2.2 SPICE Model

ISO/IEC 15504, also known as Software Process Improvement Capability Determination, SPICE, is a model for improvement, and evaluation of development processes, system information and software products maintenance [7].

ISO/IEC 15504 assessment model has 2 dimensions: process dimension and capability dimension. Process dimension consists of processes, and each process is defined in terms of its purpose and outcomes. Capability dimension defines 6 capability levels: from incomplete process (level 0) to optimizing process (level 5). Each capability level has a set of process attributes (PA) defining the particular aspects contained in process capability. The process attributes are defined by stating the goals to be achieved. The mapping should guide the "process outcomes" (level 1) and the "achievements" (levels 2-5) for each process.

The assessment model for capability levels in all processes can be from 0 and at least to level 1 of the following levels of standard capability: Level 0, Incomplete; Level 1, Performed; Level 2, Managed; Level 3, Established; Level 4, Predictable; and Level 5, Optimizing.

2.3 Knowledge Graphs

Knowledge graph is used to represent an idea, event, situation or circumstance described by a trend graph, consisting of nodes that represent concepts and links symbolizing the conceptual relationships. This theory is widely used in modeling application to information systems, natural language processing, information search and reasoning base case, and learning techniques and logic related cases [8].

According to [9], a knowledge graph can be defined as G=(V, E, L), where each vertex v ∈ V represents an entity, each e = (v_i, v_j) ∈ E represents a directed edge from vertex v_i to v_j, L(v) is the label of vertex v, and L(e) is the label of edge e.

Instances of real-world knowledge graphs include DBpedia [10], YAGO [11], Probase [12] and Freebase [13] which powers Google's knowledge graph.

As an example of the purpose of this paper, Fig. 1 describes a generated knowledge graph from the ISO/IEC 15504 model having as a filter, the domain "Acquisition preparation" belonging to the "Acquisition process" of the process dimension.

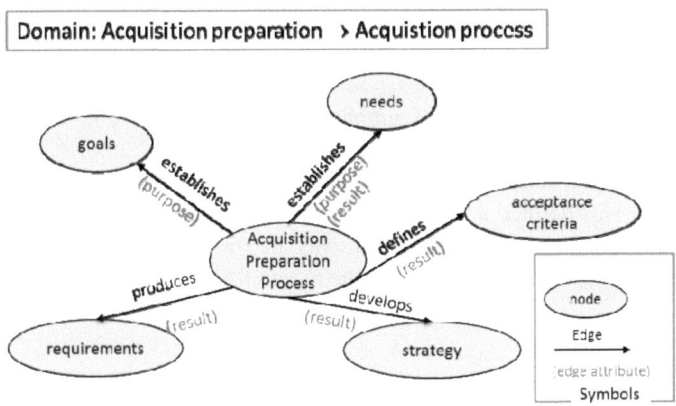

Fig. 1. An example of knowledge graph generated from the Acquisition preparation domain

3 Method

The research method used as a guide for this review is the proposed by [14]. This method starts with searching strategies definition and it is composed by several steps contained in a list.

The searching strategies definition comprises two elements: information sources and searching expressions used in the search engines, which are provided by the selected information sources. The information sources were selected, because they collect most of the scientific production, in the field of interest. The selected information sources are: ACM Digital Library, IEEE Xplore Digital Library, Science Direct and Springer.

The research method was defined as presented below:

Step 1: A set of papers were taken from the result of the search string: *"Software Process"* **AND** *"Knowledge Graph"* **AND** *"Learning"*, in the selected information sources on: title, abstract and keywords. Table 1 displays a list of synonyms and alternative spellings for the search terms.

Table 1. List of synonyms and alternative spellings.

Term	Synonyms and alternative spelling
Software process	Software development, Software development process, Software project
Knowledge graph	Knowledge diagram, Knowledge chart
Learning	Training, Teaching, Instruction, Guiding, Coaching, Preparing, Education, Studying, Understanding

The search range was between 2005-2015. Using the search equation, in the search engines of the selected information sources, we found 2,905 "potentially relevant" papers.

Step 2: After debugging the results by duplicate cleaning, a quick review of the results of step1 was performed. During the review, the papers that had relevant titles were identified. The amount of identified papers was: 146.

Step 3: Next, a second review which included the reading of keywords, abstract, introduction and conclusions was carried out. The criteria used for the selection was the pertinence among knowledge graphs, software process and software process learning. The final amount of papers was: 49.

Step 4: Finally, a full reading of the papers resulting from step3 was done. From this reading, it was defined a group of factors related to knowledge graphs applied to software process. For these papers, it was performed a quality assessment, by evaluating the objectives and context of the research within the papers.

4 Results

Table 2 shows the identified papers. The papers related to software processes have been favored from those related to learning on the industry. Many of the papers that were found refer to learning in university programs, and according to its content and relevance, some of them have been considered in the filtering.

Table 2. List of identified papers.

Group	Paper	Software process	Knowledge graph	Learning
1	[15], [16], [17], [18], [19], [20]	RUP, Software process life cycle, Iterative development models, SPICE Level 3	N/A	Instruction design, Simulation environment, Constructivism, Decision rules, Problem Based Learning, E-Learning to coach
2	[21], [22], [23], [24]	Software engineering practices, Software process improvement, Social software engineering	N/A	Game, Social software, Technology Acceptance Model (TAM) and the Theory of Planned Behavior (TPB), Tools and communities

Table 2. (*Continued*)

3	[25], [26], [27]	Competisoft, Very small software entities, Agile process	N/A	e-learning, templates, repository, Experience between industry and school, Wiki
4	[28], [29]	ACM/IEEE-CS and GSwE curriculum guidelines	N/A	Problem-based and Project-driven learning, Best practices
5	[30], [31], [32], [33], [34], [35]	N/A	Extraction, Querying, Text summarization, Identification, Information retrieval	N/A
6	[9], [36], [37]	N/A	Subgraph skyline search, Answer graph, Exploratory search, Enterprise search	N/A
7	[38], [39], [40], [41]	N/A	Extraction, Document categorization, relation detection, Concept map	Active learning, Fuzzy rules, Unsupervised learning. Course planning
8	[42], [43], [44], [45], [46], [47], [48], [49], [50]	Health and life sciences, Design rationale, Software requirements, Software patterns and design decisions, Definition of processes	Concept maps and graphs, Architectural decision model, Acyclic graph, Semantics of a design pattern, Ontology	N/A
9	[51], [52], [53], [54], [55], [56], [57], [58], [59], [60], [61], [62]	Airborne software, Reverse engineering, Requirements engineering, End-user development, Software projects, Construction of models, Collaboration management of teams, Design patterns, Development process, Software process reference models	Analysis and verification of requirements, Discussion and solution knowledge graph, Requirements diagrams in SysML, Web pages and navigational links, Semantic visualization, Transition systems, Members and interactions, Representation of patterns, Concept map, Ontology	Collaborative learning, Comprehensibility of requirements, Understanding software systems and software behavior, Visualizing group learning, Use and apply of patterns, Usability of an API, Comprehension of code, Teaching/learning process references models

The first group of papers is focused on traditional software processes, as software life cycles or iterative models. The learning in these models is achieved through constructivist techniques, problem based learning, games and simulations, and E-learning. For this group, there were not found applications that used knowledge graphs.

In the second group of papers are discussed specific software engineering practices, using models of social psychology, such as the Technology Acceptance Model (TAM) and the Theory of Planned Behavior. For this group, there were not used knowledge graphs to model the knowledge of software process.

In the third group of papers, the focus is on software processes oriented to small businesses and in the use of agile processes. The process approach for learning is based on artifacts, templates, experiences and knowledge repositories. Modeling of processes by using knowledge graphs was not applied.

The fourth group of papers contain process models oriented to software engineering processes curricula. Their learning is based on projects and problems solution. These processes curricula do not use knowledge graphs.

In the fifth group of papers, there is some use of knowledge graphs oriented to query, extraction, summarization and identification. This group is not oriented to software process learning.

In the sixth group of papers, the target is on finding and exploring knowledge graphs, emphasizing on sub-graphs for querying, also, on finding answer sub-graphs based on exploration and search. This group is not oriented to software process learning.

In the seventh group of papers, there can be found techniques for active learning, unsupervised learning and fuzzy rules for extraction; as well as, relations detection, categorization of documents and concept maps. This group is not focused on software processes.

The Eighth group of papers, there can be found some concept maps and models of decision in knowledge graphs, for specific software systems, such as personal health systems and life sciences and health. This group does not include aspects of learning.

The ninth group of papers integrate the three aspects in the discussion level and solution knowledge graphs applied to: airborne software or modeling conditions, requirements, software projects, models, patterns and process reference models using cooperative learning, understanding and teaching software process .

These groups of papers specify a set of factors, which must include a framework, to assess the knowledge of SPICE process, therefore, it has been found, that the most appropriated groups for the focus of this paper would be number 5, 6, 7, 8 and 9; having:

- Knowledge extraction process of IT workers: The framework must be able to extract (group 5) current knowledge of the IT workers about the SPICE process that applies to their organization.
- SPICE standard knowledge modeling process by extracting information (group 5) and querying organizational knowledge repository, by using search graphs (groups 6 and 7).
- Matching process of the standard SPICE graph and the user graph to determine strengths and weaknesses of user learning (groups 8 and 9).

Since the first four groups are not applied in determining factors, because they are related to general software development processes, and they do not use knowledge graphs, they are not suitable for the purposes of this paper.

5 Framework

The proposed framework (Fig. 2) presents the mechanisms to help improving the learning of the ISO/IEC 15504 model. This proposal would support organizations have a mechanism to determine IT workers' knowledge capability on the SPI model.

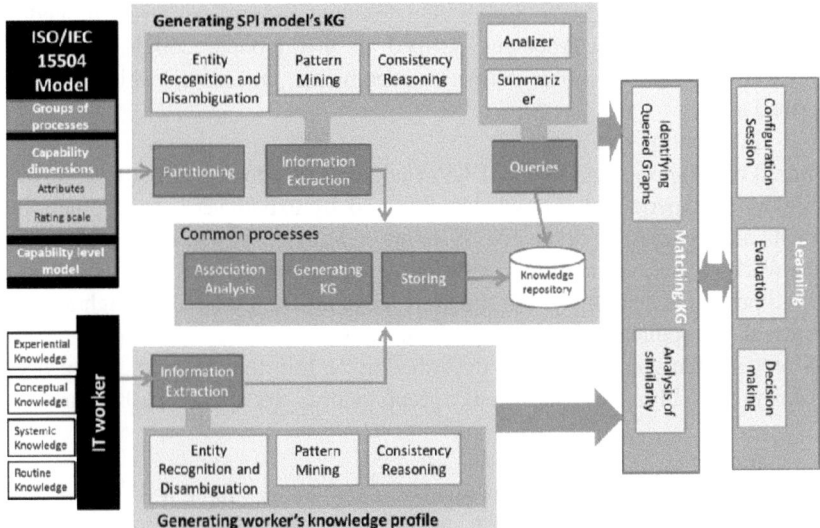

Fig. 2. A framework for supporting the learning of SPICE

This framework is composed by three modules, as explained below:

a. Generating a SPI model's knowledge graph

Information is extracted from the SPI standard and a knowledge graph is generated, with nodes representing entities, such as concepts and terms, and edges representing the semantic relations between them. The processes defined in this module are:

- Information Extraction

This process aims at gathering entities and relationships, from the SPI standard. Based on [63], some of the techniques considered to carry out this process include: 1) Entity Recognition and Disambiguation: filtering noisy sentences and obtaining typed entities; 2) Pattern Mining: identifying patterns from compiled sentences and used for filtering relationships; and 3) Consistency Reasoning: setting consistency between sentences and avoiding exclusions.

- Partitioning

A filtering activity makes a previous segmentation on the ISO 15504 document before extracting information in order to generate its knowledge graph according to a topic or domain defined.

- Queries

Queries can be formulated over the SPI model's knowledge graph. This process includes an analyzer, to discard irrelevant information, when discovering information results. Subsets of graphs returned are in order to make easy the interpretation and understanding of results.

b. Generating worker's knowledge profile

The focus of this module is on building a worker's profile about the acquired knowledge and the learning on any domain of the SPI model. As a result, it is generated a knowledge graph, which contains the concepts and terms related to the assessed domain. The processes defined in this module comprise Information Extraction, especially, those defined as common processes, which are briefly described as:

- Information Extraction

Based on [44], the categories of knowledge assets adopted to define the worker's profile were: experiential (knowledge acquired by experience), conceptual (mainly concepts and processes perceived), systemic (addressed as documentation generated by the worker), and routine (know-how and working practices carried out day-to-day). They all provide a clear insight of the knowledge profile gathered through answers, in response to the application of forms and questionnaires.

Moreover, the same techniques described in the Information Extraction process, of the Generating SPI model's knowledge graph module, are applied in this part.

c. Matching knowledge graphs

Once the worker's profile is generated as a knowledge graph, it is compared to the SPICE knowledge graph, in order to determine the degree of similarities and differences between both of them. This analysis is carried out under specific topics previously determined, in order to perform an analysis within the same semantic context. The processes considered are:

- Identifying Queried Graphs

The degree of matching is identified between the worker's knowledge graph and the one obtained from the ISO 15504 model. Mechanisms of searching sub-graphs are executed to determine similarities and differences between them based on the level of alignment of their semantic spaces.

- Analysis of similarity

Isomorphism techniques based on [9] are applied on the graphs, following the filtering and verification stages. The transformation of the analysis of entities is considered to obtain result graphs, being weights assigned to nodes and relationships. A summary graph is obtained, which preserves the semantic content of matching.

d. Analysis of learning

This module comprises the learning process followed by the IT worker, in order to achieve learning goals. The processes considered are:

- Configuration session

  A session defines the topic to be evaluated, the goals to be achieved by the IT worker and the questions to be answered. Different difficulty levels are associated to the questions according to the complexity of the analyzed knowledge domain.

- Evaluation
  Based on the matching results, this process establishes the relation between the results that were accomplished with those that were expected. As a result, it is possible to determine the strengths and weaknesses in the learning process.
- Decision making
  Taking the evaluation results, it is determined either what aspects of the SPI model need to be reinforced or what aspects are plenty learned.

As common process between both modules, we have:

- Association Analysis

This process analyzes the belonging and association, between entities by using relations. Triplets in the form of <relation_name, entity_name#1, entity_name#2> represent the graph, which must be properly evaluated to determine consistent relations and discard unnecessary information.

- Generating Knowledge Graph

A semantic space is represented by a knowledge graph. The ISO 15504 model concepts are encoded, where a node is created for each entity, based on the defined domain of the SPI document, and edges according to the semantic meaning. The attributes can be assigned both to nodes and edges, to properly enrich the graph.

- Storing

This process stores the extracted knowledge into a graph database, which is a knowledge repository based on semantic web. Graphs are stores through nodes and relations, being considered different kinds of these elements.

6 Validation

A first validation on the proposed framework was carried out, where a short course about the ISO15504 process was developed for a group of 37 students of the Software Engineering course. A kind of process learning evaluation was developed, which consisted of 25 questions about the Engineering process category of the model.

From student responses, knowledge graphs were generated on the learned process, and then they were compared to the ISO15504 knowledge graph, to evaluate the degree of learning on Engineering process category.

Table 3 shows learning outcomes obtained by the group of students in each of the engineering sub process. The scores are showed in scale of 0 to 100.

The processes with the highest score were: Development process and System and software maintenance process. These scores describe that concepts involved in these processes are high-level and easy to learn.´

The processes with the lowest score were: System requirements analysis and design process and Software requirements analysis process. The students had difficulty differentiating between system requirements analysis and software requirements analysis. In addition, they were unable to identify which process the system architecture belongs to.

Table 3. Learning on Engineering process category.

Process	Average	Standard deviation
Development process	75,67	15,13
System requirements analysis and design process	44,59	13,38
Software requirements analysis process	37,83	22,93
Software design process	54,05	10,0
Software construction process	49,54	10,0
Software integration process	54,05	1,0
Software testing process	60,81	1,0
System integration and testing process	54,05	1,0
System and software maintenance process	63,78	2,0

The processes: Software design, Software integration and System integration and testing process had the same score. The students know well the processes purpose but had trouble identifying the results of process implementation.

7 Conclusions and Future Researches

This paper describes a general framework, to establish the first step towards determining IT workers' knowledge capability on a SPI model, through the analysis of knowledge graphs. This proposal aims to contribute with learning of ISO 15504, as an important standard on developing software process. The framework includes modules to extract information from IT workers and the SPI model, and generate knowledge graphs to be compared and analyzed to determine the degree of learning about a predefined topic.

We conducted a proposal based on the reviewed literature, which was searched on important databases, containing most of the scientific production in the field of interest. According to the searching results, papers including research about SPI models learning using knowledge graphs were not found. Instead, their focus was mainly on querying knowledge graphs, analysis of associations between graph components, structuring and summarizing of graphs, having uncertainty in knowledge graphs, generation of graphs, and several other approaches to strengthen teaching software process.

For future works, our research will be extended towards a more detailed validation of the framework, by people working in the IT field, developing software and applying the ISO 15504 standard.

We believe that this approach assists to carefully construct the individual knowledge more quickly. Although knowledge graphs could be powerful as a tool to learn on exploratory search, they cannot replace the document search [39]. Hence, interconnections between the document of the standard and the graphs, should be considered as an extension to this framework.

Acknowledgements. The authors would like to thank ILIIET (Latin-American Institute of Innovation, Research and Technological Studies) and Web Applications and Tools research group of the Universidad Nacional de Colombia, for their support on this research.

References

1. Fuggetta, A.: Software Process: A Roadmap. In: 22nd International Conference on Software, Engineering (ICSE 2000), Future of Software. Engineering Track, Limerick, Irlanda. ACM (2000)
2. Florac, W., Park, R. Carleton, A.: Practical Software Measurement: Measuring for Process Management and Improvement, SEI Software Engineering Institute, Carnegie Mellon University, CMU/SEI-97-HB-003, Pittsburgh (1997)
3. IEEE Computer Society: SWEBOK, Guide to the Software Engineering Body of Knowledge (2004)
4. Huang, S.T., et al.: ADDIE Instruction Design and Cognitive Apprenticeship for Project-based Software Engineering Education in MIS, pp. 652–662. APSEC, IEEE Computer Society (2005)
5. Burnstein, I.: Practical software testing: A process-oriented approach, pp. 503–536. Springer Professional Computing, USA (2003)
6. Lyytinen, K., Robey, D.: Learning Failure in Information Systems Development. Information Systems Journal **9**, 85–101 (1999)
7. ISO/IEC 15504-1:2004, Information technology — Process assessment — Part 1: Concepts and vocabulary, ISO/IEC JTC1 (2004)
8. Jayara, N. et al.: Towards a Query-by-Example System for Knowledge Graphs. In: GRADES 2014 Proceedings of Workshop on Graph Data Management Experiences and Systems, pp. 1–6 (2014)
9. Zheng, W. et al.: Efficient Subgraph Skyline Search Over Large Graphs. In: CIKM 2014, Proceedings of the 23rd ACM International Conference on Conference on Information and Knowledge Management, pp. 1529–1538 (2014)
10. Auer, S. et al.: DBpedia: A nucleus for a Web of open data, In: ISWC (2007)
11. Suchanek, F.M., et al.: YAGO: a core of semantic knowledge unifying WordNet and Wikipedia. In: WWW (2007)
12. Wu, W., et al.: Probase: a probabilistic taxonomy for text understanding. In: SIGMOD, pp. 481–492 (2012)
13. Bollacker, K. et al.: Freebase: a collaboratively created graph database for structuring human knowledge. In: SIGMOD, pp. 1247–1250 (2008)
14. Kitchenham, B.: A. Guidelines for performing Systematic Literature Reviews in Software Engineering (2007)
15. Huang, S.T., et al.: ADDIE Instruction Design and Cognitive Apprenticeship for Project-based Software Education in MIS. In: Proceedings of APSEC2005, pp. 652–662. IEEE CS Press (2005)
16. Oh Navarro, E.: Design and Evaluation of an Educational Software Process Simulation Environment and Associated Model. In: 18th Conference on Software Engineering Education & Training, pp. 25–32 (2005)
17. Kuhrmann, M. et al.: Teaching software process modeling. In: ICSE 2013 Proceedings of the 2013 International Conference on Software Engineering, pp. 1138–1147 (2013)
18. Srinivasan, J., Lundqvist, K.: A Constructivist Approach to Teaching Software Processes. In: 29th International Conference on Software Engineering (2007)

19. Hogan, J.M. et al.: Tight spirals and industry clients: the modern SE education experience. In: ACE 2005 Proceedings of the 7th Australasian conference on Computing education, vol. 42, pp. 217–222 (2005)
20. Messnarz, R., et al.: SPICE Level 3 - Experience with Using E-Learning to Coach the Use of Standard System Design Best Practices in Projects. Systems, Software and Services Process Improvement, Communications in Computer and Information Science **99**, 213–221 (2010)
21. Monsalve, E.S. et al.: Teaching software engineering with SimulES-W. In: 24th IEEE-CS Conference on Software Engineering Education and Training (CSEE&T), pp. 31–40 (2011)
22. Singer, L. et al.: Influencing the adoption of software engineering methods using social software. In: 34th International Conference on Software Engineering (ICSE), pp. 1325–1328. IEEE (2012)
23. Umarji, M., Seaman, C.: Predicting acceptance of Software Process Improvement. In: Proceeding HSSE 2005 Proceedings of the 2005 Workshop on Human and Social Factors of Software Engineering, vol. 30(4), pp. 1–6 (2005)
24. Robillard, P.N.: The learning component in social software engineering. In: SSE 2011 Proceedings of the 4th International Workshop on Social Software Engineering, pp. 19–22 (2011)
25. Cruz, R., et al.: Supporting the Software Process Improvement in Very Small Entities through E-learning: The HEPALE! Project, pp. 221–231. IEEE Computer Society, ENC (2009)
26. Rong, G. et al.: Where does experience matter in software process education? An experience report. In: IEEE 27th Conference on Software Engineering Education and Training (CSEE&T), pp. 129–138 (2014)
27. Amescua, A., et al.: Knowledge repository to improve agile development processes learning. IET Software **4**(6), 434–444 (2010)
28. Tian, K. et al.: Improving Software Engineering Education through Enhanced Practical Experiences. In: IEEE/ACIS 10th International Conference on Computer and Information Science (ICIS), pp. 292–297 (2011)
29. Moreno, A.M., et al.: Process Improvement from an Academic Perspective: How Could Software Engineering Education Contribute to CMMI Practices? IEEE Software **31**(4), 91–97 (2014)
30. Desarkar, M.S., et al.: Med-Tree: A user knowledge graph framework for medical applications. In: IEEE 13th International Conference on Bioinformatics and Bioengineering (BIBE), pp. 1–4 (2013)
31. Corby, O., Zucker, F.C.: The KGRAM Abstract Machine for Knowledge Graph Querying. In: IEEE/WIC/ACM International Conference on Web Intelligence and Intelligent Agent Technology (WI-IAT), vol. 1, pp. 338–341 (2010)
32. Hulliyah, K. & Kusuma, H.T.: Application of knowledge graph for making Text Summarization (Analizing a text of educational issues). In: International Conference on Information and Communication Technology for the Muslim World (ICT4M), pp. E79–E83 (2010)
33. Jayara, N. et al.: Towards a Query-by-Example System for Knowledge Graphs. In: GRADES 2014, Proceedings of Workshop on GRAph Data management Experiences and Systems, pp. 1–6 (2014)
34. Yang, S. et al.: SLQ: a user-friendly graph querying system. In: SIGMOD 2014 Proceedings of the 2014 ACM SIGMOD International Conference on Management of Data, pp. 893–896 (2014)

35. Genest, D., Chein, M.: A content-search information retrieval process based on conceptual graphs. Knowledge and Information Systems **8**(3), 292–309 (2005)
36. Wu, Y., et al.: Summarizing answer graphs induced by keyword queries. Proceedings of the VLDB Endowment VLDB Endowment Hompage archive **6**(14), 1774–1785 (2013)
37. Kaufmann, M., Wilke, G., Portmann, E., Hinkelmann, K.: Combining bottom-up and top-down generation of interactive knowledge maps for enterprise search. In: Buchmann, R., Kifor, C.V., Yu, J. (eds.) KSEM 2014. LNCS, vol. 8793, pp. 186–197. Springer, Heidelberg (2014)
38. Bairi, R. B. et al.: Personalized classifiers: evolving a classifier from a large reference knowledge graph. In: IDEAS 2014, Proceedings of the 18th International Database Engineering & Applications Symposium, pp. 132–141 (2014)
39. Xin, W. et al.: A novel approach to concepts via knowledge graph theory and AFS theory. In: International Conference on Intelligent Control and Information Processing (ICICIP), pp. 87–92 (2010)
40. Hakkani-Tur, D. et al.: Using a knowledge graph and query click logs for unsupervised learning of relation detection. In: IEEE International Conference on Acoustics, Speech and Signal Processing (ICASSP), pp. 8327–8331 (2013)
41. Lopes, S. et al.: Making Concept Maps Available on the Web to the Students. In: Computers and Education, pp 179–188 (2008)
42. Gurupur, V.P., et al.: Semantic requirements sharing approach to develop software systems using concept maps and information entropy: A Personal Health Information System example. Advances in Engineering Software **70**, 25–35 (2014)
43. Zimmermann, O., et al.: Managing architectural decision models with dependency relations, integrity constraints, and production rules. Journal of Systems and Software **82**(8), 1249–1267 (2009)
44. Ernst, P., et al.: KnowLife: A knowledge graph for health and life sciences. In: IEEE 30th International Conference on Data Engineering (ICDE), pp. 1254–1257 (2014)
45. Bracewell, R., et al.: Capturing design rationale. Computer-Aided Design **41**(3), 173–186 (2009)
46. Hasegawa, R., et al.: Extracting Conceptual Graphs from Japanese Documents for Software Requirements Modeling. In: Proc. Sixth Asia-Pacific Conference on Conceptual Modelling (APCCM 2009), Wellington, New Zealand, pp. 87–96 (2009)
47. Di Maio, P.: 'Just enough' ontology engineering. In: Proc. International Conference on Web Intelligence, Mining and Semantics, WIMS 2011, pp. 8:1–8:10 (2011)
48. Wegeler, T., et al.: Evaluating the benefits of using domain-specific modeling languages: an experience report. In: Proc. 2013 ACM Workshop on Domain-Specific Modeling, pp. 7–12 (2013)
49. Karla, P.R., Gurupur, V.P.: C-PHIS: A Concept Map-Based Knowledge Base Framework to Develop Personal Health Information Systems. Journal of Medical System **37**, 9970 (2013)
50. Prabhakar, T.V., Kumar, K.: Design Decision Topology Model for Pattern Relationship Analysis. In: Asian PLOP 2010 Tokyo, pp. 16–17 (2010)
51. Wu, W. et al.: Formal Modeling of Airborne Software High-Level Requirements Based on Knowledge Graph. In: Buchmann, R., Kifor, C.V., Yu, J. (eds.) KSEM 2014. LNCS(LNAI), vol. 8793, Springer, Heidelberg, pp. 258–269 (2014)
52. Kakehi, M. et al.: Organization of Discussion Knowledge Graph from Collaborative Learning Record. In: Apolloni, B., Howlett, R.J. Jain, L. (eds.) KES 2007/WIRN 2007, Part III, LNCS(LNAI), vol. 4694, pp. 600–607. Springer, Heidelberg (2007)

53. Watanabe, Y. et al.: Organization of Solution Knowledge Graph from Collaborative Learning Records. In: Velásquez, J.D., Ríos, S.A., Howlett, R.J., Jain, L.C. (eds.) KES 2009, Part II. LNCS(LNAI), vol. 5712, pp. 564–571. Springer, Heidelberg (2009)
54. Scaniello, G. et al.: On the Effect of Using SysML Requirement Diagrams to Comprehend Requirements: Results from two controlled experiments. In: 18th International Conference on Evaluation and Assessment in Software Engineering, vol. 1, pp. 433–442 (2014)
55. Deufemia, V., et al.: Visually modelling data intensive web applications to assist end-user development. In: Proc. 6th International Symposium on Visual Information Communication and Interaction, pp. 17–26 (2013)
56. Kapec, P.: Visualizing software artifacts using hypergraphs. In: Proc. 26th Spring Conference on Computer Graphics, pp. 27–32 (2010)
57. Ploeger, B., Tankink, C.: Improving an Interactive Visualization of Transition Systems. In: Proc. 4th ACM Symposium on Software Visualization 2008, pp. 115–124. ACM (2008)
58. Kay, J., et al.: Visualisations for team learning: small teams working on long-term projects. In: Proc. 8th International Conference on Computer Supported Collaborative Learning, pp. 354–356 (2007)
59. Díaz, P., et al.: Visual representation of web design patterns for end-users. In: AVI 2008, Proc. Working Conference on Advanced Visual Interfaces, pp. 408–411 (2008)
60. Gerken, J., et al.: The concept maps method as a tool to evaluate the usability of APIs. In: Proc. SIGCHI Conference on Human Factors in Computing Systems, pp. 3373–3382 (2011)
61. Zhou, H., et al.: Developing Application Specific Ontology for Program Comprehension by Combining Domain Ontology with Code Ontology, Software Technol. Res. Lab., Montfort Univ., Leicester Quality Software (2008)
62. Espinosa-Curiel, I.E., et al.: Graphical Technique to Support the Teaching/Learning Process of Software Process Reference Models. In: Riel, A., O'Connor, R., Tichkiewitch, S., Messnarz, R. (eds.) EuroSPI 2010. CCIS, vol. 99, pp 13–24. Springer, Heidelberg (2010)
63. Chou, S.W., Young He, M.: Facilitating knowledge creation by knowledge assets. In: Proceedings of HICSS 37, p. 10. IEEE Computer Society (2004)

Towards a Serious Game to Teach ISO/IEC 12207 Software Lifecycle Process: An Interactive Learning Approach

Ufuk Aydan[1,2](✉), Murat Yilmaz[1,2], and Rory V. O'Connor[3]

[1] Game Research & Development Laboratory, Çankaya University, Ankara, Turkey
[2] Department of Computer Engineering, Çankaya University, Ankara, Turkey
aydanufuk@gmail.com, myilmaz@cankaya.edu.tr
[3] School of Computing, Dublin City University, Dublin, Ireland
roconnor@computing.dcu.ie

Abstract. ISO/IEC 12207 training is a key element to provide an ability to software development organizations for selecting a set of required processes, measuring the performance of these processes, and continuously improving them. Traditionally, such training is either performed by an expert individual to the software quality management personnel most likely in form of a seminar in a classroom environment. This may also be given by a qualified professional, such as a registered auditor. However, software requirements are usually subject to change, and therefore such training is not enough to teach the substantial details of the entire standard. This has led to increased reports of complications, which demotivates organization to use this standard. To improve the quality of traditional training, a 3D serious game was proposed. The preliminary idea here is that the training is utilized as a game that employs 3D office landscape to provide a realistic virtual environment for ensuring that the training will be based in a real-world-like environment. Before building a prototype for our serious game, we consulted five industrial experts whose works are related with ISO standards. To give these practitioners an opportunity to explore the conceptual design and raise some potential problems, the semi-structured interview method was used. Based on the suggestions of experts, proposed model of the serious game were revised. Taken together, initial results suggest that a serious game for teaching ISO/IEC 12207 should be useful for individuals who are interested in learning more about the standard.

1 Introduction

ISO/IEC 12207 is an international software engineering standard that defines the software engineering processes and activities, which are associated with software life cycle process from conception to the end of product [1]. This standard defines a set of suitable roles for software practitioners and follows the plan-do-check-act cycle for improving the quality of the product [2].

ISO/IEC 12207 is based on *the qualitative definitions of the processes*, and therefore there are no implementation details of defined the tasks and activities [3]. Moreover, it does not measure the quality, it does not define specifically how to do activities and tasks, and it does not prescribe to specific methods, practices or tools. Its modular structure is suitable for tailoring. Therefore, an organization can customize the necessary parts of the standard that are planned to be used based on the requirements of a software project [4]. Because of the high modularity of the standard, it is more easily to deal with factors that are affecting the software development such as complexity, schedule, cost, etc. In addition to that ISO/IEC 12207 can act as an *inventory* of processes, which give different perspectives to specific parts of the software life cycle process. These processes are categorized as organizational processes (i.e. management, infrastructure, improvement, training), supporting processes (i.e. documentation, configuration management, quality assurance, verification, validation, joint review, audit, problem resolution), and primary processes (i.e. acquisition, supply, development, operation, maintenance) [5].

ISO/IEC 12207 is a guideline based on a set of process descriptions for providing a base for adopting a role, which defines a set of constraints for selecting process, activities or tasks that are required for software development. The standard proposes a set of views that can be used to label the processes connected to a role. To this end, it offers five different viewpoints as follows: (i) contract, (ii) engineering, (iii) operating, (iv) quality management, and (v) management views [4]. Firstly, there is a contract view that includes an acquisition process (i.e. for the acquirer) and supply process (i.e. for the supplier). Secondly, there is an engineering view which has a development process for product development and a maintenance process for upkeeping the software. Thirdly, the operating view with the operation process that provides a guideline for operating the software. Fourthly, a quality management view that has six processes; (i) joint review, audit, verification, validation, quality, and problem resolution processes [4]. ISO/IEC 12207 Software Lifecycle processes can be maintained by 7 main phases by any organization which have capability to support the standard's views and ability to handle software engineering requirements. These main phases are; (i) requirements analysis, (ii) specification, (iii) design, (iv) coding, (v) verification & validation, (vi) installation, (vii) maintenance & support [6].

Despite the fact that ISO/IEC 12207 is a well-structured and detailed technical text on a complex subject, many professionals find it difficult to gain substantial information regarding to the standard. Games are found to be effective learning tools especially for teaching complex subjects. In particular, serious games are a kind of interactive computer application (i.e. computer simulations of real-life situations or processes) designed for educational purposes. As a serious game is designed to include an educational aspect [7], the learners can be challenged with possible scenarios that may found similar to a real-world problem. However, a well-designed serious game should include game playing and a set of serious aspects (e.g. teaching, learning, communication, information, etc.) where such combination should be based on an utilitarian goals [8]. In fact, this scenario should be aligned with gaming objectives that implements the dramatic elements of a game such as story, sound, rules, graphics, etc.

In light of this remarks, the goal of the study is to investigate the possibilities of a game that is designed for teaching the primary concepts of ISO/IEC 12207. The rest of the paper is organized as follows. Section 2 presents the background of the study. It details of the ISO/IEC 12207 standard and the notion of serious games. Section 3 includes a discussion about the customization of the standard. Further, it details the applications of serious games in software engineering. Next, we discuss the tentative plans for an ideal game. Lastly, paper concludes with conclusion and future work.

2 Background

2.1 ISO/IEC 12207

Similar to the definition of ISO/IEC 12207, definition a software life cycle starts with a requirement analysis based on a need and eventually the life cycle ends with the retirement of a product [9]. The standard has an architecture, which is built by set of interrelated processes, which are consequent to modularity and responsibility. While defining modularity under the conceptualization of the standard is about being unique with every processes and availability of being capable enough to handle all types of projects. The processes that are designed for the standard have a modular structure. From the practical point of view, the modules have the maximum cohesion and minimum coupling where each process supports unique functionalities as possible [5]. To clarify every part which is associated with the life cycle has specific and well defined responsibility to take care. However, from a traditional point of view, the modules of a life cycle should be studied distinctively.

To understand the basics of the standard, the definition of organization and party should also be elaborated. The terms organization and part are required to highlight different viewpoints that can be acquired using the standard. The term organization defines a group of persons (or authorities) with a set of responsibilities who are organized for a particular objective. However, the party defines an organization that enters into a contract, which can be either from an organization or more. The name that is given to a part is usually correlates with the name of the process it performs (e.g. an acquirer is involved with the acquisition process). There are several roles, which can be directly related with the process names from the standard such as acquirer, supplier, implementer, maintainer, and operator, etc [6].

The ISO/IEC 12207 processes can be organized into three main categories: primary processes; supporting processes; and organizational processes (see Figure 1).

Primary processes described by the standard are (i) acquisition, (ii) supply processes, (iii) development processes, (iv) operation processes, and (v) maintenance processes. The goal of a supporting process is to support other processes

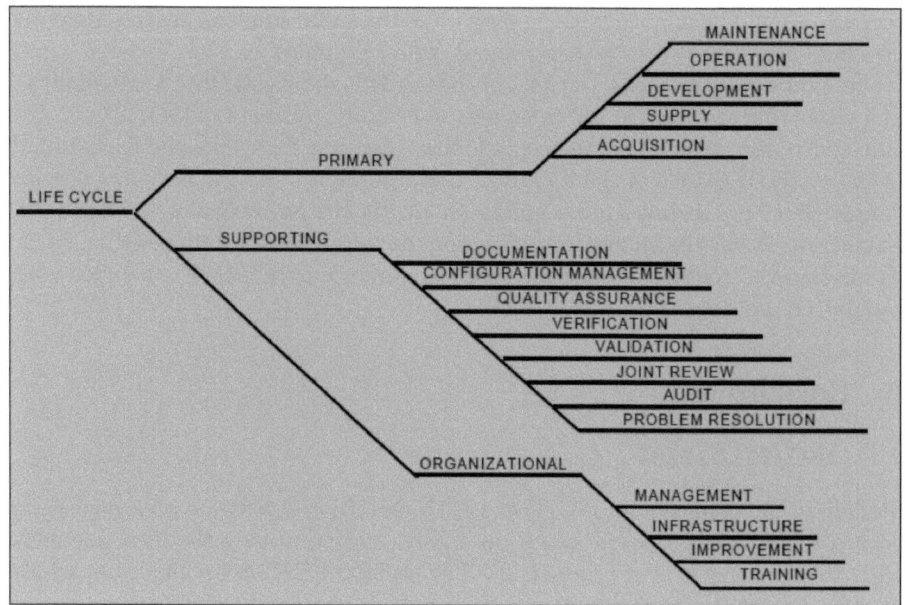

Fig. 1. The Life Cycle Processes of ISO/IEC 12207 [5]

while fulfilling a function. The supporting processes are identified as (i) documentation processes, (ii) configuration management processes, (iii) quality assurance processes, (iv) joint review processes, (v) audit processes, (vi) verification processes, (vii) validation processes, and (viii) problem resolution processes. The organization processes are employed by an organization to manage, control and improve the life cycle processes.

There are seven process groups that are defined by ISO/IEC 12207 which can be accomplished during the life cycle of a software system. Each of the life cycle processes within those groups can be defined with respect to its goals and expected outcomes. Figure 2 shows the activities and tasks that should be carry out to accomplish these outcomes [6].

(a) Agreement Processes (two processes) (subclauses 5.2.2.1.1 and 6.1)
(b) Organizational Project-Enabling Processes (five processes) (subclauses 5.2.2.1.2 and 6.2)
(c) Project Processes (seven processes) (subclauses 5.2.2.1.3 and 6.3)
(d) Technical Processes (eleven processes) (subclauses 5.2.2.1.4 and 6.4)
(e) Software Implementation Processes (seven processes) (subclauses 5.2.2.2.1and 7.1)
(f) Software Support Processes (eight processes) (subclauses 5.2.2.2.2 and 7.2)
(g) Software Reuse Processes (three processes) (subclauses 5.2.2.2.3 and 7.3).

Basically, the design of ISO/IEC 12207 software life cycle process was constituted with a set of complementary components [6]. For instance, each process has

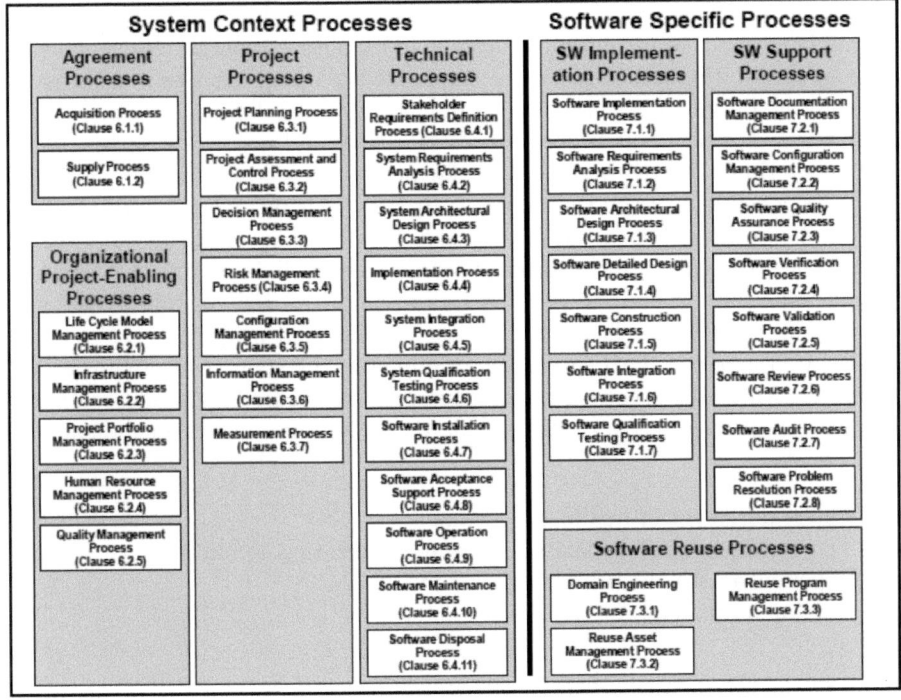

Fig. 2. Life Cycle Process Groups [6]

its own activities that cover cohesive tasks where tasks have necessary actions [5]. A task takes several type of inputs (e.g. data, information) and generate outputs (e.g. data, information). A set of verbs such as *will* (for declaration of purpose), *shall* (for binding provision), *should* (for recommendation) is used to express requirements, recommendations or acceptable actions.

The standard utilizes the fundamentals of quality management techniques which are the integral and indispensable parts of the total life cycle. Therefore, each process is a basic implementation of plan-do-check-act (PDCA) cycle. To implement ISO/IEC 12207 properly, it is important to know that each process and individuals who are in charge of related processes must be aware of their particular roles and responsibilities in all processes. Based on the assigned roles, evaluations of particular tasks have to be carried out properly within the software development organization [10].

ISO/IEC 12207 requires outputs and these outputs have to be documented, but there is no specific or predefined format for any types of output to be documented. The organization can use their documentation methods also get benefit from standards. In addition to documentation base-lining is important issue. The standard requires the baselines of software related tasks and activities such as software requirements, software design, and coding. Baselining is a process in which quality and effectiveness of a method assessed by comparing before and after a change. The idea of *baselining* can be considered as an effective method to mitigate risks that establish certainty in milestones, to control costs and deadlines by prohibiting unnecessary (i.e. unplanned or open) changes in all parts of the software development life cycle [5]. In particular, baselining can happen while joint review (or an audit process) so as to clarify and acquirer-supplier understandings. However, it is not necessary for projects to perform baselining, which is the responsibility of the Development Process. It is not related with Configuration Management Process and it is not a must. Consequently, ISO/IEC 12207 covers the total software development life cycle and it is relatively a complex process especially when it is based on a viewpoint of variety of stakeholders who are working together in the same software development project.

However, the standard should be examined in the context of organizational objectives where the requirements of a project may hinder a solid interpretation. To avoid improper usage of the standard, these prerequisites below shall be met [5]:

(a) The requirement of qualified personnel;
(b) The requirement of understanding the organization's policies;
(c) Experience with the project's environment;
(d) Develop an understanding of the standard.

2.2 Customization of ISO/IEC 12207

Although ISO/IEC 12207 software lifecycle standard shows a set of agreements of experts on some procedures for software development, there is no one-size-fits-all type of selection and tailoring of processes. However, the responsibilities of both acquirer and supplier are considerably important in the tailoring process. According to the *acquisition process* defined by ISO/IEC 12207, *"success of the supplier depends largely on explicit definition of the acquirer's expectations, in terms of system requirements and with respect to the software development process"* [11].

There is a common point of view to the quality of any software product largely depends on the quality of the software development process [12]. In fact, all successful companies in any size should follow well-defined activities and tasks. Another factor that increase the success of further development and reduce the current project's problems is receiving adequate feedback from both user and prior projects. To accomplish these factors and to improve the development process, companies should invest on software process improvement activities, however a number of companies still rely on the success of the employment of ad-hoc processes, which relies on individual's skills. Such processes are very difficult to reuse. In addition, they may have an adverse effect on the quality, maintainability, cost of a product [11]. Moreover, too many reasons can be stated for a failure of process because of the absence of enough knowledge, lack of customer feedback and market related problems.

To overcome risks, problems, and inadequate development process and to improve the quality, there is a strong need to follow some standardized methods.

Due to these reasons ISO/IEC 12207 is one of the recent and valid to use standard that includes the steps that should be followed by contractors. Tailoring process shows itself here more clearly at the acquisition process and acquirer has a chance to tailor ISO/IEC 12207. This process is totally good for providing guidance for quality related activities by mitigating risks and ultimately crucial to project success. Under tailoring circumstances such as novelty, size, budget, risks, technology, time etc. shall be inspected.

3 Concept of Serious Games and Examples

A serious game is an interactive approach, which is designed for a purpose other than pure entertainment [13]. A goal of a serious game is usually improving an educational aspect where participants certainly attend such activities with such an expectation. These interactive application are widely preferred in training and education for medical and military personnel. Recently, serious games become more popular and therefore they are now found in any size, complexity and platform similar to casual games. The education aspects of these interactive applications are heavily depend on the notion of play which is an important factor for individuals development and learning [7].

In addition, serious games are kind of simulations of real-world events or processes that are addressed to comprise particular problems. Therefore, they can be considered as serious activities such as exploring, training or advertising. However, they still can be entertaining, if their main purpose covers game elements well. Substantially, games have many attributes which have been seen in the case of different examples. For instance, serious games allow user to experience different learning tasks by using the elements of fun. Another example of attributes is stating how actions affect the context. Players can create artifacts or complete tasks within in the orders of a serious game serves and without the effects of real world problems and stress. This can be interpreted to resembling sand box type games. Moreover, serious games allow users have an active participation while accomplishing the main goal. In fact, games are powerful tools, because they have the ability to change human behavior [14]. Furthermore, games can help users with repetitive actions while learning certain subjects. Because particular tasks and clearly stated objectives of serious games make player easier to follow certain pathways and play their role for a set of planned behaviors. Such planned behaviors can be easily linked to the learning process where gaming may assist and ultimately create a user-oriented learning experience.

There are numerous works which are related about serious games and applications. However in the literature there are only several serious games which are related to software project management. These are; Problems and Programmers [15], SIMSOFT [16], SimSE [17], SESAM [18], DELIVER [19], ProDec [20].

Problems and Programmers [15], is an educational (serious) card game, which simulates several software engineering processes. It is designed as a teaching tool to improve the students' understanding of the software processes. The goal is to teach software processes and issues that are encountered in software development, which may not sufficiently highlighted by software engineering lectures and projects. Among computer based digital variants of serious games, Problems and Programmers is created as a non-digital card game where two or more player are trying to finish a software project. By using the benefits of card games, the game state and action of the players are always visible. The game is designed as a competitive game where participants may have a chance to learn from each other [21]. These attributes strengthen the main goal of the game and reveal the games powerful sides such as (i) covering proper use of software engineering techniques, (ii) providing clear and instant feedback of players choices and decisions towards phases, and (iii) encouraging interactions among different players and evaluating their perspectives. According to Baker, *"Because different players follow different strategies, more than one strategy is exposed per game. This allows players to not only evaluate their own strategy but to also discuss and compare strategies followed by others. As a result, players learn from each other, which enhances the educational value of Problems and Programmers"* [21].

SimSE [17] is a single player serious game that is design to software engineering in an interactive (graphical) environment. The participants take on the role of a project manager who is responsible from a team of software developers. The game allows players to manage the software engineering process by recruiting engineers, assign them to a set of tasks, monitor their progress and ultimately gain (virtual) experience on managing a software development project. A significant reason for creating educational software engineering applications is that during the courses, computer science and engineering students from are only exposed to the theoretical concepts of software engineering. There is no sufficient or relatively sufficient project which converts lectures into practices. SimSEs main goal is fulfilling this absence by providing 2D graphical virtual office where software engineering processes take place. This office scene includes many office staff such as computers, desks, employees, and artifacts. These approaches clarify the players' actions with the support of selection of the available moves and steps the player will proceed. Perhaps the most important feature of SimSE (among other variants) is that it has a model builder which allows user to create employees, artifacts, tools, projects, and customers without any need of programming skills. Bu using such a modeler, SimSE supports customization of the software processes based on real-world scenarios about software projects.

Project Decision (ProDec) is a simulation-based serious game created with the intention to train and assess students in software project management [20]. The main objective is to take advantage of the engaging nature of games to place the learners in a virtual organization where they can manage software projects and solve real-life problems in a risk-free environment [20]. The main goal of the game is to remain aware of planning, controlling, and managing a software project. The game is over to the extent permitted by the amount of budget the players have and allocated time for the project. While gameplay players need to plan to deal with obstacles which are created by unplanned events. ProDec is intended to be a collaborative game, that is, it is a game to be played by teams of players [20]. This means that the group of players works collaboratively to win the game not to compete among them [20]. After any game play, ProDec offers a complete report including the logs representing every decision the players made and the result of applying the assessment criteria provided by the trainer at the beginning of the game play [20].

Simsoft [16] is a kind of serious game which consists of two game boards, a printed board and a digital board. A printed board is used to gather participants to discuss the actual state of the game project and decide their strategies. The staff is represented by plastic counters while game chips as virtual money, which is used for resources such as project budget. The players make a set of meaningful decisions and spend their resources during the game. In addition to a printed board there is a digital game board which shows several game stats, player's history and reports. The goal is to complete a small software development project in a given set of time frame. The participants are grouped into small set of teams to manage the software development from start-up to final delivery [16]. The players have the opportunity to observe the difficulties of resource management where the skills of the hired personnel affects the outputs of a software project.

In addition, SESAM is a natural language based serious game which motivates players for learning software project management techniques. SESAM's environment consists of natural language interface, records about program and statistics about project. Lastly, DELIVER is another type of serious game which consists of a printed board. It helps students to develop controlling projects performances. Its main ambition is totally motivate students in their learning progression.

Defining a solution of improving the managerial skills in software project practitioners by using a game environment may somehow lead disagreement. Some researchers may claim that the concepts of software engineering could be hard to be thought by using a game system. However, Gee [22] suggest that *"good video games incorporate good learning principles, principles supported by current research in cognitive science."* In fact, a game may encourage the process of deep learning [23] in which participants may improve their thinking skills about a complex situation by becoming successful in a serious game. In other words, if a cycle of learning has a chance to improve itself in a more enjoyable way, the interaction process become easier to everyone. In particular, a goal of a serious game is to make people think that they can shorten their learning time in a complex topic by putting some effort into improving their skills in a video game.

4 Discussion on Planning the Ideal Game

Typical software engineering methods and principles are not quite easy to learn and implement because of the lack of motivation and absence of fine learning period in lectures. In addition to this, technical developments and evolving industry demands change rapidly and there is a need for learning broader concepts about software engineering and management tasks, rather than simply getting general knowledge that was given in every introductory level software engineering course. The problem is not simple as being only hard-to-learn. The main point is being unable to make easier to understandable for everyone either managerial or technical levels of software engineering topics in the market. Due to this no consistency of an adequate education there are too many projects have been struggling to go further.

Undoubtedly, getting the big picture of today's current circumstances and state of the software engineering and project management are difficult, but obvious thing is the failures and problems are becoming more visible for everyone to recognize. To reduce failures and problems there are crucial jobs which are waiting for project managers to accomplish. Because project management skills are the key factors which have potential to overcome risks in development environment, and this skills may lead the way of engineers, developers and even students who are the future responsible of life cycle of software. However, current view of project life cycles in any kind of software development implies that managerial skills need more practical experience to become mature enough to produce more stable projects with less risks and problems.

From the student side, this problem can be restated with similar reasons. Although being the future engineers and managers there are too many inconsistencies between market and syllabuses. In fact, software development organization desires to see better skills from university graduates while there is a lack of software engineering skills taught at university level [24]. Apparently, many software engineering concepts are given to students in a more theoretical sense. In contrast, this should be more practical with supporting projects which resemble to real life scenarios. Even they come together there is a need for in depth procedure to follow. Navarro et al. [24] states that *"In particular, lectures allow only passive learning, and the size and scope of class projects are too constrained by the academic setting to exhibit many of the fundamental characteristics of real-world software engineering processes [24]"*.

To deal with these problems one possible and feasible way is using serious games which is suitable for specific concept. Serious games are designed to teach especially educate players about desired topics in a well-defined environment [7].

To define the learning process in a clear sense, it can be repeated in any time without practicality, because in theoretical approach information is static not dynamic so there should be actions in several ways to change it to dynamic which helps to resolve the problem. No matter what the type is every game should clearly define some attributes while game play even before. This is more decisive when the serious gaming concept is under concern, because every player who is playing a serious game he/she ought to be conscious about what will he/she do, accomplish and learn. Desired commitment to the learning journey requires well defined and planned program. For instance without clearly defined characters or personalities in the game it is difficult to expect anyone to commit himself to a specific progress. Moreover the new virtual environment serves players living and acting with their commitment and this is the evident for most games success in any theme and ambition. In a software project development environment with a serious game it is necessary clarify exactly what are the characters, who are they, and what are the capabilities that they have. This clear sense is the primary factor for a player to commit himself in such an environment at first.

There is a degree of uncertainty around the terminology in being interactive with games. This shows a need to be explicit about exactly what is meant by the word interactive. Furthermore, this is more difficult for anyone at first to estimate the literal meaning of being interactive in the concept of serious game for ISO/IEC 12207. Being interactive comes from interaction so any kind of game have to provide a dialogue to player. In fact if there is no such an interaction, how do players accomplish task? The instant feedback and continuous active reactions are the wanted factors to define the term being interactive. Undoubtedly, it is believed that every subject of in any science must be readable. This is the case over years and every person accomplishes many lectures and passes their exams via reading the related resources. Text and textbooks have to be in daily life, but in wider concepts such as engineering and medicine conceptualization needs to contain more practical program. To sustain ISO/IEC 12207 in a serious game environment the ambition of being interactive is possible with dynamic reactions between players and the game rather than text based learning.

There is an increasing desire about sandbox type games recently and this is another factor how a game should be. In games, sandboxes are safe environments where everyone can improve or destruct everything they create before without any stressful decision which is about the things can go wrong because it is isolated from outside world and therefore the effects of outside world can be minimized. This is an important factor for project managers to train software practitioners with respect to various bad experiences. Serious games have a potential to enhance this practice, because while playing a game usually players create different virtual careers based on their own interests and selections. They modify the ongoing progress according to their point of view to the concept, so any practitioner could be trained in a game setting, where they can learn from virtual situations where they make meaningful choices without experiencing negative outcomes.

5 Conclusions

This preliminary study investigates the need of a serious game from an industrial perspective. Initial results from the semi-structured interviews suggest that a serious game can improve the ability of learners of ISO/IEC 12207 standard. All five interviewees (n=5) agree that an interactive learning approach should make it easier to teach the standard. Moreover, there is a consensus among the participants that such an approach will provide a better understanding of the documented concepts. One interviewee recommends that a serious game should be in a simulated office environment (by creating a set of situations) in which several complex concepts can be explained in an iterative way. One other recommends that a usability study should have to be conducted to address user perceptions of such an approach. In addition, she suggested that the potential for learning and engagement should somehow be measured. However, a major limitation of this study is the limited number of experts, therefore, caution must be applied. To evaluate the benefits of the proposed serious game, more research should be conducted on the functionality of the production process and ultimately with the end-product.

References

1. Tsui, F.F.: Essentials of software engineering. Jones & Bartlett Publishers (2014)
2. Futrell, R.T., Shafer, L.I., Shafer, D.F.: Quality software project management. Prentice Hall PTR (2001)
3. Yilmaz, M.: A software process engineering approach to understanding software productivity and team personality characteristics: an empirical investigation. PhD thesis, Dublin City University (2013)
4. Jones, A.: Iso 12207 software life cycle processes fit for purpose? Software Quality Journal **5**, 243–253 (1996)
5. Singh, R.: International standard iso/iec 12207 software life cycle processes. Software Process Improvement and Practice **2**, 35–50 (1996)
6. ISO/IEC: Amendment to ISO/IEC 12207-2008 - Systems and software engineering Software life cycle processes (2008)
7. Abt, C.: Serious games. University Press of Amer (1987)
8. Alvarez, J., Djaouti, D.: Introduction au serious game. Questions théoriques (2010)
9. Acuna, S.T., Juristo, N., Moreno, A.M., Mon, A.: A Software Process Model Handbook for Incorporating People's Capabilities. Springer-Verlag (2005)
10. Yilmaz, M., O'Connor, R.V., Clarke, P.: Software development roles: a multi-project empirical investigation. ACM SIGSOFT Software Engineering Notes **40**, 1–5 (2015)
11. Demirörs, O., Demirörs, E., Tarhan, A., Yildiz, A.: Tailoring iso/iec 12207 for instructional software development. In: Euromicro Conference, vol. 2, pp. 2300–2300. IEEE Computer Society (2000)
12. Clarke, P., O'Connor, R.V.: An approach to evaluating software process adaptation. In: O'Connor, R.V., Rout, T., McCaffery, F., Dorling, A. (eds.) SPICE 2011. CCIS, vol. 155, pp. 28–41. Springer, Heidelberg (2011)
13. Khosrow-Pour, M.: Encyclopedia of information science and technology, vol. 1. IGI Global (2008)
14. McGonigal, J.: Reality is broken: Why games make us better and how they can change the world. Penguin Pr (2011)
15. Baker, A., Navarro, E.O., Van Der Hoek, A.: An experimental card game for teaching software engineering processes. Journal of Systems and Software **75**, 3–16 (2005)
16. Caulfield, C., Veal, D., Maj, S.P.: Teaching software engineering project management-a novel approach for software engineering programs. Modern Applied Science **5**, p87 (2011)
17. Navarro, E.O., van der Hoek, A.: Simse: an interactive simulation game for software engineering education. In: CATE, pp. 12–17 (2004)
18. Drappa, A., Ludewig, J.: Simulation in software engineering training. In: Proceedings of the 22nd international conference on Software engineering, pp. 199–208. ACM (2000)
19. von Wangenheim, C.G., Savi, R., Borgatto, A.F.: Deliver!-an educational game for teaching earned value management in computing courses. Information and Software Technology **54**, 286–298 (2012)
20. Calderón, A., Ruiz, M.: Prodec: a serious game for software project management training. In: ICSEA 2013, The Eighth International Conference on Software Engineering Advances, pp. 565–570 (2013)
21. Baker, A., Navarro, E.O., Van Der Hoek, A.: An experimental card game for teaching software engineering. In: Proceedings of 16th Conference on Software Engineering Education and Training, (CSEE&T 2003), pp. 216–223. IEEE (2003)

22. Gee, J.P.: What video games have to teach us about learning and literacy. Computers in Entertainment (CIE) **1**, 20–20 (2003)
23. Gee, J.P.: What video games have to teach us about learning and literacy. Macmillan (2014)
24. Navarro, E.O., Baker, A., Van Der Hoek, A.: Teaching software engineering using simulation games. In: ICSIE04: Proceedings of the 2004 International Conference on Simulation in Education (2004)

Short Papers

An Approach for Combining SPICE and SCRUM in Software Development Projects

Detlev Hantke[✉]

Quality Assurance, Softing AG, Richard-Reitzner-Allee 6, Haar D-85540, Germany
`Detlev.Hantke@softing.com`

Abstract. In this industrial paper, an implementation of a software development process is presented that takes into account the ideas of the agile SCRUM approach as well as the SPICE requirements. With the help of a traceability matrix the process activities are related to the SCRUM and the SPICE practices, firstly to check if all SPICE base practices were considered in the process design and secondly in an approach for relating SCRUM activities to SPICE practices.

Keywords: SPICE · SCRUM · Traceability matrix · Process activities

1 Introduction

Softing is a privately owned business company with head quarter in Haar close to Munich in Germany. The main business areas are Automotive Electronics (AE) and Industrial Automation (IA) with the AE division specialized on applications for Automotive Diagnostics. For more than 5 years now, the development process in the AE division is based on Automotive SPICE, the automotive industry refinement of the SPICE framework. The process was verified successfully in several SPICE assessments by German automotive OEMs.

In the IA division, the standard process for product developments apart from the V model also takes into account the SCRUM framework. As experiences with SCRUM have been very promising here, and the project team members appreciate much more transparency, clarity and improved communication, while on the other hand the AE standard process is somewhat overloaded and not as flexible as desired, the idea came naturally to combine both worlds (SCRUM and SPICE) in the AE development process.

In this paper, first the roles, phases and activities used in the process are outlined. Second, the method for implementing the process in a first pilot project and for training the team members is described, and last, a method for evaluating the process with respect to the requirements of the SPICE and SCRUM activities is presented.

2 Process Implementation

With respect to the general process design, the idea was to take over as much as possible from the working process implementation in the IA division and to extend the process with respect to the SPICE requirements which come specifically into play from the Engineering Process Group and the SUP.1 Quality Assurance process.

On the other hand, a substantial part of the SPICE requirements on MAN.3 Project Management were already considered in the process due to the fact that SCRUM includes a good deal of the SPICE requirements on MAN.3.

To become more acquainted with the ideas of SCRUM, the team members of a pre-selected pilot project were trained externally by a SCRUM expert company, while the author and the head of the AE development department attended a seminar on ideas to combine SPICE and AGILE at KMG[1] [1].

2.1 Roles

Core of the role definition are the standard roles used in the SCRUM process, e.g. the roles of the SCRUM Master, Product Owner and the (project) Team. The roles of the Product Manager / Project Leader in product developments / customer projects, respectively, were taken over from the already existing AE standard process.

As recommended by KMG and as a necessity to account for the independence of the quality assurance, the new role of the "Quality Product Owner" (QPO) as a project-external quality assurance role was introduced. In the former AE standard process, quality assurance (QA) was divided among the roles of a Quality Internal (QAi) and a Quality External (QAe) responsible. Here, the QAi as a project team member is in charge of basic quality control activities like document reviews, code and test inspections, etc., while the QAe monitors the execution and quality of the activities, the completeness of documents and the general quality of the project.

The role definition is summarized in the table below.

Table 1. Roles used in the revised development process.

Role	Use in the AE development process
Product Owner (PO)	Organizational interface between PM / PL and the development teams.
Product Manager (PM) / Project Leader (PL)	PM / PL is the organizational interface to the customer in product developments / customer projects with respect to commercial topics and features to be implemented
Scrum Master (SM)	Responsible for the implementation of the SCRUM process in the project, moderator and coach of the team, removes impediments and makes sure that the team can work effectively.
Team (T)	The team takes also project management tasks (e.g. distribution of work tasks, organization, general decisions).
Scrum Team	Product Owner, Team and Scrum Master have a common interest in the project success, they constitute a team together in this sense.
Quality Product Owner (QPO)	Not a core part of SCRUM, was introduced to satisfy the SPICE requirements with respect to organizational independence of QA.
System Architect (SYA)	Responsible for the definition and maintenance of the system, interface and component architecture in the main product lines.

---

[1] KMG: KUGLER MAAG CIE GmbH, Leibnizstr. 11, 70806 Kornwestheim, Germany

2.2 Process

The process was defined in the BPMN notation (Business Process Modelling Notation). This method for process definition is the standard in the QM system of the company. The activities are mapped to roles that are displayed as "swim lanes" and the output work products are shown as data objects.

The process is broken down into 4 phases:

1. Phase 1: Product / Project Definition
2. Phase 2: Release Definition
3. Phase 3: Implementation
4. Phase 4: Delivery

The most interesting part here is phase 3 - implementation - as it includes the basic ideas of the SCRUM model and covers the largest part of the engineering process activities (ENG process group according to SPICE). Therefore, phase 3 is described below in more detail, whereas the activities of the other phases 1, 2, and 4 are only briefly summarized.

Phase 1: Product / Project Definition: in this initial phase, the requirements and the architecture for a new product or a product enhancement in product developments or customer projects are defined.

Phase 2: Release Definition: in this phase, project execution is divided into releases and team building starts in a release kickoff. Note, that important strategic tasks that are required by SPICE (QA strategy, integration and test strategy, etc.) are already carried out in this phase. This was a request from the management to make sure that important strategic issues are taken into account early enough in the project.

Phase 3: Implementation. Here, the development according to SCRUM is carried out in sprints. As an example, part of these activities is shown in BPMN notation in Fig. 1. A sprint starts with a planning meeting and terminates with the sprint retrospective:

1. Sprint Planning Meeting (PO, Team, SM, System Architect)
2. Daily SCRUM Meeting (daily standup, Team and SM)
3. Continuous processing of all tasks (daily work of task by the team members)
4. Sprint Review Meeting (Team, SM, PO, QPO, System Architect, optional PM / PL)
5. Sprint Retrospective (Team, SM, optional QPO and PO)
6. External QA Tasks (QPO)
7. Reporting and Escalation (QPO)
8. Information Exchange PO - PM

Most of the SPICE practices for the engineering processes are considered in activity 3 (Continuous processing of all tasks). Here, the necessary work is described as tasks in more detail. Activity 3 is broken down further into the following tasks:

1. Update of Integration and Test Strategy
2. Creation / Update of Test Specifications
3. Component Design
4. Software Coding
5. Software Test
6. Reviews
7. User and additional Documentation
8. Configuration Management
9. Internal Quality Assurance
10. Problem and Change Management

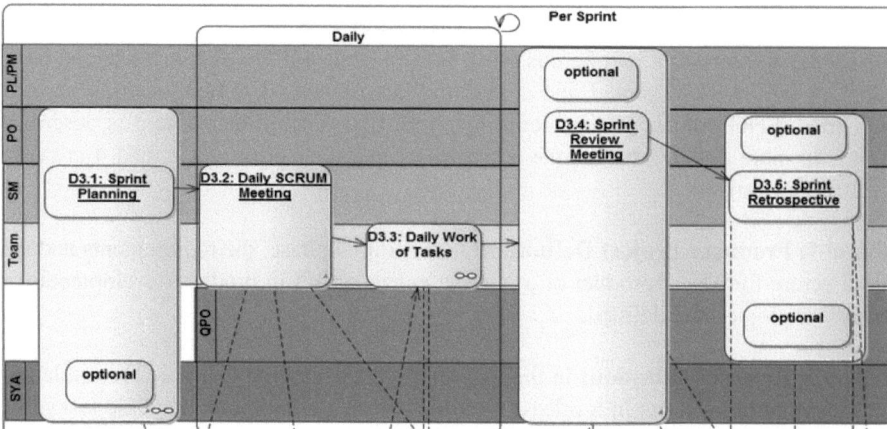

Fig. 1. Part of phase 3 in the development process: Implementation phase. The roles involved are, from top to bottom: PL/PM, PO, SM, Team, QPO, SYA, see section 2.1.

Phase 4: Delivery. After the last sprint for a release, the product is delivered by PO to PM/PL and to the external customer.

3 Training and Continuous Improvement

After the completion of the process design, a pilot project was defined and the process was presented to the team in a common work shop. Open issues with respect to the process realization were recorded in an open issue list and tracked continuously. The project was then started with a formal kick off. During the first sprint, all activities for the current week were prepared and discussed in a weekly regular meeting with the PO and the SM who then instructed the team members accordingly. After the first sprint, this weekly regular meeting was continued to address the continuous improvement, especially with respect to the process and the team performance.

The main sources for potential improvement were found to be the sprint review and the retrospective at the end of the sprints. As an example it was the observed that in the first sprint no business requirement could be completed by the team because miscellaneous unplanned activities like e.g. tool setups, configuration activities, installation procedures, etc., had to be carried out. Consequently, the process was modified in a way that for a new product development an "initial sprint" is carried out with a set of standard user stories addressing these preparatory activities.

4 SPICE and SCRUM Coverage

The process coverage with respect to the SPICE and SCRUM practices may be checked with a traceability matrix, see the examples in Tables 2 and 3 for ENG.8 and ENG.4. In the 3rd column, Px.y(.z) denotes phase x, activity y, (task z in phase 3), see section 2.1. With respect to ENG.8 (see Table 2), the SCRUM activities in phase 3 cover a large fraction of the SPICE practices. On the other hand, the coverage of the SCRUM activities with respect to ENG.4 (Table 3) is a little lower than for ENG.8. This is probably mainly an artefact of the specific process design as the ENG.4 activities are distributed on the various process phases (see column 3 in the tables below).

Table 2. SPICE / SCRUM traceability matrix for ENG.8 – Software Testing.

SPICE Base Practices					SCRUM practices					
ID Base Practice	Base Practice	Activities in Development Process	Comments	Coverage of BP in Activity in %	Release Planning	Sprint Planning	Daily Standup	Backlog Refinement	Sprint Review	Retrospective
ENG.8.BP1	SW Test Strategy	P2.4, P3.3.1, P3.3.2, P3.1, P2.5	documented in Integration & Test Plan (based on Template)	100%	x	x			x	
ENG.8.BP2	SW Test Specification	P3.3.2, P3.2	New test case for every requirement/bug in test specifications, presented in daily standup	100%			x			
ENG.8.BP3	Verification of Integrated SW	P3.3.5, P3.4	Automated tests => test results shown in Sprint Review	100%					x	
ENG.8.BP4	Record Result of SW Test	P3.3.5, P3.4	Test Results shown in Sprint Review	100%					x	
ENG.8.BP5	Traceability of SW Test to SW Requirements	P3.3.2, P3.3.5, P3.4	Update of Traceability Matrix is user story for every sprint, Traceability Matrix shown in Sprint Review	100%					x	
ENG.8.BP6	SW Regression Test Strategy and Regression Testing	P2.4, P3.3.1, P3.3.5, P3.4	SW Regression Test Strategy included in I&Test Plan, Regression Testing in nightly builds and at end of sprint, results presented in Sprint Review	100%					x	

Table 3. SPICE / SCRUM traceability matrix for ENG.4 – Software Requirements Analysis.

SPICE Base Practices					SCRUM practices					
ID Base Practice	Base Practice	Activities in Development Process	Comments	Coverage of BP in Activity in %	Release Planning	Sprint Planning	Daily Standup	Backlog Refinement	Sprint Review	Retrospective
ENG.4.BP1	Identify SW Requirements	P1.1, P2.1	carried out in several phases: product backlog, release backlog	100%	x					
ENG.4.BP2	Analyze SW Requirements	P1.3, P 2.11, P3.1.1	estimation in early phase, Backlog Refinement Meeting, detailed analysis in Sprint Planning Meeting	100%		x		x		
ENG.4.BP3	Impact on Operating Environment	P3.1.1	also carried out in Sprint Planning Meeting	100%		x				
ENG.4.BP4	Prioritize / categorize SW Reqs	P1.1, P2.1, P2.4 P2.11, P3.1.1	also carried out in several phases as above, Release Kickoff carried out in P2.4 (mapping to releases)	100%	x	x		x		
ENG.4.BP5	Evaluate / Update SW Requirements	P1.1, P2.1, P2.11, P3.1.1, P3.4	as above carried out in several phases	100%	x	x		x	x	
ENG.4.BP6	Traceability System Reqs to SW Requirements	P1.1, P2.1, P2.11	Traceability to Customer Requirements recorded in used database	100%	x					
ENG.4.BP8	Communicate SW Requirements	P1.1, P2.1, P2.4 P2.11, P3.1.1, P3.4	Dissemination and update to all relevant parties, as above	100%	x	x			x	x

For the analyzed processes, the score for the coverage of the SPICE practices by the SCRUM activities was the lowest in the SUP.1 Quality Assurance process[2].

5 Conclusions

An implementation of a development process that includes both the requirements of SCRUM and SPICE shows first promising results in a pilot project: requirements became clearer and more transparent, team communication, interaction and spirit were improved and the project goals were better understood by the team.

The coverage of the SPICE practices by the SCRUM activities was found to be relatively large in all practices that require communication, evaluation or review by the stakeholders (see examples ENG.4.BP5, ENG.4.BP9, ENG.8.BP4, ENG.8.BP6 as shown in chapter 4). Most of the work required by the engineering group (ENG) processes is however actually carried out as project specific tasks in the sprints by the team. These tasks are based on the business requirements in the project and are discussed in the daily standup meetings. Strategic topics as e.g. the definition of the quality assurance or test strategy are prepared quite early in the process before the sprint cycles start and are then completed in the sprint tasks.

In future projects (see chapter 3) an initial sprint will be carried out in which mostly installation, configuration and setup tasks are performed.

A lessons-learnt workshop in which the experiences in the pilot project are discussed in detail will be carried out shortly.

Reference

1. Agile in Automotive, Pocket Guide SCRUM & KANBAN, Kugler Maag CIE GmbH, Leibnizstr. 11, 70806 Kornwestheim, ISBN 978-3-945547-07-6

---

[2] The corresponding traceability matrix for SUP.1 may be obtained from the author.

A Layered Framework for Managing Access to Customer-provided Process Requirements

Ricardo Eíto-Brun[✉]

Universidad Carlos III de Madrid, Madrid, Spain
reito@bib.uc3m.es

Abstract. This paper describes an approach to support the tailoring of process models in response to Customer-requirements in software development. The approach consist of a conceptual infrastructure made up of three layers that represent: a) the process characteristics extracted from the ISO/IEC 29110 international standard, b) the tailoring of the standard processes made at the corporate level, and c) an additional tailoring made in response to client or project-specific requirements. The tailoring extends and refines the process definitions at the previous levels by incorporating additional requirements and practices. Requirements are contextualized in process definitions by linking them to activities, tasks and work products. Software engineers have at their disposal a single point of access to all the process-related information they need to complete their work, avoiding the risk of missing relevant information when completing a particular task or working on a project deliverable. The resulting product is implemented on top of the Semantic Wiki content management platform.

Keywords: ISO/IEC 29110 · Software Process Tailoring · Process requirements · Semantic Wiki · SPEM

1 Introduction

ISO/IEC 29110 "Software engineering -- Lifecycle profiles for Very Small Entities (VSEs)" [1] provides organizations with a prescriptive process model adapted to the needs of VSEs (Very Small Entities), defined as companies with less than twenty five employees. The Basic profile establishes two processes - Project Management (PM) and Software Implementation (SI) -, with their activities, tasks, inputs and outputs and roles. With this standard, VSEs have at their disposal guidelines on how to develop software and a reference to conduct improvement activities. The importance of ISO/IEC 29110 has been widely discussed in the professional literature [2] [3]. These companies do not have at their disposal the resources needed to deploy more complex improvement models like CMMI or SPICE. This makes difficult to demonstrate their capability to develop reliable software following standard life cycle processes and industrial best practices. For large companies subcontracting software development activities to SMEs, the lack of models tailored to SMEs characteristics makes also difficult to plan and conduct assessments to assess their capabilities as subcontractors. ISO/IEC 29100 applicablity also extends to system engineering activities [4] [5].

It is expected that companies adopting the ISO/IEC 29110 processes model will make some kind of adaptation or tailoring on the standard. As an example, the process model can be applied to different life cycles (waterfall, incremental, etc.), or adapted to agile practices. In other cases, it may be necessary to give a more precise meaning to some of the activities and work products described in the standard. For example, internal or external reporting, or the use of software engineering tools may require further explanations and details, as companies may follow different practices, tools, templates or techniques to execute the same task.

At this stage, the process definitions available in the standard need some kind of adaptation or tailoring to the corporate practices. This tailoring shall be applicable to all the projects completed by the organization. The main advantage of doing this tailoring on the process model defined in a standard like ISO/IEC 29110, is the fact that the company ensures the harmonization across projects and, at the same time, the fulfillment of the international standard requirements.

Tailoring needs may require an additional step in response to customer requirements. In some situations, project teams need to:

- include additional tasks, activities and work products to those defined in the standard and corporate gruidelines, or
- review and adapt the corporate procedures to accomodate customer requirements that affect either managerial or engineering activities and work products.

These customer requirements introduce an additional level of complexity in the process model tailored at the corporate level, and require an additional level of adaptation. As an example, a standard or the corporate methodology may request the regular reporting of the project status to the project's stakeholders; this general tasks may be affected by particular, customer requirements, that impose constraints on the frequency of the activity, the format and layout to use, or the data that need to be provided in the reports.

Software engineers and project managers not only need to know the corporate, organizational guidelines. They also need to pay significant attention to their customer's requirements. This paper describes the implementation of a tool that offers a single point of access to software processes' descriptions tailored to corporate guidelines and to customer or project-specific requirements. The tool is built on top of the SemanticWiki content management tool, and makes use of the SPEM (Software Process Engineering Metamodel) modeling language to represent the processes.

2 Process Model Tailoring and Customization

A three-layered approach for software process modeling is proposed. The first, layer consist of the processes (including tasks and work products) defined in the ISO/IEC 29110 standard. In particular, the Basic profile, that corresponds to companies that develop non-critical software -, has been taken as a reference. The second layer represents the tailoring or adaptation made by the company when adopting the international standard. This second layer provides the guidelines to be applied for all the projects completed by the company, and defines corporate policies and work procedures. The third and final layer represents the adaptation or tailoring of the corporate processes to the specific requirements imposed by the customer or the stakeholders for particular projects.

As stated, ISO/IEC 29110 sits at the core of the proposed framework. This standard provides the main elements in the model, that are further refined to establish the corporate processes and procedures. As ISO/IEC 29110 offers a mininum set of elements for just two processes (Project Management and Software Implementation), tailoring is expected to emphasize those tasks that add more value to the corporate business and incorporate additional practices, tools and methods [6]. The second layer of the tailoring gives the organization a common set of guidelines on how to develop projects, ensures harmonization and a common understanding of the processes across the different teams, staff and projects completed at different periods.

This adaptation of the processes defined in ISO/IEC 29110 may be directly enacted in projects whose customers or stakeholders do not ask for additional process-related requirements. In other cases, the customer may impose additional management or engineering requirements that make necessary to further adapt the corporate processes, moving to a third layer of tailoring. In general, project specific requirements may ask for additional tasks and work products, or impose constraints on existing work products or tasks already defined at the corporate processes. Particular requirements may refer to the use of a particular templace, to the need of adding some information to an existing work product, or completing an activity under some parameters to ensure completeness, efficiency or effectiveness.

This tailoring of the company corporate processes in response to Client requirements and project characteristics may be understood as a sign of maturity, as they demonstrate the capability of the company to adapt their corporate processes to fulfill the particular needs of different types of projects [7].

3   Implementation of the Tailored Process Model

The most important objective of the proposed research is giving staff involved in software development a single point of access to all the requirements and constraints they need to know when planning, executing or evaluating the status of a particular tasks or work product. Applicable requirements may be spread across multiple specifications and documents, what makes necessary to facilitate engineers a unique location where they can easily find the requirements impacting a particular activity or work product. In the proposed implementation, this place consist of a web-site built on top of the SemanticWiki platform that contains a „process description" with links to all the process requirements and constraints. With this information, it is possible to gve answer to questions similar to the following ones:

- Which content is expected for a particular document or deliverable?
- Is there any requirement on how to conduct particular activities (e.g. reporting, unit testing, etc.)?
- Which is the format and delivery method for distributing the software and related documentation?

- Which are the expected diagrams that need to be included in the design documentation?
- Which coding standards need to be enforced?

To demonstrate the feasibility of the proposed approach, a practical implementation has been completed with data provided by a real company. The implementation resulted in a „tailored process model" built as a Semantic Wiki site. In the practical experience described in this paper, Semantic Wiki has demonstrated its capability to support the generation and dynamic publication of a complex set of interrelated pages indexed with controlled terms. The capability of tagging the different types of relationships or links between pages representing different types of data is another of the advantages offered by the tool.

The site with the process model has been built folllowing these steps:

- A visual representation of the ISO/IEC 29100 PM and SI processes (as defined in the Basic profile of the standard) has been elaborated using the SPEM modeling notation. The resulting diagrams and the description of the processes, roles and work products extracted from the standard were uploaded into the Semantic Wiki site.
- Task and work products defined in ISO/IEC 29110 were tailored to the corporate needs of a company using the SPEM extension and customisation capabilities. Updated content was also uploaded into the Semantic Wiki site, and links were created between the content extracted from the standard (first or core layer) and the content obtained as a result of the corporate tailoring (second layer).

  Individual base practices from the corporate procedures were uploaded as separate units and tagged with the names of the activities, tasks and work products they impacted on. An additional tag was used to indicate the level of tailoring (corporate, that is to say, common to all the projects).
- Finally, a set of technical and management requirements extracted from two different specifications provided by one client were extracted and stored as independent units in the Semantic Wiki site.

  These requirements were tagged with the names of the task(s) - or activities - and work product(s) on which they had an impact. For these project-specific requirements, new tags were used to indicate that they belonged to the third layer (project-specific requirements) and to indicate the project where they were applicable and the specification document they were extracted from.

The resulting web site combines the visual representation of the processes with their tailoring at two different levels: corporate and project specific. For example, the SI.6.6 task defined in ISO/IEC 29110, „Perform delivery according to Delivery Instructions" was further refined through links to different requirerements from the corporate procedures or from project specifications.

3.1 The Role of SPEM in Process Modeling and Tailoring

The synthesis of the different layers of tailoring of the software development process defined by ISO/IEC 29110 requires a sound conceptual framework. To develop this tailoring the SPEM modeling framework was selected. SPEM is a MOF-based metamodel and conceptual framework published by the Object Management Group (OMG) that provides concepts and notations to represent, exchange, publish and enact different types of processes (not only those related to software development). The scope of SPEM consist of "the minimal elements needed to define any process and accommodate a large range of development methods and processes of different styles, cultural backgrounds, levels of formalism, life cycle models and communities.".

3.2 The role of Semantic Wiki.

Semantic Wiki is a content management platform that offers the functions available in traditional or standard Wiki sites, plus the capability of adding properties and metadata to the pages and links in the wiki. These custom properties give the possibility of tagging the content of the items, making explicit their meaning or "semantics".

In Semantic Wiki, it is possible to use both categories (also available in standard wikis) with properties. There are separate, independent pages for each property, and all the pages for properties are grouped in a common namespace. Properties are not predefined, so it is possible to define and use different properties and metadata at each implementation. There are anyway initiatives to propose a common, general set of properties for tagging Semantic Wiki content: SWiVT, and it is also possible to establish equivalences between the custom properties and metadata defined in other schemas like Dublin Core or FOAF. Although out of the scope of the present research, the ability to work with custom properties in Semantic Wiki opens a wide range of possibilities to define and use vocabularies and ontologies defined for the software engineering field. Properties can be attached both to the textual content of pages and to the links between pages. This makes possible to establish equivalence between the Semantic Wiki and the RDF-based model based on triples made up of subject, predicate and object. In Semantic Wiki, the subject shall correspond to the entity to which the page containing the link refers; the predicate shall correspond to the property, and the object to the page acting as the target of the link. The annotated links between pages in the Semantic Wiki are created using this syntax:

```
[[propertyName::targetPage]]
```

Using these properties it is possible to distinguish different types of links between the pages in the Wiki, what it is not possible in a conventional wiki. In the particular case of the process model description, different properties are used to differentiate the relationships between processes, activities, tasks, roles and work products. Besides tagging the links with custom properties, Semantic Wiki allows attaching properties in the textual content of the pages. These properties are added using the same syntax used for the links but adding their data type to avoid the Wiki engine interpreting them as links.

4 Conclusions

Standards like ISO/IEC 29110 provides a process map and processes descriptions that are the basis for establishing more detailed work procedures at the corporate level. But in some cases, software development companies need to combine and further extend these process descriptions to cover additional requirements coming from their customers. The tasks and work products defined in the standards are affected by additional requirements that are usually spread through different specifications and documents provided by the Client as part of the tender conditions or the statement of work. Dealing with requirements coming from different sources implies a risk, as staff involved in project planning and execution may disregard relevant requirements and information. In addition, dealing with separate documents and standards has a negative impact on productivity, due to the difficulties to remember at a given time all the applicable constraints. The proposed solution ensures a single, shared point of access to search and browse applicable requirements – whatever their source - and assess their impact on activities and work products. When working on a specific deliverable or tasks, engineers can get the list of requirements that need to be considered.

References

1. International Organization for Standardization (2012) ISO/IEC TR 29110-5-1-1 Software Engineering – Lifecycle profiles for Very Small Entities (VSEs) – Part 5-1-1: Management and Engineering Guide – Entry Profile
2. O'Connor, R.V., Laporte, C.Y.: Software project management in very small entities with ISO/IEC 29110. In: Winkler, D., O'Connor, R.V., Messnarz, R. (eds.) EuroSPI 2012. CCIS, vol. 301, pp. 330–341. Springer, Heidelberg (2012)
3. Ribaud, V., Saliou, P., O'Connor, R.V., Laporte, C.Y.: Software engineering support activities for very small entities. In: Riel, A., O'Connor, R., Tichkiewitch, S., Messnarz, R. (eds.) EuroSPI 2010. CCIS, vol. 99, pp. 165–176. Springer, Heidelberg (2010)
4. Laporte, C., Fanmuy, G., Ptack, K.: The development of systems engineering international standards and support tools for very small enterprises. In: 22nd Annual International Symposium of the International Council on Systems Engineering, INCOSE 2012 and the 8th Biennial European Systems Engineering Conference, vol. 3, pp. 1563–1590 (2012)
5. Laporte, C., O'Connor, R., Fanmuy, G.: International systems and software engineering standards for very small entities. CrossTalk **26**(3), 28–33 (2013)
6. Boucher, Q., Perrouin, G., Deprez, J.-C., Heymans, P.: Towards configurable ISO/IEC 29110-compliant software development processes for very small entities. In: Winkler, D., O'Connor, R.V., Messnarz, R. (eds.) EuroSPI 2012. CCIS, vol. 301, pp. 169–180. Springer, Heidelberg (2012)
7. Alexis, O.: Rationale modeling for software process evolution. Software Process: Improvement and Practice **14**(2), 85–105 (2009)

How to Certify the Very Small Entity Software Processes Using ISO/IEC 29110

Patricia Rodríguez-Dapena[1(✉)] and Miguel Francisco Buitrago-Botero[2]

[1] Softwcare SL, CEO, Vigo, Spain
rodriguezdapena@softwcare.com
[2] SEQUAL S.A., CEO & President, Medellin, Colombia
miguel.buitrago@sequal.com.co

Abstract. A large majority of enterprises worldwide are VSEs (Very Small Entities). Like for any business, VSEs in the IT business sector face a challenging and strong competition. Adopting "best practices", standardizing processes and obtaining an international recognition or certification, are key factors for success. This paper introduces a new and cost/effective alternative for international recognition of small SMEs (VSEs), as good quality software producers. The new standard is VSE tailor-made, lightweight, certifiable and compatible with traditional models such as CMMI [2], ISO330xx [15], or ISO 9000. New standards are on their way to internationally harmonize these conformity assessments and certificates for VSEs.

Keywords: Process assessment · Conformity assessment · VSE · ISO/IEC 29110

1 Introduction

According to the very new ISO series standard, ISO/IEC 29110 [6], an enterprise comprising 25 people or less is called Very Small Entities, or VSEs, for its acronym in English. The name not only refers to companies, but also serves to reference an organizational or project area comprised of 25 people or less. In some way, the term VSEs keeps relationship with the common term SMEs (Small and Medium-sized Enterprises) for micro and small SMEs. Overall, SMEs accounted for 99.8% of all enterprises active in the EU28 nonfinancial business sector, 66.8% of total employment and 58.1% of the value added (as in the EU28 in 2013 [1]). In Europe, for instance, over 92% of enterprises have up to 9 employees [1]. These figures are similar worldwide. Like for any business, VSEs in the IT sector face a challenging and strong competition. Adopting "best practices", standardizing processes and obtaining an international recognition or certification, in addition to improving productivity, competitiveness and organizational climate, help retaining customers, and also establishing new inter-business relationships. However, most international standards and models were initially designed thinking on large software organizations; although it is possible to adapt such models to the small and often growing companies, it consumes an important amount of extra time and effort.

ISO JTC1/SC7 has created a working group (WG24) mandated to develop a set of tailored-made standards and guides to drive VSEs through a scalable, cost effective, less time consuming and manageable step by step approach in adopting and using world class Software Engineering practices. As a result of the ISO SC7 WG24 work, the incremental profiles under definition are:

- entry profile intended to be the starting point of process approach and improvement
- basic profile intended to include basic processes and to be certified.
- organizational profile intended to be the improvement path to high mature processes.

The profiles are proposed to use a Process Reference Model, defined according with ISO/IEC 24744 [8], to be easily understood, and to facilitate both their implementation (with the use of the guides available in ISO 29110) and also for their assessment as well as their conformance /recognition (or certification). The processes goals are expressed via sentences with 'shalls' (in the process outcomes). The requirements or "shall" sentences are included in the new draft ISO/IEC 29110-4-1 standard. The processes are proposed to be defined with purpose and outcome.

2   Conformity Assessment of VSE Profiles

The new draft of ISO 29110-4-1 requirements [6] are required in a profile definition to be observed by IT systems claiming conformance to the profile. The conformance evaluation or certification can be achieved through either process assessment or audit both by an officially accredited body. Certification is the process of confirming that a system or component complies with its specified requirements and is acceptable for operational use [9]. Certification can: (1) provide acquirers with confidence in the suppliers, products or services they use; (2) help businesses be competitive; and (3) facilitate trade and marketing.

2.1   Accredited Certification Body

According to ISO, "...when choosing a certification body, one should: (a) Evaluate several certification bodies; (b) Check if the certification body uses the relevant CASCO standard (e.g. ISO 170xx standards) and (c) Check if it is accredited. Accreditation is not compulsory, and non-accreditation does not necessarily mean it is not reputable, but it does provide independent confirmation of competence. To find an accredited certification body, contact the national accreditation body(ies) in ones' country or visit the International Accreditation Forum..."

Accreditation is an on-going process of assessment of a conformity assessment body to ensure that its performance is: impartial, technically competent, to the required standard, appropriately resourced, and can be sustained [11]. For example in Europe, since 1 January 2010 it has been a requirement that every EU Member State

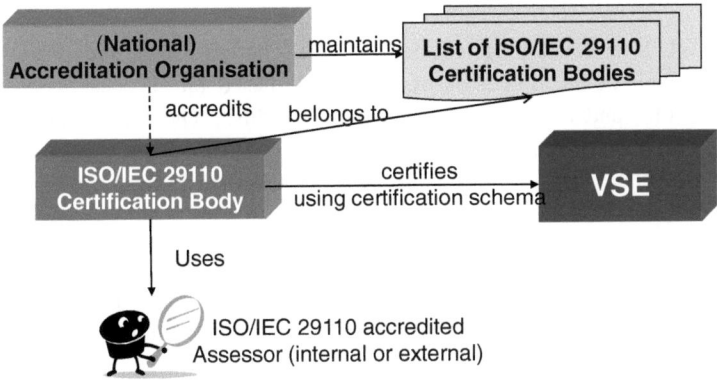

Fig. 1. Certification process main roles

should formally appoint a single National Accreditation Body to be the sole provider of accreditation services for that country. Each National Accreditation Bodies are organized under the auspices of the European co-operation for Accreditation (EA). EA members may also be members of the two organizations with worldwide representation—the International Laboratory Accreditation Cooperation (ILAC), and the International Accreditation Forum (IAF).

Accreditation has multiple benefits among which the following can be mentioned:

• Accreditation provides confidence in the competence and consistency of conformity assessment activities that can be used to support the implementation of requirements and regulations.

• Accreditation is objective proof that conformity assessment organizations conform to recognized standards. It is the internationally recognized system that is used to develop and sustain high standards of performance.

• Accredited conformity assessment is essential for decision-making and risk management. Organizations can save time and money by selecting accredited and therefore competent conformity assessment services.

• Accredited conformity assessment can provide a competitive advantage and facilitates access to export markets with the aim of 'tested or certified once, accepted everywhere [12].

An accredited certification body, from a list of possible certification bodies, using accredited assessors, will perform the conformity assessment to independently/as third party recognize the profiles of a VSE.

2.2 Certification Schema

ISO SC7 WG24 is developing two certification schemas for the independent conformity assessment of the processes of VSEs: one based on "Process assessment and maturity levels" and the other one based on "Audits". The certification body shall fulfill a specific set of requirements to be entitled as a certification body to these new schemas for VSEs. These requirements will be published in the following standards, still under preparation in ISO [6]:

- ISO/IEC 29110-3-3 Systems and software engineering -- Lifecycle profiles for Very Small Entities (VSEs) -- Part 3-3: Certification requirements for conformity assessments of VSE profiles using process assessment and maturity levels
- ISO/IEC 29110-3-2 Software engineering -- Lifecycle profiles for Very Small Entities (VSEs) -- Part 3-2: Conformity Audit.

Table 1. Comparing "Process assessment and maturity levels" and "Audit"

Issue of comparison	Process assessment and Maturity Levels	Audit
Known	It is a new method for ISO certifications/conformity assessments, but has strong similarity with similar good experiences and well valuated assessment schemas such as SCAMPI (the CMMI appraisal method)	Certification/conformity assessments method already used for other schemas
Criteria	Indicators publicly available, therefore everyone will know the detailed criteria the evaluators will use	'Checklist' or evaluation criteria unknown and open for interpretation
Assessors training	Existing internationally recognized schemas for assessor accreditation, knowledgeable in the entity business area	'Accredited' auditors are not always required to know about the business area of the entity assessed
Improvements for the VSE	Method well supporting incremental profile assessments and improvement paths for VSEs	Not intended to be used for incremental profile assessments nor for improvement purposes
Certification bodies	There are not yet certification bodies accredited to the ISO/IEC 29110-3-3 [6] requirements not to the general ISO/IEC 29169 [10] standard, both still to be published.	Existing certification bodies using audits as the method, accredited to assess other requirements: like ISO 9001, etc. The risk is that existing certification bodies using audits will perform these VSE conformity assessments without being accredited for this schema in particular.
Time consuming	A little more time consuming than a traditional audit, even though it analyses a detailed set of publicly available indicators.	Time spent in interviews (oral evidence) and in reviewing documents without the possibility to corroborate them with correlated evidence.

Table 2. (*Continued*)

Cost	A good cost/benefits ratio. The cost includes the appraiser, the collection evidence process and the on-site period, even though it analyses a detailed set of publicly available indicators.	Could be a little bit cheaper because the less time used to evidence collect and analyses.
Objectivity	Besides interviews, the method includes objective evidence collection, such as documents, presentation and work products..	High degree of dependency on interviews, oral evidences and no cross check document review
Repeatability	Easily repeatable as the set of indicators is known and detailed enough and the standard process assessment process is detailed	Hardly repeatable because of the considerable amount oral evidence.
Credibility	Good level of credibility in similar Process assessment methods such as SCAMPI (the CMMI appraisal method)	Eventual credibility issues because of the oral evidences dependability

2.3 Detailed Set of Indicators for Repeatability and Objectivity

As mentioned above, the accredited assessor, through the Certification Body uses a certification schema for the conformity assessment of the VSE profiles. This section is intended to present an example of the set in detailed indicators to be used when performing the conformity assessments using process assessment and maturity level schemas. Every aspect to be assessed (each process attribute) will need to be assessed at least twice for each process within a VSE (for two instances of the same process) and using a detailed set of indicators, for which all evidences will be recorded and mapped to each indicator. Making the assessment objective and repeatable. The Basic Profile for VSEs mentioned above (soon to be published in ISO/IEC 29110-3-1 [6]): By reporting all evidences found for each of above indicators for the two process instances to be assessed, the results of the assessment can be repeatable and objective.

2.4 Accreditation of VSE Process Assessors

VSE certifications, as many other certifications, will need to be performed by 'Accredited Assessors' from (or subcontracted by) the accredited certification bodies. The meaning of 'Accredited Assessors' is that these conformity assessments shall be performed by trained and qualified individuals who are trained by an 'authorized' training organization, and who have the education, competencies and working and practical experience to be able to perform these assessments, in particular using the process assessment and maturity level schema.

As in the CMMI schema [2] and the ISO 15504-5 (new ISO/IEC 330xx [15]), an "ISO/IEC 29110 Accredited Assessor" needs Software Engineering specific knowledge, enough field experience, some ISO/IEC 29110 training and skills and qualification to conduct properly an VSE assessment and certify, for example and in particular, its ISO/IEC 29110-4-1 software basic profile fulfillment. The organization training and accrediting assessors will need to comply with ISO/IEC 17024 [14] which contains the principles and requirements for a body certifying persons against specific requirements, and includes the development and maintenance of a certification scheme for persons. One example of an international organization performing this assessor's competencies accreditation role is INTRSA [13], certifying as *competent*, process assessors trained and qualified in the principles and practices of assessing processes with the requirements ISO/IEC 330xx [15] (former ISO/IEC 15504). Assessor accreditation schemas for each specific process assessment model may need to come soon to be publicly in place.

Figure 2 below shows the different roles for the assessor accreditation. To become an accredited process assessor, and specifically for VSE profiles, one would need to demonstrate:

- He is trained in the process assessment process and in the specific process assessment model to be used (e.g. in our case the ones included in ISO 29110).
- He has the working experience, to be an assessor knowledgeable in the required area of expertise to be assessed. For example, for the assessment of VSE's processes, the applicant will need to demonstrate he has relevant work experience in the system and/or software industry, including in system and/or software development life cycle processes functions, within system and/or software development or maintenance, inspection or enforcement, or the equivalent.
- He has practical assessment experience in using the assessment schema and performing process assessments (measured mainly through the number of performed assessment hours and the number of assessments). The applicant will need to demonstrate he has performed system and/or software processes assessments in organizations under the leadership of a qualified assessor.

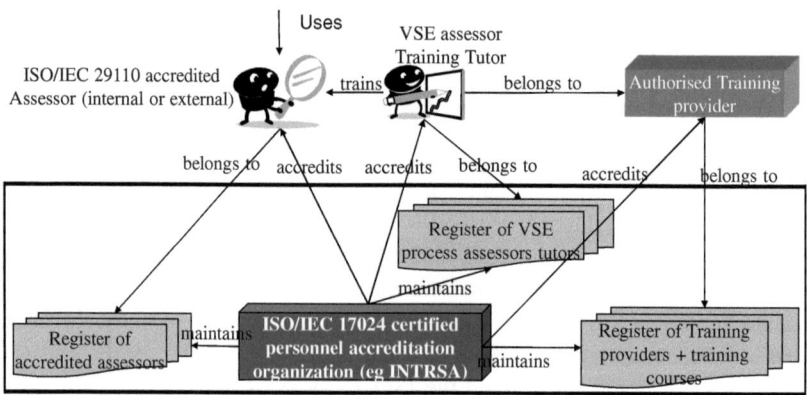

Fig. 2. Assessor accreditation main roles

With all this information the applicant may be granted with the accreditation of being an assessor or a principal assessor depending on the expertise and practical assessment performances, in particular for VSE profiles/processes. These accreditations are to be renewed periodically, and for example in INTRSA (www.intrsa.org) [13], for ISO/IEC 15504-5 assessors it is every three years.

3   Conclusions

This paper has presented an overview of new and cost/effective ways for international recognition to small VSEs (VSEs), tailor-made, lightweight, certifiable and compatible with traditional models. Like for any business, VSEs in the IT business sector face a challenging and strong competition. Adopting "best practices", standardizing processes and obtaining an international recognition or certification, are key factors for success. New standards like the ISO/IEC 29110 series are on their way to internationally harmonize these conformity assessments and certificates for VSEs.

The status is still very incipient but fast moving into the right direction. In one hand, industry needs to get all VSE profiles published from ISO, together with all their process assessment models. The guides that are defined together with the profiles by ISO will serve to support the implementation of these profiles. In the other hand, and in order to be able to get recognition of VSEs excellence, first, the different Countries need to adopt the "Process assessment and maturity levels" certification schema based on ISO/IEC 29169 and the coming ISO/IEC 29110-3-3, so that they can accredit certification bodies. In turn, these certification bodies need 'accredited' assessors. Therefore, in parallel, process assessors need to be trained by an 'authorized' training organization, which recognize they have the education, competencies and working and practical experience to be able to perform these assessments.

References

1. Laporte, C.Y., Alexandre, S., O'Connor, R.: A software engineering lifecycle standard for very small enterprises. In: O'Connor, R.V., Baddoo, N., Smolander, K., Messnarz, R. (eds.) EuroSPI 2008. CCIS, vol. 16, pp. 129–141. Springer, Heidelberg (2008)
2. CMMI® for Development, Version 1.3. November 2010 CMU/SEI-2010-TR-033 ESC-TR-2010-033
3. ISO/IEC 12207. Systems and software engineering - Software life cycle processes. Geneva, Switzerland: (ISO). New version in preparation (2008)
4. ISO/IEC 15288. Systems engineering - Systems life cycle processes. Geneva, Switzerland: (ISO). New version in preparation (2008)
5. ISO/IEC 15289. Systems and software engineering - Content of systems and software life cycle process information products. Geneva, Switzerland: International Organization for Standardization (ISO) (2011)
6. ISO/IEC 29110 - parts. Systems and Software engineering - Lifecycle profiles for Very Small Entities (VSEs). Geneva, Switzerland: International Organization for Standardization (ISO). Including new drafts for 29110-3-1, 29110-3-3 29110-4-1

7. ISO/IEC JTC1/SC7 N3288 New Work Item Proposal – Software Life Cycles for Very Small Enterprises, 21-06-2005
8. ISO/IEC TR 24774 Systems and software engineering — Life cycle management — Guidelines for process description, 2nd edn. 15-09-2010
9. ISO/IEC 24765. Systems and software engineering–Vocabulary, Geneva, Switzerland: International Organization for Standardization (ISO) (2010)
10. ISO/IEC 29169. Information technology - Process assessment - The application of conformity assessment methodology to the assessment of process quality characteristics and organizational maturity
11. Accreditation in Europe. Facilitating regulatory compliance and international trade. www.european-accreditation.org. EA (2013)
12. Conformity Assessment and Accreditation policy in the UK. Department for Business, Innovation and Skills. UK government, April 2012
13. IntRSA. International Registration Scheme for Assessors. http://www.intrsa.org
14. ISO/IEC 17024:2012 Conformity assessment – General requirements for bodies operating certification of persons. ISO
15. ISO/IEC 330xx Information technology – Process assessment

Author Index

Angarita, Leonardo Bermón 203
Aydan, Ufuk 217

Barafort, Béatrix 188
Bergdahl, Daniel 58
Bosch, Jan 58
Buitrago-Botero, Miguel Francisco 245

Cairns, Paul 159
Cater-Steel, Aileen 72
Clarke, Paul 13
Colomo-Palacios, Ricardo 114
Cortina, Stéphane 188

Del Carpio, Alvaro Fernández 203
Demirörs, Onur 100, 145, 177
Doğanay, Betül 131
Dorling, Alec 13

Eíto-Brun, Ricardo 239

Falcini, Fabio 3
Flood, Derek 19, 45

Gökalp, Ebru 100

Hantke, Detlev 233

İnal, Ayhan 131

Johansson, Enrico 58

Lami, Giuseppe 3
Lepmets, Marion 13

Matalonga, Santiago 33
McCaffery, Fergal 13, 19, 45
Miyoshi, Takeshige 87

O'Connor, Rory V. 114, 217
Olsson, Helena Holmström 58
Ozcan-Top, Ozden 145

Paige, Richard 159

Regan, Gilbert 45
Renault, Alain 188
Rodrigues, Felyppe 33
Rodríguez-Dapena, Patricia 245
Rout, Terry 72
Rust, Peter 19

Salah, Dina 159
Sanchez-Gordon, Mary-Luz 114
Shrestha, Anup 72

Tekbulut, Tuğrul 131
Toleman, Mark 72
Travassos, Guilherme H. 33

Uskarci, Algan 177

Yilmaz, Murat 217

MIX
Papier aus verantwortungsvollen Quellen
Paper from responsible sources
FSC® C105338

If you have any concerns about our products,
you can contact us on
ProductSafety@springernature.com

In case Publisher is established outside the EU,
the EU authorized representative is:
**Springer Nature Customer Service Center GmbH
Europaplatz 3, 69115 Heidelberg, Germany**

Printed by Libri Plureos GmbH
in Hamburg, Germany